Arts and Business

Arts and Business aims at bringing arts and business scholars together in a dialogue about a number of key topics that today form different understandings in the two disciplines. Arts and business are, many times, positioned as opposites. Where one is providing symbolic and aesthetic immersion, the other is creating goods for a market and markets for a good. They often deal and struggle with the same issues, framing it differently and finding different solutions.

This book has the potential of offering both critical theoretical and empirical understandings of these subjects and guiding further exploration and research into this field. Although this dichotomy has a well-documented existence, it is reconstructed through the writing out of business in art and vice versa.

This edited volume distinguishes itself from other writings aimed at closing the gap between art and business, as it does not have a firm standpoint in one of these fields, but treats them as symmetrical and equal. It is our belief that by giving art and business an equal weight, we the editors also create the opportunity to communicate to a wider audience and construct a path forward for art and business to coexist.

Elena Raviola is an Associate Professor at the School of Business, Economics and Law at the University of Gothenburg, Sweden, and works also in the Department of Organization at Copenhagen Business School, Denmark.

Peter Zackariasson is an Associate Professor in Marketing at the School of Business, Economics and Law at the University of Gothenburg, Sweden.

Routledge Research in Creative and Cultural Industries Management

Edited by Ruth Rentschler,
University of South Australia Business School, Australia

For a full list of titles in this series, please visit www.routledge.com

Routledge Research in Creative and Cultural Industries Management provides a forum for the publication of original research in cultural and creative industries, from a management perspective. It reflects the multiple and inter-disciplinary forms of cultural and creative industries and the expanding roles which they perform in an increasing number of countries.

As the discipline expands, there is a pressing a need to disseminate academic research, and this series provides a platform to publish this research, setting the agenda of cultural and creative industries from a managerial perspective, as an academic discipline.

The aim is to chart developments in contemporary cultural and creative industries thinking around the world, with a view to shaping future agendas reflecting the expanding significance of the cultural and creative industries in a globalized world.

Published titles in this series include:

Arts Governance
People, Passion, Performance
Ruth Rentschler

Building Better Arts Facilities
Lessons from a U.S. National Study
Joanna Woronkowicz, D. Carroll Joynes, and Norman M. Bradburn

Artistic Interventions in Organizations
Research, Theory and Practice
Edited by Ulla Johannson Sköldberg, Jill Woodilla and Ariane Berthoin Antal

Rethinking Strategy for Creative Industries
Innovation and Interaction
Milan Todorovic with Ali Bakir

Performing Arts Center Management
Edited by Patricia Dewey Lambert and Robyn Williams

Arts and Business
Building a Common Ground for Understanding Society
Edited by Elena Raviola and Peter Zackariasson

Arts and Business

Building a Common Ground for Understanding Society

Edited by Elena Raviola and
Peter Zackariasson

LONDON AND NEW YORK

First published 2017 by Routledge

2 Park Square, Milton Park, Abingdon, Oxfordshire OX14 4RN
711 Third Avenue, New York, NY 10017

Routledge is an imprint of the Taylor & Francis Group, an informa business

First issued in paperback 2018

Library of Congress Cataloging-in-Publication Data
Names: Raviola, Elena, editor. | Zackariasson, Peter, 1972– editor.
Title: Arts and business : building a common ground for understanding
    society / edited by Elena Raviola and Peter Zackariasson.
Description: New York : Routledge, 2016. | Includes bibliographical
    references and index.
Identifiers: LCCN 2016014006 | ISBN 9781138887442 (cloth :
    alk. paper) | ISBN 9781315714110 (ebook)
Subjects: LCSH: Art and business.
Classification: LCC N72.B87 A79 2016 | DDC 701/.03—dc23
LC record available at http://lccn.loc.gov/2016014006

ISBN: 978-1-138-88744-2 (hbk)
ISBN: 978-1-138-61685-1 (pbk)

Typeset in Sabon
by Apex CoVantage, LLC

The Editors would like to acknowledge and sincerely thank the donation
of Torsten Söderberg Foundation, which financed Elena Raviola's editorial
work for this volume.

Contents

Images

Introduction

Elena Raviola and Peter Zackariasson

The Idea

Arts and commerce is what this book promises a common ground for. A ground for scholarly conversation between the field of the arts and the field of business studies about contemporary societal issues. Far from the desire to appropriate a territory in one way or the other, our approach is rather directed towards the framing of a space for trading and forming ideas in peer relationships.

The idea of business and the arts coming together is in many ways not new, neither in practice nor in academia, as many of the authors in this volume remind us. In business practice, designers have been used in organizations in different ways, from working on advertising to designing products and organizational charts, at least since the beginning of the 20th century (Czarniawska, 2016; Johansson-Sköldberg et al., 2016). Not alien to new public management, a lot of attempts have been made to put business thinking into the art world (see, for example, the emergence of cultural management and cultural entrepreneurship as new areas of practice). In academia, ideas bringing arts and humanities into business research and education (e.g., Strati, 1992; Czarniawska and Guillet de Monthoux, 1994;Czarniawska, 1997; Hatch, 1998; Guillet de Monthoux, 2004; Adler, 2006; Czarniawska and Gagliardi, 2006; Barry and Meisiek, 2010) have been discussed for quite a while, with a recent acceleration due to the publication of the Carnegie report on the future of education (see Statler and Guillet de Monthoux, 2015; Steyaert et al., 2016).

In many ways, the project of this book is enormously indebted to these discussions and positions itself in close relationship with them. In one way, however, it attempts to open a new path and thus to contribute originally to these discussions. Its main goal is, in fact, to construct a space for the development of an academic conversation between the disciplines of business and the arts on even grounds.

Developing the Idea Into an Edited Book

It was in Iceland that we started thinking about this project. In August 2013, at the biannual conference of the Nordic Academy of Management, then held in Reykjavik, we organized a track called "Changing practiced of cultural industries: exploring the grey zone between culture & commerce". We not always easy nor probably successfully, we have tried to move away from the "taking without giving" (Brown, 2016: 148) that often characterizes the disciplinary approach. When arts and business come to discuss on even grounds, we have seen that the common roots come across and disciplinary boundaries disappear in favour of the interest for the topic at hand.

Thirdly, the chapters present a wide variation in terms of format. While some of them seem to be a traditional text, others experiment with the idea of dialogue and boundaries between disciplines. In several chapters, the dialogues are staged with a reference to theatre in a more or less explicit way. We think this is a very interesting development in the common land of business and the arts, and we hope that textual and other experiments will continue beyond this volume.

Structuring and Reading the Book

We have structured them in five sections: Arts and Business; Organizing Collaboration; Performing Values; Leadership and Power; Learning, Knowledge and Thinking. Each section includes conceptual, experience-based and case-based chapters and is preceded by a short introduction to the theme of the section as well as to the chapters included.

These sections are our suggestion for reading the contributions to this volume. However, as mentioned earlier, there is no grand narrative throughout all the chapters and discussions develop widely across chapters and sections, while some of them are unique for each chapter. It is thus left to the reader to read this book however she or he pleases and finds most convenient.

References

Adler, Nancy (2006). The arts & leadership: Now that we can do anything, what will we do? *Academy of Management Learning & Education*, 5(4):486–499.

Barry, Dave and Meisiek, Stefan (2010). Seeing more and seeing differently: Sensemaking, mindfulness, and the workarts. *Organization Studies*, 31(11):1505–1530.

Brown, Steven D. (2016). They have escaped the weight of darkness: The problem space of Michel Serres, in: Chris Steyaert, Beyes, Timon and Martin Parker (eds.). *The Routledge Companion to Reinventing Management Education*, pp. 144–160. New York: Routledge.

Czarniawska, Barbara (1997). *Narrating the Organization: Dramas of Institutional Identity*. Chicago: University of Chicago Press.

Czarniawska, Barbara (2016). Postlude, in: Ulla Johansson Sköldberg, Woodilla, Jill and Ariane Berthoin Antal (eds.). *Artistic Interventions in Organizations: Research, Theory and Practice*, pp: 250–252 New York: Routledge.

Czarniawska, Barbara and Guillet de Monthoux, Pierre (1994). *Good Novels, Better Management: Reading Organizational Realities*. Chur: Harwood Academic Publishers.

Gagliardi, Pasquale and Czarniawska, Barbara (Eds.) (2006). *Management Education and Humanities*. Cheltenham, UK: Edward Elgar.

Galison, Peter (2010). Trading with the Enemy, in: Michael E. Gorman (ed.). *Trading Zones and Interactional Expertise*, pp: 25–52. Cambridge: MIT Press.

Gherardi, Silvia and Nicolini, Davide (2005). Actors-Networks: Ecology and Entrepreneurs, in: Barbara Czarniawska and Tor Herner (eds.). *Actor-Network Theory and Organizing*, pp. 285–306. Malmö: Liber/CBS.

Gorman, Michael E. (2010). *Trading Zones and Interactional Expertise*. Cambridge: MIT Press.

Guillet de Monthoux, P. (2004) *The art firm: Aesthetic management and metaphysical marketing*. Stanford, CA: Stanford University Press.

Helin, Jenny (2015). Wiring process after reading Bakhtin: From theorized plots to unfinalizable "Living" events. *Journal of Management Inquiry*, 24(2):174–185.

Hatch, Mary Jo (1998). Jazz as a metaphor for organizing in the 21st century. *Organization Studies*, 5:556–558.

Johansson-Sköldberg, U., Woodilla, J. and Berthoin Antal, A. (2016) *Artistic Interventions iN Organizations. Research, theory and practice*. New York and London: Routledge.

Statler, Matt and Guillet de Monthoux, Pierre (2015). Humanities and arts in management education: The emerging Carnegie paradigm. *Journal of Management Education*, 39(1):3–15.

Steyaert, Chris, Beyes, Timon and Parker, Martin (2016). *The Routledge Companion to Reinventing Management Education*. New York: Routledge.

Strati, Antonio (1992). Aesthetic understanding of organizational life. *Academy of Management Review*, 17(3):568–581.

About the Editors

Elena Raviola is an Associate Professor at the School of Business, Economics and Law, University of Gothenburg, and works also in the Department of Organization at Copenhagen Business School. Her research focuses on cultural industries, with particular interest in news organizations and the transformation of news production and journalism in relation to digitization. She is particularly interested in the relationship between management and other logics, like journalism and culture. She has conducted ethnographic studies in several news organizations in Italy, Sweden and France. Her research has been published in *Organization Studies*, the *Journal of Change Management*, *Information, Communication and Society*, the *Journal of Media Business Studies* and the *International Journal of Media Management*, as well as in several edited volumes.

Peter Zackariasson is an Associate Professor in Marketing at the University of Gothenburg, School of Business, Economics and Law. Since 2001, he has studied cultural industries and their production and consumption. The results of this research have been published in international journals and books.

About the Contributors

Ester Barinaga is a Professor of Social Entrepreneurship in the Department of Management, Politics and Philosophy at Copenhagen Business School. She has published articles in *Geoforum, Human Relations, Ethnicities* and the *Journal of Social Entrepreneurship*. Her latest books are *Social Entrepreneurship: Cases and Concepts* (2014) and *Betongen berättar: Handbok för muralaktivister* (2015). Her work focuses on concepts and strategies that may help us better design organizations aiming at social change in general and the dissolution of the immigrant condition in particular. In 2010, Ester founded *Förorten i Centrum*, a venture based in Stockholm that uses collective mural art to empower communities burdened by stigmatization.

Aleksandra Bida has a PhD in communication and culture from the joint programme at Ryerson and York Universities in Toronto, Canada. Her research looks at the concept of value in late capitalism in an increasingly global and digital age, primarily through the lens of contemporary film and literature. She currently teaches in the Department of English at Ryerson.

Nina Bozic Yams is a PhD student in Innovation and Design at the School for Innovation, Design and Engineering, Mälardalen University, Eskilstuna, Sweden. Her research focuses on exploring how knowledge and methods from contemporary dance practice can be applied in organizations to enable innovation. Her research and teaching are influenced by her experience in both dance and business and her belief in emergent, people-driven processes. Prior to her PhD studies, she worked as a manager, consultant and trainer in the areas of management, creativity, innovation and entrepreneurship in both the public and private sectors.

Dorina Coste has had a long career in enterprise as designer and is currently at the origin of graphic design courses in school, which was her research field for a PhD in sociology obtained at Paris 1 Panthéon-Sorbonne in 2012. Her research continues focusing on students' perceptions as to ethical issues through graphic arts.

Ravi Dar is a lecturer in informatics and a scholar of business studies at Uppsala University in Sweden. His area of interest has circled around management and organizational aspects of information technology. His recent research is focused on valuation processes of information technology 'solutions' within different contexts.

Daniel Ericsson received his PhD from the Stockholm School of Economics and is now an associate professor at Linnaéus University. He is particularly interested in understanding how creativity is constructed and organized in society and in different ways of rewriting management.

Magnus Eriksson is Senior Lecturer in the artistic basis of creative writing at Linnaéus University, where he mainly focuses on critical and essayistic writing.

Marianela Fornerino obtained a PhD degree from the University of Grenoble in 1982. She teaches in the fields of marketing, market research and consumer behavior. She publishes in the areas of experiential marketing, brand management and new product management.

Pierre Guillet de Monthoux is a Professor of Philosophy and Management at Copenhagen Business School (CBS) and a guest professor at the Center for Art Business and Culture at the Stockholm School of Economics. He is also the director of CBS Art Initiative. He is currently engaged in integrating art and aesthetics as a critical resource in management education and research. He sees art as the main gateway to philosophizing about action and enterprise in the mood of speculative realism and continental philosophy. Art is about Reality!

Kent Hansen's work highlights the operative value of the object status that comes out of the tradition of monochromatic painting. In conceiving the art object and media as working artefacts, he is coining the critical potentials of collective production.

Since 1998, he has initiatied and facilitated projects, cross-sector collaborations and public debates in the interplay between visual fine art and organizations. He has at times been affiliated with the Centre for Art and Leadership and Department of Management, Politics and Philosophy, Copenhagen Business School, Denmark on the Danish Art Council's grant for 'artists as visiting professors'.

Tracy Harwood is a Senior Research Fellow at the Institute of Creative Technologies. Her research focuses on consumer behaviour/technology/usability in emerging contexts, including virtual/augmented and online environments.

Elisabeth Helldorff is a PhD student in cultural management at the University of Hildesheim and the School of Design Thinking, Hasso Plattner Institute Potsdam, Germany. She grew up in a family which placed importance both on fine arts and techniques. Even though she put her focus on becoming a professional cellist, she never lost interest in how to implement artistic thinking in non-artistic areas. Her profession turned out to be one of a business coach for artistic and design thinking. Since 2010, she has been the head of Schwarz+Weiss, a consultancy with a focus on arts-based trainings and artistic interventions.

Maeve Houlihan is a Senior Lecturer in work and organizational behaviour at UCD Business, University College Dublin, Ireland, and a long-standing contributor to the UCD MA in Cultural Policy and Arts Management. She completed her PhD at Lancaster University Management School, published in journals including *Work, Employment and Society*, *Work and Occupations* and the *Journal of Business Ethics* and is a joint editor of *Searching for the Human in HRM* (Palgrave 2007) and *Work Matters* (Palgrave, 2009). Maeve is currently a Vice Principal for Teaching and Learning at UCD Business.

Katja Lindqvist, PhD, is a Reader (Associate Professor) in the Department of Service Management and Service Studies, Lund University. She conducts research on art management, art entrepreneurship and governance of the arts and culture and publishes in international, high-ranked journals. She cooperates with government agencies at the national, regional and local levels in Sweden regarding cultural policy evaluation. She was a co-founder of the master's programme Curating Art at Stockholm University in 2003.

Michael MacDonnell is the former Dean and Director of the Quinn School of Business at University College Dublin. The Quinn School of Business is the leading undergraduate business school in Ireland. It combines the excitement of university life with one of the most progressive education programmes in the world. The school is also the only Irish school to hold both the AACSB (International) accreditation and the top European accreditation, EQUIS.

Michael is an experienced manager in both academia and industry and has published widely in the fields of supply chain management and inventory control.

Philippe Mairesse, artist and researcher, wrote a PhD on the sharing of speech in organization as an aesthetic and political experience. A long-time professional in introducing new forms of art interventions within organizations, he is actively involved in international research projects on how art can help think and act organizational mutations. He currently leads an experimental and research program for Paris Dauphine University about rethinking management and accounting pedagogy based on art and art making.

Kerry McCall is Director of Academic Affairs in Uversity, Dublin. She specializes in teaching arts and cultural management and has been a Lecturer in the Institute of Art and Design, Dun Laoghaire, University College, Dublin, Queen's University Belfast and is Affiliate Faculty, LEAP Institute for the Arts at Colorado State University, USA. Kerry is a founding editor of the *Irish Journal of Arts Management and Cultural Policy* and co-founder of Cultural Policy Observatory Ireland: an all island research network. With colleagues in the USA and Germany, Kerry coordinates the Arts Management Studies Research Stream (RS01) of the European Sociological Association.

Alison Minkus first trained as a concert pianist and collaborative artist, completing a BMus in piano performance. She then completed the MBA program in international business followed by the PhD in organizational analysis at the University of Alberta. Her current research draws from institutional theory, with a focus on both artistic and historical contexts, including maintenance and disruption at the New York Philharmonic Orchestra, art programs of the Canadian Pacific Railway in the late 19th century and the impact of power and influence of the Medici banking family in 17th-century Florence.

Isabelle Né has had the opportunity to work in many different organizations, both in France or abroad. This experience was the basis for her DBA (Grenoble Ecole de Management, 2011) on the topic of management relationship efficacy *versus* the corporate culture. She continues her research on discrimination and careers, as well as on humor at work.

Janina Panizza has worked as a professional in the performing arts industry for over thirty years. Her experiences include involvement in the successful delivery of globally recognized events such as the *Lord of the Rings* premieres to national and international tours by the New Zealand Symphony Orchestra and from one-man shows to stadium performances.

Andrew Power is the Head of the Faculty of Film, Arts and Creative Technologies at the Institute of Art Design and Technology (IADT). IADT is the leading Irish educator for the cultural, digital media and film sectors. The faculty is focused on creating a rich interdisciplinary environment drawing on the strengths and synergies of these fields and growing a research culture in both traditional and practice-based subject areas.

Andrew is an active researcher and has authored or co-authored three books, seven book chapters and numerous articles in the last four years.

Chloe Preece is a Lecturer in Marketing at Royal Holloway, University of London. Her research is in the field of marketing, specifically marketing within the arts and creative industries. To date, this research has focused on production and consumption issues in the visual arts and how this translates into social, cultural and economic value.

Pauline Quantin graduated both from Sciences Po Paris and from Master 2 "Cultural Management in Europe" of l'Institut d'études européennes (Paris 8 Saint-Denis).
   She worked in cultural structures such as the Théâtre de Chelles to reinforce the links with the audience. Then she was in charge of the contemporary circus companies Circo Aereo and the association W for their administration and their diffusion on a national and international scale. In 2008, she co-founded the mixed-arts festival Brise-Glace in Reims. From 2009–2010, she was commissioned by the city of Reims to imagine and implement the prefiguration of the "Seamtress" (la Fileuse- Friche artistique de Reims), an ex-factory for artists to work at. She was the head of that structure from 2012 to 2015. Today, she lives in Tours, and she is still active in bringing culture and society together.

Emilie Reinhold, PhD in management studies (Paris-Dauphine 2014), is a Franco-Swedish researcher based at the interdisciplinary research center GRI, Göteborg and at Stockholm Business School. She is concerned with the aesthetics of the organization and its link to ethics and politics. Her PhD was about dancers doing an intervention in an investment bank, interrupting the share of the sensible through the exposure of their bodies and the difficult solicitation of participants. To overcome her passion for contemporary artists and her love/hate relationship with Italy, she is currently working on an essay about the body's economy.

Elen Riot works as an ethnographer in the laboratoire REGARDS. She is mostly interested in the role of art, artists and artistic work in society. This social role of art leads her to study various fields where art is especially present as a frame for actions and representations such as business organizations.

Dr. Kahena Sanaâ, PhD in visual arts and aesthetics (La Sorbonne Paris 2015), is an active member of *Laboratoire du geste*, a platform for experimental practices and theoretical reflections about live arts and performance. She is also a member of the ESPAS team at Paris 1 University. Her thesis is called "*Déplacement, emplacement, replacement. Poïétiques visuelles du corps urbain*". She investigates how the foreign artistic subject succeeds in taking a 'place' in his/her immediate urban environment, taking into consideration the relation between performance as an act of presence and its visual and audio recording as a postponed act.

Pamela Schultz Nybacka holds a PhD in business studies from Stockholm University and is a Senior Lecturer at Södertörn University. Since her thesis "*Bookonomy. The Consumption Practice and Value of Book Reading*" (2011), she has explored topics of organizing art in public spaces, libraries and the intersection of popular literature and consumer culture. She is the head of the Cultural Management programme at Södertörn University, and of courses in Publishing Studies and Art Management in the international Curating Art master programme at Stockholm University. She is currently working with the research project "Brands resonating co-authors" funded by the Foundation for Baltic and East European Studies.

Claudia Schnugg is curating, producing and researching in the field of art and science collaborations in the transdisciplinary field of art, technology and society as the head of the Ars Electronica Residency Network. She holds a PhD in social and economic sciences from the University of Linz. Her doctoral dissertation was conceptualized as an interdisciplinary at Johannes Kepler University, Linz, and the University of Art and Design, Linz. Before she started working at the Ars Electronica Futurelab, she worked as an assistant professor at Johannes Kepler University, Linz, and as a visiting researcher at the Copenhagen Business School.

Yuliya Shymko is an Assistant Professor of Strategy and International Management in Vlerick Business School (Belgium) and a visiting professor of sociology at IE University (Spain). She has a helpful mix of academic and managerial backgrounds. Trained as an economist with the specialization in international relations, she has also dedicated her time to research the socio-political and cultural reality of post-Soviet republics in affiliation with the University of Alberta (Canada). Her current academic interests include the application of feminist theories to business ethics, corporate philanthropy in cultural industries, and organizational justice.

Sophy Smith is a Reader at the Institute of Creative Technologies, De Montfort University, where her research focuses on creative collaboration, primarily in relation to professional arts practice and social media. She is the co-director of the live art company Assault Events.

David Stewart is a Senior Lecturer in the School of Management, Victoria University of Wellington. He is a co-author of *The Marketing Pathfinder* and has published in numerous journals. He has also conducted courses for Saatchi & Saatchi, Ogilvy and Mather and Television New Zealand.

Anke Strauß is a researcher at the European University Viadrina. She is interested in relationships between the art and the business sphere. After her PhD at the University of Essex, she worked at the WZB Berlin Social

Science Centre. Here she researched processes and dynamics of artistic interventions in organizations and issues of evaluating such initiatives, as well as intermediaries at work. Her book on the concept of dialogue between art and business is in preparation. Together with performance artist Christina Ciupke, she is currently working on artist-run organizations and the performativity of utopian thinking for (re-)organizing cultural labor.

Victoria Vesna is an Artist and Professor at the UCLA Department of Design Media Arts and is the Director of the UCLA Art|Sci center and a Visiting Professor at the University of Tsukuba, Japan. With her installations, she investigates how communication technologies affect collective behavior and perceptions of identity shift in relation to scientific innovation (PhD, University of Wales, 2000). Her work involves long-term collaborations with composers, nano-scientists, neuroscientists and evolutionary biologists and she brings this experience to students. Victoria has exhibited her work in 20+ solo exhibitions, 70+ group shows, has been published in 20+ papers and gave 100+ invited talks in the last decade.

Section I

The Arts and Business
Contemporary and Historical Dialogues

The first section is about the definition of the arts and business and their relationship. Of the three chapters included in this section, the first two offer contemporary views and present the format of dialogues between the authors. The last one builds on a historical perspective to then analyze a recently developed art form and is shaped around one unified voice summarizing both sides of the dialogue.

The opening chapter takes us through the dialogue between the business scholar **Pierre Guillet de Monthoux** and the artist and researcher **Philippe Mairesse**. Their 15-year history of common interactions and their common interests in the arts and organization shape this to be a dialogue between peers without disciplinary belonging, taking at times unexpected routes, deeply engaging in understanding the other's view and experience. We wanted to open this edited volume with this chapter for two reasons. First of all, it raises issues that come back in many following chapters and that are at the heart of our idea, such as research and art, aesthetics, organization, being critical, using arts in business education. Secondly, in a way it represents the shape of the trading zone that has emerged in this volume: a messy, somewhat loud, undefined but very engaged and open conversation between researchers that formally happen to belong to different disciplines.

In the second chapter, the critical management scholar **Daniel Ericsson** and the literary critic **Magnus Eriksson** focus on question of 'being critical' and offer a partially different answer to this question than Pierre Guillet de Monthoux and Philippe Mairesse developed in the previous chapter. They depart from the impression that these traditions are very different, yet are not convinced of their opposition. Their well-reasoned and engaged dialogue takes them to discuss issues such as loyalty and disloyalty to interpretation and emancipation as central ideas of being critical in their respective fields, the relationship between author and text and the relationship between theory and interpretation or understanding. In a very interesting and honest way, this dialogue leads them to conclude that the two traditions offer two incommensurable perspectives on what it means to be critical.

The third chapter, by business scholar **Claudia Schnugg** and media artist **Victoria Vesna**, takes up the question of what art is and what relationship it has with business and technology. Claudia Schnugg and Victoria Vesna dig into art history to argue that the definition of art has always been related to the form and state of economy in the contemporary society of the time. A very important point they make for purpose of our project is that the conception of l'art pour l'art, which is the basis for the autonomy of art, is a modernist idea, defined in time and space and not at all universal nor eternal. They then take the recently developed media art as an example in which art, business and technology are entangled from the very definition and emergence of this art form.

1 Aesthetics of Collective Action

Φ and Π in a Twisted Impromptu on Art and Research by Operational Aesthetics

*Pierre Guillet de Monthoux and
Philippe Mairesse*

Philippe ("Φ") is an artist and a researcher both doing and reflecting on artistic interventions in organizations, and Pierre ("Π") is a business researcher fascinated with exploring the role of art and artists in the study of business organizations. Let each of them tell what they do and find out how the two perspectives might interact. This seemed an easy piece, given that both Pierre (Π) and Philippe (Φ) had a fifteen-year history of common interaction. So writing this up seemed such a simple, straightforward thing to do!

In July 2015, we met in the small French village of Gattières. We talked, taped and transcribed the talk that at first glance seemed a pretty smooth exchange between two guys from different corners. Pierre wrote it down but when Philippe got the transcription he responded not by simply editing the dialogue but by taking the whole text, remixing the material in a "meta-letter" and commenting on what he thought we really had been up to in France that summer day. Not only did things that had been luring in an obscure background pop up, making the initial starting points less and less obvious: what you are about to read is no longer a conversational exchange between two given positions. Sometimes the voices are in harmony; sometimes they break off in a new key in an intricate, interactive reshaping of who is an artist engaged in interventionist research and who is a researcher engaged in art-based approaches. Our cooperation blurred the original idea and what we now have, our correspondence, indicates the mysterious things that happen when art opens up to organization research and vice versa. Pierre and Philippe pretended to the editors of this volume, that they would act out a neat conversation between two ideal types: the art and the business scholar. Instead you get an honest and messy account for subjectivation, struggles and deconstructive butchery of neat identities or art, artist, scholarship and research.

Let the curtain rise!

Characters:

Φ (Phi): The artist, Philippe, who for at least fifteen years has been engaged in making art inspired by organizational action research and has recently complied his view on organizational art intervention in a PhD thesis.

Π (Pi): The researcher, Pierre has spent his time as a professor of business philosophy exploring how aesthetics might help grasp the impact and emergence of art in organizational contexts.

of philosophy we use to call aesthetics. If artists are scholars, they are doing aesthetics. Winnicot, from deep inside his psychoanalytical position, develops the meaning of this 'Third Realm' or the 'Zone' very similar to the 'Play Drive' so central to Schiller's classical rendering of the Kantian aesthetics. If you go for Winnicot, I go for Schiller!

Φ to Π: Do you know that the same Schiller is also Rancière's muse, though in a radically different sense? Rancière refers to "Letters on the aesthetic education of man" in order to support his political stance about anybody's equal capacity to see things differently—and to reconfigure the social scenes of power. Seeing differently, seeing more (Barry and Meisiek, 2010)? Or seeing less? The issue is not rhetoric. It is about the operationality of the stranger—'a man without a history' to the members he approaches. Schütz (1944:503) describes "an unconcerned onlooker [willing to] transform into a would-be member of the approached group". More radically, Nietzsche saw the arts as the visionary dancer which could set a new humanity by questioning the taken for granted. The interpretation in organizational research of the artist's position seems rather Nietzschean: a concerned onlooker unwilling to become a member and confronting the strange organizational patterns with curiosity—she deliberately 'stranges' the taken for granted. So we have two visions of the artist-in-the-organizations: on the one hand, a newcomer strives at becoming a member—and by so doing is forced to questions any admitted pattern, his as well as theirs. On the other hand, a visionary has the power to transform routines into strangeness—critical integration or opening through critique? What operates the rapprochement of art and aesthetics with organization, the Schützean desire to belong or the Nietzschean destruction of 'truths'?

Π to Φ: You art scholar artist! So now you toss in Nietzsche, too! I sense that your way of being an artist, of wanting to be an artist/researcher, is closely connected to our suspicion of the hierarchical and management as ways to hierarchize. I remember the fantastic show you put on 2013 in Paris called *Restructuration*, where you injected aesthetics by images and performances into a conference on putting people on the dole. Almost a decade after the Product/Vision exhibition in Berlin, where you emphasized the dyad of artist/consultant, you now declared that you as an artist preferred to work in a triad with artist/consultant/researcher! This to me indicates that artists in a sense are aesthetic researchers, scholars if you want! But what about the Nietzschean innovating artist frightening off his audience by arrogance and irony of the kind dear old Freddy was feared for?

Φ to Π: Fear or care. It was one of the hottest days in Gattières last summer, but your house was cool, and I remember saying, "All this connects to the concept of the disseminated self, a phase where things are both in and out, where things are both given and created. This inner-out experience is a mood that makes it possible to open up the boxes one into another. It is your projection of the world, but as Rancière helps us see, the world is also made by this. So the aesthetic experience of perceiving is also forming the world in that moment".

Π to Φ: Aha, you are really an art(ist) scholar! I had the pleasure of hearing you defend your doctoral thesis "Reversal" (Mairesse, 2014) in a medieval university in the Netherlands. Your thesis accounts for several of your own interventions, and Jacques Rancière is central to your way of conceiving how art and business organizations can open up and pave the way to an acceptance of ambiguity, dissensus and conflict. As one of the external examiners, I asked you how you would design an executive education for managers. What would you like art to contribute to business? And you immediately proposed a pedagogy that makes us accept and live with complexities and ambiguity instead of attempting to find methods that do away with these messy aspects of reality. The world is messy, and this even makes it beautiful. Anyway, that was what you meant in Berlin: "beauty is irregular and asymmetric", you said then! Perfection and equilibrium are not the hallmarks of the aesthetic!

Φ to Π: Right now I don't know: it depends on what you mean by "aesthetics". Apart from aesthetics as the study of forms and their meaning and mutual influences, one way is to consider how 'aesthetic' characterizes the lived experience of the organization members and its embodied quality. Often focused on the central role of the senses for action and decision, it points to a specific form of knowledge called 'sensible knowledge' at the intersection of the body and cognition—you and Strati (Strati and Guillet de Monthoux, 2002) wrote about that. In this perspective, art in organizations is considered as a knowledge and research approach: "imaginative and aesthetic practices as knowledge-producing resources for organizing and social change" (Harter et al. 2008). Another way is proposed by Rancière (2001), who defines another kind of aesthetics: the equally distributed capacity of ordering the world, which he attributes to logos. Any human being, because she is a 'speaking animal', has the power to (re)-order the world by means of thinking, speaking and doing. She can read or invent an order, a reason, a meaning to the disparateness of the world in an aesthetic vision that characterizes the political dimension of Rancière's perspective. 'Aesthetic' here not only comes for 'capacity of ordering by reason' but as esthetical action: Rancière argues that art and artists show the way to a critical re-configuration of any given order, opening the path for a new 'political aesthetics' far from aesthetic as knowledge. Rather than a theory or knowledge, aesthetic practice, typical of modernity, tends towards critically confronting any established given division of things and people.

Π to Φ: The chapter we are supposed to write for this book should be the exchange between art and business scholars, what they can learn from each other. I clearly understand how important the scholarly side is to your own practice as an artist. You share this kind of practical scholarship with other artists who have written academic works rooted in their art. In the field of business and organization, Armin Chodzinski (2007), Henrik Schrat (2010) and Anna Scalfi Enghenter (2014) come to my mind, but I daresay your dissertation addresses the relation between art and researchers in the field of management and organization as the operationality of aesthetics in a very special way. And obviously, Rancière helps you grasping this in a rather original way.

Φ to Π: Rancière thinks this way of confronting social reality is giving way to another worldview he calls the 'aesthetic regime'. In the mimetic world, organization comes first and gives meaning. In the aesthetic regime, according to Rancière, we are in a situation where we can collectively build new orders, where organization does not make sense, meaning or value if you want, but meaning makes organizations. In the first cultural regime, value depends on the faculty of resembling something or someone else; the regime is based on accepting a set of rules and on the exclusion of others models based on different rules. The second aesthetic regime is based on what Rancière calls dissensus. Being different here is what links people through a kind of 'similarity of dissimilarities', an equivalence of orderings typical of the aesthetic regime—and thus is deeply political: aesthetics means the possibility for anyone to re-order any social situation in a different way.

Π to Φ: Can we say that what Rancière helps us discern is a difference between 'culture' and 'aesthetics'? Culture would be more a matter of order and organization, something important to maintain. Culture is based on 'either/or' and hinges on its contrast, namely 'nature'. We study and defend culture by conjuring its opposites, like the 'foreigner' or 'stranger' who in turn will have 'adaption' or 'civilization' as her main ambition if she does not opt for 'resistance' or 'counter-cultures'. Aesthetics, on the other hand, simply 'is'! It is not a phenomenon coming out of conscious organization that can be perfected with the help of social studies of symbolic orders. Such studies, usually labeled 'social science' in its most mainstream rendering, rather block our access to the 'aesthetic', for it is completely dependent on the idea that something can be observed in practice, on one hand, and then generate theory, on the other. Social science is rooted in the representational dichotomy; it is the ideological, or perhaps the liturgical, workshop for 'culture' where organizational instruments are improved and experimented. Am I in tune with what you mean, dear Philippe?

Φ to Π: I completely agree with you, dear Pierre! But there is no pure aesthetic and pure an-aesthetic action: it is a matter of degree. There are plenty of discreet or even invisible ways to do art in society and have a transformative effect on it; some call it 'dark matter' (Sholette, 2011). Jacques Ranciere is of great help reminding us of that fact by making us see aesthetic action as something beyond the opposition between art and business.

Π to Φ: The managers we business scholars attempt to understand might also be of a different kind than the ones organizing the art world. There is actually another French word for manager often forgotten today: cadre. The French word 'cadre' comes from the world of art, for it literally means 'frame'. How does the competence of a 'cadre' differ from that of managers? Maybe a cadre is more like a companion opening up paths to explore with his team rather than a controller organizing the work of others—two references to different kind of artists: the star for the latter, the craftsman for the previous?

Φ to Π: Right, organizing has to be revisited from the aesthetic point of view opened by Rancière. But it is important not again to fall in traps of dualism. There will always be hierarchies and processes of the old kind in both art and business. We can never completely escape culture and the hierarchies, what Ranciere calls the 'police' way of ordering things and imposing power from above. The critical stance in art aims at denouncing these practices, detecting and fighting exploitation and defending the exploited. Utopia is the core of this critical approach, in the tradition of the Marxist critique of capitalism and the socialist utopias, revisited by the contemporary reorientation of critique after its postmodern semi-failure. Common among artists and the art world, this approach fosters a revival of the 'artist critique' (Boltanski and Chiapello, 2005) opposing liberalism and is grounded in the romantic idea of freedom and individual freewill. Both culture and its critique are part and parcel of both art and business. But again, they are in close interaction by being their mutual opposites.

Besides police constraints or utopic resistance, organizing (or re-ordering) by aesthetics indicates a third possible way which connects to Rancière's (2001; 2012) idea of equality of intelligences. To the extent that Rancière's political aesthetics keeps with the tradition of Marxist critique, one could of course debate if he really opens up to a third way or if he actually contributes to a revival of the 'artist critique' by vitalizing the egalitarian assumption. Would the 'third way' only be an escape, what you spotted accurately by suspecting me of "softly annihilating the hierarchies of establishment by simply neglecting them"?

But as we know, Rancière split up early with his philosophy master Louis Althusser and turned to a more anarchist kind of French artistic leftism balancing between freedom and democracy. For Rancière, the aesthetic regime of the arts enacts the effort and realizes the possible re-configuration of the given order by anybody—and in any new one—but already immediately falling into the realm of a new order. Hope and failure in Rancière's work are two faces of the same coin: you cannot choose. Freedom and slavery together resolve in fight, effort and will.

Π to Φ: The first time I met you, in 2005, was at the Product/Vision show we spoke about. Next time we met, you demonstrated the importance you give to materiality in an experiment staged at the European Academy of Management conference of 2004 in Oslo on "Managing Human resources in the High Tech Companies". You then staged an experiment in communication by means of microphones and headsets around a large conference table. The technology used had a visual analogue archaic touch that to me was Philippe's slap in the face to the digital electronic culture; the table we sat at was a mess of cables, old-fashioned headsets and clumsy microphones and looked like some strange installation with hidden references to Jules Verne's mechanical fantasies and Stanley Milgram's[1] classical laboratory equipment. We were all struck by the aesthetic appeal of the settings. At the *Art and Restructuration* arts-conference show in Paris, you directed a two-day event where the visual and material were mixed and blended with texts written by business scholars. Your aim was to help the 'visualization' of the sociological research in the shape of an art show with seminars included.

Your visual and performance art is integrated in your scholarship. Like Bruno Latour, Francois Lyotard or Paul Virilio, you are engaged in curating art shows as a deeper necessity to work with art, like Andy Warhol and Michelangelo Pistoletto, both participants in the pop art movement, who had their training, not in art, but in advertising and marketing. Carsten Höller is a trained biologist and you are a telecom engineer.

Φ to Π: With my background as a telecommunications engineer, my main interest is not so much action as inter-action. I go to organizations, for I am interested in facing the fact that value is created in interaction and not by individual purely idealistic action. I act in the intersection of individual action and collective value making. That is how I got hooked on the theme of organization. Not art about organization, but art made by organizations, collectives not only of artists, but with business scholars and practitioners as well.

The artistic communication device you just mentioned works as a performance, a group discussion letting anyone's voice into the conversation without permission. The system is based on the principle of "you can choose who you listen to, you cannot choose who you talk to". It was thought of as a way to let people listen to one another, but it revealed that listening is also deeply authoritarian: choosing who is worth listening to and excluding others. What in fact matters is the possibility to listen to a space where the voices of all can be heard simultaneously and separately at the same time. An 'undifferentiated listening', consisting of first an indifference to the loudest voices trying to occult the weak ones, then in an equally differentiated attention to every single voice in the hubbub. Learning to listen in this equally differentiated way appears to be the main lesson art can bring into organizing, and into research as well, where the rule is to listen only to the 'bests': non-hierarchical but not anarchy, not a dis-organizing and not a re-organizing, a third way toward transformative action.

Π to Φ: So when you enter a business firm and make your Access Local performance as a consultant in a client company, you intervene by injecting aesthetic organizing in a social organization already subject to cultural and industrial methods of organization. They already have techniques and instruments of organizing, but now you offer them something else: aesthetic transformation. I feel this is happening when you set up your conference table and have people play with this intricate communication machine or when you subsequently cut up their transcribed conversations and rearrange them as lettrist collages on the walls of the firm. Is that how you provide solutions to their managerial problems?

Φ to Π: In practice, it is never as clear. The client firms usually have an 'organization' that works on a functional level: they produce and sell and have money to hire me, for instance. So you have to dive in to find the detailed problems they spur when contacting you. Like a physiological therapist, I try to find the fossilized spot in the organization. But I do not work on this spot as would a doctor or physiotherapist. That is what normal consultants do. They spot the deadlocks of organizing, and then they work on it. I rather go for what works, what is healthy, and I do NOT dwell on what does not work. Let us go ahead doing what works and try to circumnavigate your bottleneck and enter the sound living places of your organization, avoiding directly confronting the ill spots.

It is not a question of despising and ignoring the bottlenecks and focusing on 'positive thinking' or actions. The idea is that, like a painter, you can deal with painful issues without 'curing' them. How a painter would 'cure' the edge issue? When you think of it, dealing with the edge is not easy: is your painting limited to the inside of the canvas? If so, where does the 'inside' start? If the edge is already the core of your painting, why paint the middle? Why not paint outside the canvas, directly on the walls, or paint 'all over' (a painting style initiated by Pollock)? Painters deal with this difficult and classical issue by . . . painting, and inventing a way to paint: they draw on their resources and knowledge and circumscribe the issue, then propose a kind of 'painting' (organizing their action) which 'solves' the issue, which means they propose a painting where the edge issue is changed (and may become a dripping issue or an abstraction issue).

It suggests an active way to do art-in-organizations, leaving critique and instead turning to transformative practices. "[T]there is an urgent need to correct the one-sided emphasis on unmasking, and we can do this by reorienting critique to the practice of individual and social transformation" (Kompridis, 2000) close to the artist's reason to practice his art. "Why should a painter work if he is not transformed by his own painting?" (Foucault, 1984:35). Beyond self's transformation, art proposes new ways for 'inhabiting the world' (Bourriaud, 2002). The 'relational' artists immerse themselves in 'real organizational life', acting like action-researchers, with the conviction that they can change it more or less deeply.

Π to Φ: So operational aesthetics is less leaning towards critique or critical management than toward transformative action as basically interaction but with material elements. All is not chitchat, seminars and hot air conversations like the one we're having now. The reason you make collages and performances is to show gained power by concreteness. Your most recent experience teaching business students, more precisely in accounting and finance at the Dauphine University in Paris, seems to provide an example of how this might work. In an intense one-week workshop, you invite them to materialize their favorite themes in accounting in objects. At the end of the week, the objects are presented at an opening in an art space. You told me that you consciously avoided all talk about art. References to art history are taboo. As I understood it, this exercise was much liked by the accounting and finance students. One group focusing on the working of international accounting standards produced a glittering steel sculpture of very sharp and dangerous knives embodying the danger, risks and need for careful precision in matters of applying and interpreting financial standards. As a result, students familiar with only discursive textual work found themselves enjoying and engaging in making objects that generated ways of understanding they would otherwise have missed and never discussed. Art worked with the students, too.

Φ to Π: And in doing such things together, we experience how the material and the symbolic work together in unpredictable ways. Doing art like that would constitute an alternative to the dualistic tradition of opposing art as pure aesthetics to art as political critique, or art as knowledge of a superior kind to art as expression and realization of individual freedom: beyond art as wisdom or art as revolution, the third trend proposes art as a transformative practice enabling us to deal with issues we constantly face in organizational situations but try to avoid.

Active, immersed in non-arts organizations and not isolated in the protected areas of the art world, the artist proposes her relational, deconstructionist and paradoxical talents like a consultant, as methods for imagining and creating a different organizing. S/he is an interventionist, convinced that her/his impact onto the host organization will last—the longer the better. The remaining question is, of course: which impact?

The first immediate answer coming to mind is: subversion. Researchers often see art as subverting the organizations by surprise—perhaps because it is what they would love to do? Art-in-organization would be a way to introduce unpredictability, multiplicity, polyphony, heterogeneity, diversity and subvert a system which aims at stabilizing, regulating, controlling and repeating. It would mean a turn in the critical stance: instead of questioning power, it claims to 'forget the power and act'. But such transformative action has to be differentiated from freedom of action. The avant-gardes Dada and Fluxus with the concept of happening in modern art were able to foster the subversive quality of free action because they were independent and opposed to any kind of institution, contrary to art-in-organization, which cannot any more pretend to be subversive in a revolutionary way—like the art-in-org researcher who should forget her dream of subverting or transcending the order.

Rather than sub-vert, con-vert could be the right term, focusing on the idea of change. I am convinced that people can only engage in their work if it is meaningful to them. They can only get there if they can 'invent the job' from the inside. They have to have the freedom space inside the job, be it advanced or just seemingly a task on the conveyer belt. Factory workers can, for instance, talk to you about the 'choreography' of the job as a dance. If people lack aesthetic autonomy, they get depressed and do a bad job. In any activity, you have to be able to activate the level where you reconfigure, reshape, reconsider activities. And for this you need to enable transformative aesthetics, which artist-consultant-resarchers can help with. This is my way of reading and doing Rancière.

Π to Φ: So what became clear to me in our conversation is that we hardly fit the ideal types of artists or researchers. I go on talking to you as 'the artist', which you for good reasons you have here explained that you are a bit reluctant to accept. We are both academicians, we both teach students and you are probably more familiar than I with interacting with people in organizations.

At the same time, we both seem skeptical to compare doing art in organizations to some method of social science. You also refuse to present yourself as a classical artist or engage in cultivated talks on art history with people in organizations. When we have been exchanging philosophical readings and had you not been around I am sure I would not have sensed the practical use and operationality of, say, Jacques Rancière. It is about immerging in an artful practice by refusing any shortcuts via either 'theorizing' or 'historizing'. To me, the accounts of your practice are of great importance signaling such new paths for art and management to interact in the future. The kind of practical, intellectually reflected scholarship you embody anyway makes clear to me that what seems to bring out fascination is something neither sociological nor historical. For it is not by teaching the history of art or inventing new methods that we will perform transformative operational aesthetics. Better look and engage in objects as the one on your invitation to the *Art & Facts* (Mairesse, 2016) show.

Note

1   Stanley Milgram was a psychologist who performed a much-debated spectacular experiment on obedience to authority in the early 1960s.

References

Barry, Daved and Meisiek, Stefan (2010). Seeing more and seeing differently: Sensemaking, mindfulness, and the workarts. *Organization Studies*, 31(11):1505–1530.

Boltanski, L. and Chiapello, E. (2005). *The New Spirit of Capitalism*. London: Verso Books.

Bourriaud, Nicolas (2002). *Relational Aesthetics*. Dijon: Les Presses du réel.

Brellochs, Mari and Schrat Henrik, eds. (2006). *Produkt und Vision, Katalogband*. Berlin: Kadmos Kulturverlag.

Chodzinski, A. (2007). *Kunst und Wirtschaft, Peter Behrens, Emil Rathenau und der dm-drogerie markt*. Berlin: Kulturverlag Kadmos.

Foucault, Michel (1984). What Is Enlightment, in: Rabinov, Paul (ed.). *The Foucault Reader*, pp: 32–50. New York: Pantheon.

Harter, L. M., Leeman, M., Norander, S., Young, S. L. and Rawlins, W. K. (2008). The intermingling of aesthetic sensibilities and instrumental rationalities in a collaborative arts studio. *Management Communication Quarterly*, 21:423–453.

Kompridis, N. (2000). Reorienting critique: From ironist theory to transformative practice. *Philosophy & Social Criticism*, 26:23–47.

Mairesse, P. (2016). Learning by Art-Making: The Inner-Outer Experience: An Experiment within a Master Course in Audit, Control, and Accounting, in: Charles Wankel and Wankel, Laura eds. *Integrating Curricular and Co-Curricular Endeavors to Enhance Student Outcomes*, pp: 67–98New York: Routledge.

Mairesse, P. (2014). *Reversal, le partage de la parole comme expérience sensible, esthétique, et politique*. Paris: Editions Accès Local.

Rancière, J. (2012). *La Méthode de l'égalité, Entretien avec Laurent Jeanpierre et Dork Zabunyan*. Paris: Bayard.

Rancière, J. (2001). *Le Partage du sensible*. Paris: La Fabrique.

Schrat, H. (2010). *Meanwhile . . . Wham!, Comic and Its Communication Value in Organizational Context*. Doctoral dissertation for PhD, University of Essex, UK.

Scalfi Eghenter, A. (2014). *Organization and the Work of Art*. Doctoral dissertation for PhD, University of Essex, UK.

Schütz, Alfred (1944). The stranger: An essay in social psychology. *The American Journal of Sociology*, 49(4):499–507.

Sholette, G. (2011). *Dark Matter: Art and Politics in the Age of Enterprise Culture.* New York: Pluto Press.

Strati, A. and Guillet de Monthoux, P. (2002). Introduction: Organizing aesthetics. *Human Relations*, 55(7):755–766.

Strauss, Anke (2012). *Reseachers, Models and Dancing Itches, Tracing Dialogue between Art and Business*. Doctoral dissertation, University of Essex.

Winnicott, D. W. (1971). *Playing & Reality*. London: Tavistock Institute.

opening
The Master Contrôle Audit Reporting, Parcours 124, University
Paris-Dauphine
presents
in partnership with the National Superior Fine Arts School in
Paris (ENSBA),

ART&FACTS

Friday, September 4th, 2015
4 pm–8 pm

*We're being repeatedly told innovation is the only way out of the
crisis.*
*What about accountants? What kind of innovation? Knowing
how to de-center? Through art?*
Exhibition of artworks created by Paris Dauphine Accounting
master's students and by young artists from the National Fine Art
School in Paris.

2 The Art and Business of 'Being Critical'

Daniel Ericsson and Magnus Eriksson

Introduction

Being critical within academia is a matter of the utmost importance. It could be regarded as the primary means of scientific production as well as a scientific end in itself, but it could also be conceptualized as a necessary scientific condition in the sense that science without it probably would not qualify as science at all. With reference to the institutionalized imperatives Merton (1942/1973) outlined to encircle research, one could even argue that being critical forms a crucial and unescapable part of the modernistic scientific ethos together with other highly valued principles, such as communalism, universalism and disinterestedness.

What it means to be critical, however, does not have a clear-cut answer. Different scholarly traditions embrace different notions of science and consequently uphold different understandings of critique. Within a Mertonian (ibid.) frame of reference, for example, being critical is most often knitted together with scepticism, a rather positivistic mindset implying the pursuit of truth by means of rational reason and doubt, whereas many non-positivists within the social sciences and the humanities endow being critical with emancipatory ideas and ambitions.

'Being critical' (and the meanings attached to it) thus comes in many shapes and colours. It might be a matter of *how* you think or it might be a matter of *what* you think—or it might be a matter of how you think in relation to what you think; it might be a matter without any other cause than itself or it might be a matter with a specific cause; and it might be a matter of epistemology and method or it might be a matter of ontology and theory. The specific shape and colour it acquires depends on the tradition at hand.

In this chapter, two seemingly very different traditions are approached: Critical Management Studies (CMS) and Literary Criticism. Whereas the former addresses managerial practices in everyday life, the latter concentrates upon the interpretation of literary texts. How is 'being critical' construed within these traditions? Are there any differences between the two in terms of agenda and agency?

Critical Management Studies vs. Literary Criticism

To be frank, there is most certainly no chasm between CMS and Literary Criticism. Both traditions are more or less cut from the same cloth of continental philosophy (cf. Marxism, structuralism and post-structuralism). The discursive and narrative turns of the 80s and 90s brought them together in a highly productive manner (cf. Czarniawska, 1999). Within both traditions, 'text' is in focus as the primary empirical material to direct critical attention to, and within both traditions, the same kind of theories are often employed (cf. narratology, genre theory and discourse analysis). This does not mean, however, that there are no differences between the two traditions. Above all, they differ in theoretical agenda, scope and method.

CMS, as outlined by Alvesson and Wilmott (1992), rests firmly on Critical Theory, i.e., the intellectual orientation of the Frankfurt School (cf. Horkheimer and Adorno, 1944/72) and its subsequent followers, such as Habermas (1971) and Bernstein (1976). The overarching agenda of this schooling is emancipation, the freeing of the individual who, enslaved by totalitarian regimes and ideologies, lives in a state of false consciousness. The overarching means to achieve emancipation are on one hand the illumination of societal deficiencies and power asymmetries coupled with the identification of hidden and unrealized potentials, and on the other to engage in 'free dialogue', in which distortive ideas and beliefs are confronted.

Being critical within this frame of reference means to represent "an intellectual counterforce to the ego administration of modern, advanced industrial society" (Alvesson and Wilmott, 1992:9). It means to systematically question what is taken for granted and 'natural' within hegemonic discourse and point to alternative ways of organizing and managing social life, but it also means to give voice to the subaltern.

In comparison with CMS, Literary Criticism is not explicitly oriented towards emancipation. There are no malignant opponents to conquer and there are no imprisoned individuals to set free, even if there still are traces to be found of the romantic idea that certain literature could have an elevating function, taking the reader into a higher state of consciousness, into the sublime. Instead of emancipation, the overarching agenda among literary critics is to describe, interpret and evaluate texts. No more, no less. As for how this is to be done, however, there are different views and opinions (cf. Culler, 1992): Some argue that interpreting a text is a matter of understanding the intention of the writer, some highlight the subjective reader response as the epistemological ground for textual interpretation and yet some interrogates the triptych of author, text and reader in order to understand the meaning horizon of the text at hand.

Perhaps the most influential view within the tradition of Literary Criticism, however, is the one proposed by the New Criticism (cf. Ransom, 1941/1979): The meaning of a text, it is argued, is acquired by a close reading of it in which its content is related to its form and in which great attention is paid to details, such as the choice of ideas, words, syntax, etc. etc.

Within this strand of Literary Criticism, the work of art is considered to be a coherent and autonomous whole, and as such, it is not supposed to be contextualized in relation to the author, readers or society at large.

What follows is a discussion between a scholar working in the field of CMS (Daniel Ericsson, "DE" in the following) and a literary critic (Magnus Eriksson, "ME" in the following) on the idea of 'being critical' and how different notions of 'criticism' are set to work in the two fields.

Loyal and Disloyal Interpretative Strategies in Literary Criticism (ME)

To begin our discussion, I would like to go back to the introduction where we state that "[i]n comparison with CMS, Literary Criticism is not explicitly oriented towards emancipation". The word 'explicitly' suggests that we nevertheless could detect different levels of interpretation, of which some might be considered emancipatory on an implicit level of understanding. This question could thus be posed: does Literary Criticism nurture an idea of social relevance and emancipation, i.e., a utopian idea of interpretation? Not primarily, I would say, although some schools of interpretation no doubt would make such claims.

In Literary Criticism, we can detect two main attitudes to the interpretative methods involved: one that is loyal to the text, and one that is disloyal. The latter attitude draws on the ideas of Marx, Nietzsche and Freud, Paul Ricoeur labeled it 'the school of suspicion'; we could also call it 'the hermeneutics of suspicion' (Ricoeur, 1965). The idea is to read beyond, or beneath (spatial metaphors are recurrent in the description of relations between the text and its different layers of meaning), the text in order to disclose hidden ideas and even hidden agendas.

In this respect, deconstruction might be regarded a radicalization of the tradition, but it also turns the tradition in a new direction. What earlier was considered a methodological issue becomes an ontological one, since deconstruction claims that the authorial intention and control over the text is an illusion. No writer—whether a philosopher, a novelist or an economist—knows all the implications of the text, and they cannot know them since the process of detecting meaning in a text implies both to 'differ' and to 'defer' (Hoy, 1978; Culler, 1982).

Other schools of interpretation claim a loyal attitude, according to which the reader does not have to see through the text. It makes perfect sense just to see the text, but to see it in all its semantic and figurative nuances, in all its layers of meaning, i.e., to see the text as a text in its own right, as a verbal artifact that can be interpreted and understood in the three dimensions of classic hermeneutics: 'intelligendi', 'explixandi' and 'applicandi' (Hoy, 1978). When we read, we reach an immediate understanding of the text, 'intelligendi'. From this we move on to an 'explication du texte', i.e., an analysis of its internal structures in order to form a more precise understanding.

But the hermeneutical object is never fully understood until it has been confronted by the interpreter's own horizon of understanding in an act of 'applicandi', which I in this context prefer to regard a mainly subconscious process; the alternative would be too technical an act, although theological and judicial hermeneutics necessarily deals with 'applicandi' on a practical level, since their task is to apply the sacred text or the law to a problem, a situation or an existential experience.

A central issue in 'loyal' hermeneutics is where we find the norm of interpretation, i.e., how we determine the correct understanding of the text. Before New Criticism, the authorial intention was the norm. But, as the new critics pointed out in the 1920s, we can only reach this through the text. If we have access to external documentation of what the author meant, this can only qualify or disqualify the intention of the text. In the latter case, the only information given by the external documentation is that the author failed to fulfill his intention. Almost parallel to New Criticism, Russian formalism and Czech structuralism worked with analogous presuppositions, although these schools—as well as French structuralism later on—rather dealt with recurring patterns than the uniqueness of the individual literary work (Wellek and Warren, 1949; Erlich, 1980).

During the 1900s, we see a shift from writer to text—and then to reader, even if most reader-response criticism takes refuge in a rather static idea of the text read; the main exceptions would be Norman Holland's (1975) analysis of idiosyncratic readings and Stanley Fish's (1980) pseudo-prophetic fight-song 'Is there a text in this class?'

The general view would in any case be that the aim of Literary Criticism is the interpretation and understanding of the literary work. If we compare this to the procedures of CMS, it is obvious that mainstream Literary Criticism is not a utopian or emancipatory discourse. The main issue was rather to emancipate the text from the author, either as a matter of methodology (New Criticism) or as a matter of ontologic necessity (deconstruction).

In this respect, we could, however, detect a difference between the loyal and disloyal schools of literary interpretation. Where the loyal methodologies focus on the text as a hermeneutical object in its own right, the disloyal attitude might very well harmonize with an idea of interpretation as an emancipatory, critical act. This could be described as a detection of repressive structures as in Freud, or of philosophical and linguistic constraints as in Nietzsche or as emancipation from socio-economic oppression as in Marx. But we could pose the question of whether this should be considered a part of the critical act or a result stemming from it. In any case, a dialogue between Literary Criticism and CMS should rather proceed from the disloyal schools of criticism than from the loyal ones.

Disloyal Loyalty for Emancipation? (DE)

From a CMS perspective, one could indeed say that the tradition is part of the 'hermeneutics of suspicion'. Disloyalty to managerial structures of domination is more or less taken for granted as the primary means to reach emancipation, and as such, it tends to both precede interpretation (as part of a Marxist theoretical pre-understanding of capitalist society) and to be a result from the interpretative act (in terms of the formulation of utopian alternatives). This is not, however, to say that disloyalty necessarily is—or could function as—an eligible bridge between CMS and Literary Criticism. As I see it, there are at least two obstacles to be dealt with before one could arrive at such a conclusion.

The first is to be found in the dilemma that CMS researchers most often face: criticizing existing oppressive management structures, yet at the same time setting out to convince actors within management—who, by theoretical definition, are the beneficiaries of the prevailing system—to bring about the preferable changes. Part of this dilemma is of course pedagogical as well as political and rhetoric in character, but it is also a question of striking a balance between two opposing views on subjectivity and agency. On one hand, actors within the system are seen as ideological 'dopes' who act without any discretion at all, yet on the other, the very same actors are ascribed great agency potentials (at least, once they are emancipated from the ideology keeping them hostages in 'false consciousness').

A common way for CMS scholars to reconcile this opposition is to discriminate between managerial actions and actors, or rather between managerial functions and functionaries, and to stress that it is management (in terms of structured and/or typical managerial practices) and not managers that are under scrutiny (cf. Alvesson and Willmott, 1992). This distinction is especially important to make for the empirically oriented CMS researcher, who out in the field is confronted with actors deeply intertwined with the capitalist system. Not only must the CMS researcher here conduct boundary work in order to chisel out suitable objects of interpretation, i.e., what is to be seen as 'author' and 'text'. In doing this, s/he must also relate to people of flesh and blood who most certainly, due to the very 'false consciousness' of theirs, will object to any disloyal attitudes and biases from the researcher. And to my mind, this is the second obstacle to solely pursuing a disloyal line of inquiry: If loyalty is not paid to the empirical actors, the emancipatory project will fail due to either a lack of empirical access and/or a lack of 'communicative validity'.

The distinction between management and managers thus makes it possible for CMS scholars to be disloyal to management without being disloyal to managers, and as I see it, this is a very important distinction, because without it, CMS research would run the risk of ending up in blaming and shrill polemic (Adler, 2004), lacking in both relevance and support from the people addressed. In other words, unless the disloyalty to the system is coupled with loyalty to the actors of the system, the emancipatory project of the CMS scholars might very well be undermined by negativity (cf. Adler, Forbes and Willmott, 2007).

Literary critics, I guess, do not face empirical challenges like these. The objects of interpretation, and the relation between them, are already given, and they do not have to take their relation to the author into account in the same way as CMS scholars do. For the literary critic, the interpretation of a literary work therefore basically could be seen as a remote activity, whereas CMS scholars, who are forced to engage in a face-to-face interaction with empirical actors, rather engage in proximal acts of interpretation.

It goes without saying that remoteness speaks in favor of disloyalty in the same sense that proximity is biased towards loyalty. But having said this, I find it particularly interesting that emancipation in the realm of Literary Criticism is said to be about emancipating the text from the author. For CMS researchers, I reckon it is the other way round: the manager (i.e., 'the author', as long as s/he is not approached discursively as 'text' to be interpreted) must be freed and dissociated from his/her actions (i.e., 'the text') as well as from their consequences if the proximal acts of interpretation will enable 'real' emancipation. The overarching imperative for the CMS researcher therefore is to be loyal to the author so that the author can become disloyal to the text s/he is producing.

I guess that this kind of 'disloyalty in disguise' is not part of the literary critic's 'hermeneutics of suspicion', but even if the text is emancipated from the author and even if authorial intentions are put within brackets, the literary criticist through her/his interpretation establishes a relation to the author, albeit of a remote and an implicit character. Is this relation characterized by loyality or disloyality? And can it—depending on its characterization—affect, or even undermine, the interpretative acts?

The Rift Between Author and Text: An Ontological Necessity? (ME)

In the critical analysis, I would say that the literary critic does not establish a relation to the author, but rather to the author's work. The relationship you outline between the function and the functionaries in the analysis of a CMS scholar is not directly equivalent to the relation between an author and his work, at least not in the theoretical framework of New Criticism, structuralism or post-structuralism. The object of analysis in CMS seems to be a unity of actor and structure. It is thus context-bound in a way that is more similar to a speech-act analysis than to Literary Criticism.

In another, and perhaps more traditional, critical context, we could, however, argue that a biographical, a psychological or a comparative analysis of literature works within a unified context of author and text, i.e., it interprets the text as a source of information about the author's life or psyche or, in the comparative case, detects a relation between the author's reading and his work.

This praxis was under attack during the 1900s, even if a biographical analysis has its proponents, most notably E.D. Hirsch, Jr. (cf. Hirsch, 1967). A central issue in this criticism has been to determine whether the disrupture of the author-text connection should be regarded a matter of methodological choice or of ontological necessity. Whereas New Criticism claimed that the analysis of the author's intention did not give any information relevant to interpretation, a theorist such as Paul Ricoeur claimed the impossibility of such an analysis. Through the distanciation of the text as meaning from the primary context of the author, it is severed from the primary sources of information, i.e., its reference to the authorial context. The severed text meets the reader as decontextualized meaning. In the reading, a new frame of reference is at work, the reader's horizon of understanding, which gives the text new significance (Ricoeur, 1970).

Conflicts of interpretation can often be analyzed as conflicts between different sets of referential ideas and experience. Thus, there is a conflict between, e.g., a psychoanalytical reading of a text and a social-historical understanding of it. But the same mechanism of distanciation is at work in both cases. The text as meaning is interpreted according to a theory or situated in an intellectual framework chosen by the interpreter, but this choice is always made within the reader's referential context, which never can be identical to the author's context.

A main difference between CMS and Literary Criticism is to be found in this idea of distanciation. Whereas the former is an analytical activity within a common context, the latter, at least if understood according to Ricoeur's idea of the text as radically distanciated from the authorial context, deals with an ontological rift that separates text from author, or 'function' from 'functionary'. The 'face-to-face interaction with empirical actors' rather connects CMS to a speech-act analysis. The actor and analyst share a common context, or a speech act-like situation, in which a critical dialogue might arise.

One parallel in Literary Criticism could be the reviews of new books in daily papers. The reader/reviewer and author seem to have a common frame of reference, at least if they live in the same country and share language. But according to Ricoeur, and also to deconstruction for that matter, this is illusory. Both author and interpreter are idiosyncratic in their understanding of the text, and they can never share a common context. But, in connection to this, one could ask if the CMS supposition of an analysis where the scholar, the agent and the structures form a common frame of reference is in a similar way an illusion, a veil that covers a rift that is as much of an ontological, or analytical, necessity as the rift between text and author in Literary Criticism.

Knitting Text and Author Back Again: An Emancipatory Necessity? (DE)

Many within CMS, especially post-structuralists following disloyal paths of interpretation, would certainly object to non-idiosyncratic interpretations of the relations between reader, text and author, accentuating the incommensurability of contexts and arguing for diversity. However, sticking to the Marxist legacy and embracing Critical Theory's ideas of false consciousness and emancipation, the notion of an illusory common context becomes nothing but an illusion in itself, a mere product of capitalist society. And, as such, it could be understood as a smokescreen designed to obfuscate the inescapable Marxist fact of life, i.e., that we are all slaves to the capitalist mode of production.

Following this materialistic line of thought (cf. Adler et al, 2007, p. 155), post-structuralist-oriented CMS scholars who ground their interpretations ontologically upon a rift between text and author sooner or later need to knit text and author (back) together in order to be able to reach their emancipatory goals. Otherwise, their interpretations risk becoming free-floating intellectual endeavors without any other cause—and context—than itself. In the words of Alvesson and Willmott (1992, p. 18), such " '[s]ociologism' must be resisted in critical management studies. If CT (read: Critical Theory) is to engage in a successful, although 'modest', managerial turn, idealized and abstract models of the good society or ideal communicative action must be confronted and complemented with understandings that are fully attentive to the material and technical organization of modern society".

Is Literary Criticism an example of such 'sociologism'? Indeed, it seems as if one can question the point of pursuing disloyal readings of text detached from the author if there are neither emancipatory ambitions nor any utopian ideals to strive for, and it seems as if one indeed can question the point of explication and/or application in the absence of a commonality between reader and author. Taking the ontological assumption of a rift between text, author and text to the extreme, one could even argue that Literary Criticism seems to lead to a kind of solipsist position from which dialogue seems rather unnecessary, not to say impossible because of incommensurable referential assumptions.

In light of literary critics' canonical readings of canonical texts, solipsism does not, however, seem to be the case. Just as researchers within CMS discriminate between 'good' and 'bad' management, literary critics—especially when it comes to the practice of reviewing books—discriminate between 'good' and 'bad' literature. But how is this done? And—more intriguing—*why* is it done? Isn't the canonical work carried out by literary criticists aiming at improving or altering literary performances? Not even the slightest?

Proponents of CMS do not beat about the bush when it comes to their motives and normative ideals: they want a break with existing oppressive management practices in favor of non-alienating ones. Theoretically as well as ethically, one could thus say that they are biased in their readings and interpretations of management, but this is not to be construed as a 'problem' of epistemology. For the CMS researcher, there are no value-free or objective ways of knowing—and consequently no value-free or objective ways of offering critique. One should, however, argue the proponents of CMS should be aware of their biases and actively reflect upon their critical consequences (cf. Alvesson and Sköldberg, 2000; Johnson and Duberley, 2000).

So, how does a literary criticist know when s/he has produced a good critical interpretation of a text? And what is critical about it?

Theory and Interpretation (ME)

A disloyal reading does not automatically follow from the idea of an onto-logical rift between the author's context and the reader's context, or between author and text. The disloyal reading is a matter of ideological and norma-tive choice, at least in the tradition of a hermeneutics of suspicion. A reading based on the idea of the rift might as well be loyal, although not to a meta-physical idea of authorial intention. The endeavor to detect different layers of meaning available to interpretation can be loyal to the idea of a critical discourse or to the idea of the text as vehicle of meaning and understanding: linguistic, social, psychological or existential.

A critical reading of this kind cannot, of course, be verified in a positiv-ist meaning of the word. But it can be found valid according to criteria based on general and shared ideas in the interpretative community regard-ing the relation between text and interpretation, between textual symbols and strategies and the interpretation's capacity to deepen the understanding of how these work within the text. This kind of interpretation is loyal to the text, not disloyal, since it regards the text in terms of unity, structure and coherence, i.e., it shares the assumptions of New Criticism rather than of deconstruction.

The same goes for the evaluation of a literary work. Its aim is not primar-ily to improve literature. That would be the author's task. Literary Criti-cism, or its reviewing avatar, reads, interprets and evaluates the work of literature. It is an activity directed to existing works, not to the ones that have not yet been written. The latter would be an inappropriate act of liter-ary politics; criticism should not state norms for works to come.

In the process of interpretation, different methodologies could be used. These should be regarded as tools for detecting or supplying meaning in/ to the text, but they are not necessary for interpretation as such. They are connected to different ideas of the text and suppositions of what kinds of meaning it yields to interpretation. A psychoanalytical theory connects the text to subconscious layers of meaning; a social theory connects the text to political and social ideas or structures, just to mention a few possibilities for theory-based interpretation.

In this respect, a Marxist understanding is one interpretation of many. The claim that "the notion of an illusory common context becomes noth-ing but an illusion in itself, a mere product of capitalist society" reflects an attempt to put forward a certain theory as a master theory or a meta-theory which works on a general level which subordinates other theories—or just another instance of the Platonistic tradition of 'the metaphysics of presence'.

Maybe we should regard theory as an umbilical cord. It works in con-necting mother to child, or theory to the interpreted phenomenon, but it might as well be severed in order to reach a certain level of independence. It is nothing wrong with "free-floating intellectual endeavors without any other cause—and context—than itself". Critical discourse could very well be the aim of criticism—if the critic so wishes.

Theory vs. Understanding and Overstanding (DE)

From relativistic and pragmatist positions, paradigmatic accounts on 'what is' and 'what ought to be' of course are troublesome. To refute such accounts in terms of belonging to a master theory of subordination, however, is to somewhat miss the point: CMS scholars working within a Marxist frame of reference *do* follow a master theory. But so do researchers pertaining to a relativist and/or pragmatic paradigm as well. Theirs is just a different master theory cut out of a different paradigmatic cloth.

Notwithstanding these paradigmatic differences between CMS and Literary Criticism, the suggested metaphor of the umbilical cord is an interesting one. It reveals a specific understanding of the relation between theory and the interpreted phenomenon which in turn accommodates a specific take on criticism slightly at odds with the one most often enacted within mainstream CMS. Whereas these researchers stick true to their theoretical heritage and come up with interpretations heavily laden with theory, a literary critic's interpretation seems to be an interpretation that at least to some extent shows independency towards the theoretical context. To be critical within the field of Literary Criticism, one thus seems to exact double disloyalties, towards the text but also towards the theoretical tradition at hand.

Since emancipation most often functions as both theory of interpretation and method within the CMS community, disloyalty towards the theoretical tradition could easily jeopardize the research's emancipatory potential. Criticality within CMS, therefore, has less to do with emancipation from the theoretical traditional. To once again use the metaphor of the umbilical cord metaphor, but alter the homology: if the theoretical tradition is the mother, then the researcher is the child. And it is not necessarily virtuous to cut the cord.

Keeping the cord intact indeed has its advantages: the interpretations are, so to speak, 'pre-validated' by the community and do need to be subjected to the arbitrariness of social 'validation' ex post. In addition, such consensual readings tend to direct attention to—and benefit—the emancipatory actions sought for. On the other hand, a too-strong loyalty with the tradition is an easy target for ideological opponents who criticize CMS for being too political (leftist) and too much of a player-piano kind of instrument. Ontologically as well as epistemologically, such critique certainly is unwarranted, but it can nevertheless confer illegitimate connotations to CMS research.

Another disadvantage of keeping the cord uncut is problems associated with the strength of the tradition's power of thought. A tradition-oriented interpretation could very well result in myopia and self-fulfilling prophecies unless coupled with a self-reflexive stance. In this regard, it might be that literary critics who cut the cord between theory and empirical phenomenon have a greater potential to engage in overstanding as opposed to understanding (cf. Culler, 1992): Instead of asking a text what it (or the theory) insists upon being asked, there is a propensity for asking a text what it (or the theory) resists to being asked.

Standing over the text and tradition in such a critical manner is perhaps a dimension that is somewhat lacking in CMS.

Discussion

We started our discussion from the premise that there 'most certainly' is no huge chasm between CMS and Literary Criticism. The two traditions are not mutually exclusive, as many other scientific disciplines are, in the sense that they both encompass traditions that cut across academic discourses. However, sticking to some of the more vividly embraced ideas in each tradition—'emancipation' within Critical Management Studies and 'hermeneutics of suspicion' within Literary Criticism—two more or less incommensurable distinctions emerge regarding each tradition's notion of what it means to 'be critical'.

The first distinction regards spatial and temporal aspects. Critique within Literary Criticism is construed as a matter of uncovering what is hidden 'here and now', whereas critique within CMS is oriented towards changing and developing the future, once the current state of affairs has been exposed or revealed. To accentuate this difference, one could say that it is a matter of excavation in the present tense vs. progression in the future tense.

Secondly, the two traditions display different kinds of loyalties and disloyalties towards empirical materials on the one hand and theories of interpretation on the other. The emancipatory imperative of CMS necessitates a division between the managerial function and functionaries which in turn necessitates the researcher to employ a 'disloyalty in disguise', and the very same imperative pushes researchers within CMS to pay loyalty to the theoretical tradition. Literary criticists in this regard, not embracing emancipation as an interpretative end, do not need to separate the authors from the authorial function or be loyal to the authors when interpreting texts in the same sense. Critique within the realm of the Literary Critic therefore could be conceptualized as less bounded by empirical and theoretical contexts than within CMS.

Given these differences, the commensurability between the two traditions' takes on criticality indeed could be questioned. 'Being critical' is constructed differently within the two traditions, and the constructions revolve around different assumptions about the world and different ways of knowing. Nevertheless, we acknowledge our discussion as a productive one: we have identified cracks and openings in our respective traditions, and we have capitalized upon these by confronting each other with interpretations and metaphors that are not necessarily part of the discourses we 'normally' engage in. This could, of course, be seen as a critical endeavor, but in order to fully appreciate such criticality, we guess we need to put our paradigmatic controversies within brackets.

References

Adler, P. S. (2004). Skill Trends under Capitalism and the Relations of Production, in: Warhurst, C., I. Grugulis, and E. Keep (eds.). *The Skills That Matter*, pp: 242–260. London. Palgrave.
Adler, P. S., Forbes, L. C. and Willmott, H. (2007). 3 Critical management studies. *The Academy of Management Annals*, 1(1):119–179.Alvesson, M. and Sköldberg, K. (2000). *Reflexive Methodology: New Vistas for Qualitative Research*. London: Sage.
Alvesson, M. and Willmott, H. (1992). *Critical Management Studies*. London: Sage.
Bernstein, R. J. (1976). *The Restructuring of Social and Political Theory*. Oxford: Blackwell.
Culler, J. (1992). In Defence of Overinterpretation, in: S. Collini (ed.). *Interpretation and Overinterpretation*, pp: 109–124.Cambridge: Cambridge University Press.
Culler, J. (1982). *On Deconstruction: Theory and Criticism after Structuralism*. Ithaca: Cornell University Press.
Czarniawska, B. (1999). *Writing Management: Organization Theory as a Literary Genre*. Oxford: Oxford University Press.
Erlich, V. (1980). *Russian Formalism*. The Hague: Mouton.
Fish, S. (1980). *Is There a Text in This Class? The Authority of Interpretive Communities*. Cambridge, MA: Harvard University Press.
Habermas, J. (1971). *Toward a Rational Society*. London: Heinemann.
Hirsch, Jr., E. D. (1967). *The Validity of Interpretation*. New Haven: Yale University Press.
Holland, N. (1975). *Five Readers' Reading*. New Haven & London: Yale University Press.
Horkheimer, M. and Adorno, T. (1944/1972) *The Dialectic of Enlightenment*. London: Verso.
Hoy, D. C. (1978). *The Critical Circle: Literature and History in Contemporary Hermeneutics*. Berkeley, CA: University of California Press.
Johnson, P. and Duberley, J. (2000). *Understanding Management Research: An Introduction to Epistemology*. London: Sage.
Merton, R. K. (1942/1973). *The Sociology of Science: Theoretical and Empirical Investigations*, Chicago: University of Chicago Press.
Ransom, J. C. (1941/1979). *The New Criticism*. Westport: Greenwood Press.
Ricoeur, P. (1965). Qu'est-ce qu'un Texte? Expliquer et comprendre, in Rüdiger Bubner (ed.) *Hermeneutik und Dialektik*, II, pp: 181–200.Tübingen: J. C. B. Mohr.
Ricoeur, P. (1965). *De l'interprétation: essai sur Freud*. Paris: Le Seuil. English translation *Freud and Philosophy: An Essay on Interpretation*, 1970b. New Haven: Yale University Press.
Wellek, R. and Warren, A. (1949). *Theory of Literature*. New York: Harcourt.

3 Media Art in the Context of Art, Science and the Market

A Historical Perspective

Claudia Schnugg and Victoria Vesna

From a historical perspective on how art and business as well as art and technology are related, we discuss art in relation to business and show the potential of how the interplay of seemingly unrelated fields can trigger social, technological and economic development and innovation. After starting off with a historical perspective on how art is and has been conceived over time in both the art world and the economic world, we will then use media arts as an example of the relation between art conception and economy.

Recently, there has been a proliferation of management and organization studies on how artists work, create and intervene in business organizations (e.g., Berthoin-Antal, 2009; Taylor and Ladkin, 2009; Barry and Meisiek, 2010; Schnugg, 2010, 2014; Schiuma, 2011;). Although bringing art and artists into organizations might seem like a new thing, it has actually a long history. For example, in 1907, German machinery and appliances manufacturer AEG appointed the renowned artist and architect Peter Behrens as its artistic advisor (Chodzinski, 2007). Similarly, at AT&T, the potential of exploring technology through pairing engineers with artists was explored. Artists like John Cage, Lucinda Childs and Robert Rauschenberg worked together with engineers like Billie Kluver from the Bell Telephone Laboratories. From this, in the mid-1960s, Experiments in Art and Technology emerged where art and technology should create input for each other (Shanken, 2002). This movement was also recognized within the artistic community, and in 1968, the Los Angeles County Museum of Art started the Art & Technology Program, which enabled pairings of artists like Andy Warhol and James Turrell with Californian organizations like Walt Disney, the RAND Corporation and psychologists working for NASA missions. In this tradition of experimenting with art and technology, an artistic residency program named PAIR (the Xerox PARC Art in-Residence program) was run during the 1990s (Gold, 1999). Moreover, diverse art movements triggered initiatives where artists and business organizations mingled: in 1966, British artists John Latham and Barbara Steveni pioneered a new approach by bringing fine arts instead of applied arts (or design) into organizations by founding the Artist Placement Group, which arranged artist-in-residence programs in industrial and governmental organizations in order to explore the potentials for cross-fertilization (Slater, 2000). This also triggered scholarly interest in this topic: in 1978, Scotese published an article claiming that managers could gain three 'obvious benefits' from closer contact with the arts: 1) due to artists' sensitivity to societal trends, artworks serve as 'a window to the future'; 2) art experience heightens aesthetic sensibility and, in turn, perceptive, expressive and creative skills; and 3) through the experience of art, managers can improve their own sensitivity for societal trends (Scotese, 1978). Similarly, the *Buchberger Kunstgespräche*, a pioneering arts and cultural studies conference in Austria in 1986, addressed the potential of art in management (Haschek, 1986). Picking up one of these dimensions, academic management research firstly turned to the aesthetic dimension of management and organization. Building on social constructionism and research in organizational culture, scholars began exploring how individuals' perceptions of an organization's physical manifestations (e.g., rituals and artifacts) informs sense making in organizations. The 1985 Standing Conference of Organizational Symbolism marked the beginning of organizational aesthetics as a legitimate field (Strati, 2009).

We want to look at art from a historical and theoretical perspective to reflect upon these proposed functions. These functions span from bringing in artistic perspectives (e.g., Barry and Meisik, 2010, who frame it as "seeing more and seeing differently"), fostering creativity and innovation to more detailed contributions to organizational, human resource, team and product development (e.g., Berthoin-Antal, 2009; Taylor and Ladkin, 2009; Schnugg, 2010; Schiuma, 2011). We will refer to digital media art as a recent example of the interplay between art and business and how this exchange can trigger developments in as well as the fusion of both fields: art and in business.

Exploring Art: Shortcut Throughout History

From an early historical perspective, the artwork and the understanding of what is art have long been determined through the practice of its production process (one could also break this down as its craft). This is dating back to the Greek roots of art in technē. Technē can be understood as art and craft and may be interpreted as the roots of both art and craft in one, or as the craft of an artist's practice. Thus, the history of the term and the concept 'art' show not the final artwork or product-defined art, but the production and manufacturing process (Heidenreich, 1998). Thus, an artist was a person who mastered the craft and thus was able to create extraordinary works. Also, artistic exploration of technologies was part of artistic work during this time. Thus, the camera obscura and reflections on other physical phenomena by the use of technological devices first were found in artists' workshops or even as part of the art collections of the aristocracy and clergy.

But throughout history, art hasn't always been as free, and artists couldn't work as self-determined as they do today. There have been monetary dependencies on clergy, aristocracy and other wealthy families who were patrons and commissioners, and there have been dependencies and rules for commissions, as any other craftsperson has. There were mainly two turns in history in which artists freed themselves from external influences: the first one was around 1500, the second one around 1800. The first freedom went along with an important development that was triggered in 1435 by Leon Battista Alberti and his writing 'Della Pittura'. Alberti formulated a theory of art that marked the starting point of art academia. For the first time, a consciousness of peculiarity and a certain status of art were coined through defining what an artwork is, which rules an artist has to follow, as well as which knowledge the artist has to have about other artworks, techniques and strategies to reach the aim of demonstrating something with the artwork. This created a first theoretical reflection on *"Sinn and Zweck"*[1] of the artistic practice.

The academic system also dealt with an artist as someone producing a body of work in the course of a career and thus provided a rational alternative to the focus on singular paintings. In this development, at the roots of the 19th-century arts machine, the artist developed from a low caste worker or part of a guild to a learned man (or woman), as the development of art in academia at this time becomes evident. For example, by the year 1786, there were 33 art academies in France (White and White, 1965:5ff).

The second turning point is marked by Kant's seminal work *Critique of Judgment* (1790). This went along with freeing artists from the ties to aristocrats and wealthy families which had been created by their financial situation in the beginning of the 1800s. The argument of the aesthetic and the sense of beauty as not based in copying nature but in art and composition legitimates works without "practical" purpose. Thus, as Kant's book was used to free art from the necessity to be purposeful or to copy and praise nature, artists were also able to liberate themselves from the necessity of working for somebody and started to explore aesthetics, beauty and later materials and contexts on their own, led by aesthetic judgment and academic contextualization (Busch, 1987b:200).

From the second turn on, the ideological framework of what art is and who an artist is changed rapidly. During the Middle Ages, art was still closely connected to the clerical system—beauty and utility or goodness were basically two sides of the same coin. In the course of the Enlightenment, the reflection on beauty and aesthetics attempted to free art and beauty from the clerical and spiritual supremacy, from popular common sense and passion and from clerical financial capacity. In the following decades, the 'l'art pour l'art' movement acted as the establishment of the artist as a Semi-Divine Genius who must be protected from all mundane activities in order to carry out the refined technique and talent (Lucas, 1961; Busch, 1987a; Friis Møller, 2012). Suddenly, artists were no longer bound by the formal traditional expectations of a guild, or of academia or by the substantive and financial boundaries of patrons and the church. Artists were now completely sovereign in what they wanted to create without being subject to specific goals of other fields (Lucas, 1961).

'L'art pour l'art' mainly states the *purposelessness (Zweckfreiheit)* of art and is the basis for the autonomy of art. Although this is based on a misinterpretation of Kant's writings on art—taking the word purposelessness literally and shifting the focus from the admirer of the artwork to the actual artwork itself[2]—it becomes a program for artists and intellectuals all over Europe (Wilcox, 1953; Friis Møller, 2012). Initially, 'purposelessness' meant that art wasn't a means to an end, then in modernism, the term was used as a way of thinking about art as focusing on aesthetics, colors and materials (Ullrich, 2005).

The focus in understanding the definition of art shifted from mastering the craft that enables extraordinary (good) works to the sublime feature of the artwork that also may lie in the basic idea of its creation. The opening for this institutional perspective (Groys, 1992) on art mainly started with the readymade works by Marcel Duchamp and *Black Square* by Kazimir Malevich, contextualized in museums at the beginning of the 20th century. From this moment on, texts by artists and theorists about the context of artwork started to play a major role in considering art production. Archiving and contextualization in a museum of aesthetic objects were fundamental for the creation of art. The museum as an institution was now co-responsible for this circle of creating and pronouncing something as art (Heidenreich, 1998). This shift and the introduction of a very conceptual approach to art opened up the way for artists to develop new art movements in which artists also started to reflect on social developments and new technologies and to innovative ideas in a more conceptual and non-material way. This contextualization implies that there is something about art that goes beyond aesthetic and verbal language. Art is not reduced to symbols depicted in the works or as linguistic metaphors, but is also considered closely connected to its social and cultural environment (Meinhard, 1994).

Entangling Art and Business: The Example of Media Art

A huge part of the research on art and business focuses on what art and artists can do for business. Such publications ask what effects scholars and practitioners see in cases of artistic interventions in (mainly business) organizations or how to integrate arts-based learning (e.g., Taylor and Ladkin, 2009; Barry and Meisiek, 2010; Schnugg, 2010; Schiuma, 2011; Berthoin Antal and Strauß, 2014; Seifter et al., 2015). Beginning with the question, "What an artist can do for the organization?" implies that there is something commissioned or especially created to contribute to a certain development of or in the organization. This would imply that the artist is not free or self-determined, but a teacher, consultant or designer. Moreover, many of these analysed effects refer to different approaches to art and are reflected in the different roles of artists and art throughout history—often outdated conceptions of art. For example, there is a close connection between standards in society and culture that represent expectations on how artists work (the autonomous artist, the creative and innovative artist, the artist as part of a guild or dependent on clergy or the aristocracy) as well as what content they tackle (e.g., aesthetic values, social questions, depict religious motives) with how these art and business case studies are analysed. So the conception of art and the artist from the perspective of those who analyse the effects of arts-based initiatives is a very economic one in terms of 'what is the contribution' and 'how is it contributed'. Moreover, it is a mixed understanding of the functions of art throughout history and art theory, picking the necessary aspects of each historical era and theoretical approach, combining them to create a flexible counterpart with whom the business world can deal as a supplier from the service sector. This mixed conception could be interesting for artists and would be something relevant for developing positions as an artist, as contemporary artists often are challenged by more complex issues and it is difficult to establish such a position as an autonomous artist and make a living from the art at the same time, but this is not an easily accepted conception of art and artists in the artworld. There is a clearly defined art market which is dominated by gallerists, art institutions and artists selling artworks to an audience that decouples the (free) artistic production from actually making the money. But if as in arts-based initiatives and their proposed effects, the process, certain artistic skills and perspectives are sold, it is way more difficult for artists to such a project as valid artistic doing within the artworld. Exactly this point is also bringing artists into the position that they divide their work into two different spheres: their artistic work, which is free and self-determined, and their 'creative' contributions to companies where they use their artistic skills and knowledge for commissioned 'creative work'. This also makes it difficult for especially upcoming artists to position their work with organizations as part of their work as an artist.

We bring media art to discuss the encounter of the art and business worlds, as it is a currently developed artform where artists have to engage in the artworld and the business world and their borders are often blurred. Artists who are trained in the field of media art often work in companies as graphical designers, coders, game developers, interface designers or other digital media experts. Sometimes they do artistic production in the course of their work or in their free time next to their 'normal' job. This is the case because technological experimentation and digital media artworks aren't easily sold by a gallery or have any other economic distribution channel on the art market. Moreover, media art is related to these ideas and expresses how artists work with new technologies, push boundaries and trespass certain limits to explore new territories that lead to new art forms or artistic professions. This can give input to organizations, but also can lead to the development of new branches in industry and business. Moreover, media art is an interesting example for discussing the understanding of art in the art world and the business world, as media artists are often connected to both worlds and are pushing the boundaries of the understanding of art. First, we will start with an exploration of what media art is and how it developed. Next, we will explore how media art is entangled with new technologies and branches in industry and business. This close entanglement again leads to a very volatile understanding of media art and the position of media artists in both the art world and the business world. It will also show that the boundaries are fluid, as something may start as art, lead to technological innovations and a few years later be conceived as an important industrial branch.

Media art has an uneasy status within the contemporary art world as new media and their exploration often result in something that is not tangible for gallerists and museums and introduces new forms of working. As everything from a color pencil to a photograph or a computer is a medium, it is difficult to specify what media art is. As a continuously evolving field, its "lowest common denominator [. . .] seems to be its computability, the fact that it is digital and based on algorithms. Other descriptive adjectives commonly used for characterizing new media art are—process-oriented, time-based, dynamic, and real-time; participatory, collaborative, and performative; modular, variable, generative, and customizable" (Paul, 2007:253). But new media is not only opening up creative activity to people with a background that is new to art, it also exerts a general influence on forms of perceiving space, objects, symbols and time, and thus (artistic) media are inextricably tied to the evolution of the sense faculties (Grau, 2007:140).

An important reflection on new media's impact on art and thus a turning point in its development was the international exhibition of cybernetic art curated by Jasia Reichardt, *Cybernetic Serendipity*, which took place in 1968 at the Institute of Contemporary Arts in London. In the tradition of art that explores up-to-date scientific fields and the latest technologies, the exhibition dealt broadly with the demonstration of the use of computers and new technology in order "to extend creativity and inventiveness" as well as "the artists' involvement with science, and the scientists' involvement with the arts". It aimed at an overview of what is artistically and aesthetically possible and interesting to approach with the newly emerging medium of the computer as all new media and systems emerging throughout the history of art inevitably altered the shape, characteristics and content of the respective art form. Such new media always add new possibilities and make creating art accessible for new groups of people to become involved. For this, the exhibition was divided in three sections: 1) computer-generated graphics, computer-animated films, computer-composed and -played music and computer poems and texts; 2) cybernetic devices as works of art, cybernetic environments, remote-controlled robots and painting machines; and 3) machines demonstrating the uses of computers and an environment dealing with the history of cybernetics. In these sections, the curators aimed to show the "links between the random systems employed by artists, composers and poets, and those involved in the making and the use of cybernetic devices" (Reichardt, 1968:5).

This early collection of computer-generated aesthetic works that was meant to provide an overview of niche works which demonstrate how new technological possibilities could be used for artistic or aesthetic production resembles a broader understanding of art and design production. In a recently upcoming art form in media art, 'device art'—the interdependence of art and technology and its blurred lines to design, games and technology industrial branches —is clearly demonstrated. Device art is reflecting upon the essence of technology through the use of newly developed materials and mechatronic devices heavy on design. Characteristically, the created devices themselves that are the content of the art piece are often very playful items that sometimes could be commercialized into devices or gadgets for use in everyday life.

As the computer becomes more integrated into our daily lives, however, there is a major shift happening that is blurring the line of the established art world, design and the technology and creative industries. Moreover, the previously artistic exploration of computer-animated films, computer-generated graphics and computer-generated and -played music developed into well-known art forms, mainstream applications and branches within the (not only creative) industries: e.g., digital music and films are now important industrial factors and changed the landscape of technological and entertainment production; computer-generated visuals and graphics that have been subject to artistic investigation in the early decades of computer application have now developed into the main forces of design production (e.g., product design, corporate design and marketing, using the virtual environment for product development), scientific visualization or communication tools. And artists go on exploring newly developed technologies (e.g., virtual environment glasses, motion-capturing sensors, open-source hardware and software, measurement technologies, UAVs,[3] robots) by exploring new possibilities of how to use them and reflecting on fields in science and society. This artistic research and investigation is also important for gaining new inputs for science, research and innovation.

Computer technology has contributed to breaking down the barriers and the artificial divisions of art and science, a heritage of the industrial age. This ubiquitous technology is also behind the emergence of new sciences that would not be in existence without the computing power—nanotechnology and biotechnology in particular—but it goes beyond these new fields to influence pretty much all the sciences. The same is true for media arts—this fluid, experimental art form would not be in existence if there was no computer to experiment with and also inspire artists to question and tinker, even hack the technology that is often seen in its extremes—as a utopian answer to all or a dystopian vision of artificial intelligence taking over the world. Ultimately, we are entering a networked age where all borders are dissolving and our collective perception of the world as we know it is shifting radically.

Media artists intensely contribute to these social, scientific and economic developments by creating new insights as well as raising new possibilities with their artistic production through bringing in their perspective that is not bound to traditional ideas and methods within science and technology and their imaginative approaches and aesthetic abilities. They are constantly pushing borders, creating changes and enabling the invention of innovative applications or even inventions. But media artists are not only pushing borders by what they are doing, they are also working within this interdisciplinary field, wandering with their doing in different professional groups and addressing different audiences. In addition to the computing technologies blurring the lines between art, technology and science, there is a significant shift to the collective, collaborative social networks influencing artistic and aesthetic production. This leads to a separation of who is perceived as an artist and who is perceived as a creative professional, both within the artworld as well as from the perspective of society and business organizations.

All these different aspects of media art make it very difficult for the artworld to integrate it into its own realm, but also somehow resemble the blurred situation and conception of art in the discussion of arts-based initiatives and how artists can contribute something to business organizations— and if this is still artistic work. Media artists have to deal with these questions daily. They are linked to so many diverse fields, and it seems that after graduation from art programs, they have to decide if they want to work as an artist—though there is no traditional gallery art market for media arts— or define themselves as predominantly designers, creative workers, creative programmers or creative technologists. Taking this problematic situation of media artists as an example, it is important to ask how this blurring of lines between the fields demonstrates that this current interest of business in organizations is also part of a development within the art world. Furthermore, it shows that it is not only interesting to ask what art can do for business, but also how this interest may trigger the development of a new era of perception of art and artists within society and moreover, in the artworld.

Paradigm shifts are known to be a major disruptive force in the human consciousness, and we are not able to predict or control the future, no matter how hard we try. We can, however, comment and bring to the attention of the public what is taking place and perhaps in a modest way influence the tides of change. Media artists play this role and are increasingly active in ways that do not neatly fit into the existing (corporate) market structure of the established art market. With the increasing number of media artists working in scientific laboratories, collaborating with scientists, we see a potential for the shift of reductionist scientific methodologies, which could result in many new innovations and certainly change the way we see artists in our social realm. Thus, what these individuals are doing is also challenging the currently established definitions of what is art, who is an artist, a designer, an entertainer, a programmer or part of the creative industries, what artistic research is and how it differs from traditional research. This makes it difficult for artists who work in this field to position themselves in the market structure as artists in the established art world. An important aspect as media art becomes close to other fields, especially industries is how media artists can keep their integrity as artists. This raises questions—from an art definition perspective—of why artists should not sell their artistic production on a well-paid market outside the art market or do marketing on mass scale. Seen from the perspective of an artist working in the field of media art, the artworld is possibly the slowest to move with the current economies, and there has yet to be a market for new media arts. Questions about the value of digital currency go hand in hand with the positioning of new media art in society today. The established artworld does not reflect the networked, collaborative world we are living in and is designed for the elitist groups who are closely tied to equally established corporate business models.

This situation is not only something that has to be tackled from an art theoretical and cultural science perspective. It also raises questions about the perception of art on the market by putting the art market in a broader context. It seems that the economic usability of the artistic production process and the artistic outcome is also influencing its perception as art or a product positioned outside of the art world. There is still a perceivable difference in what is defined as art and sold on the art market and those artistically produced outcomes that are sold on a market within the service sector or industries, although the issue of the blurred lines between economy and art was already raised by artists decades ago. Art, and culture at large, can serve as a mirror of societal values especially because of its position that is inherently immaterial and not necessary to base survival. We are now witnessing a culture that it dictated by the corporate bottom line and artwork that is valued for strictly material purposes, similar to a financial exchange market, where the exchange is abstracted from the social reality. This way of functioning is unsustainable, as is evidenced in the progressively turbulent and confused societies. The wealthy one percent are in a way similar to the small number of galleries and dealers that cater to them and ignore the crowd that is collaborating, sharing, working on the web and creating work that does not fit into the established system. Developing a new marketplace is a creative endeavor that is already happening in many fields, and it is a particular challenge for the media artists.

Conclusion

This glimpse into the development of media art as it is closely related to societal, technological and industrial changes in the last few decades shows that there is more than reflection on current developments by artists outside of the hermetic space of the artworld. The difficulty of media art fitting into a clear conception of art in today's artworld shows that these changes in the conception of art go slow. But as there is an inherent interconnectedness between what artists do and how parts of society live and work, there has to be not only a next step in the conception of art, but also the interest in artistic contribution to business that looks at artists through the lens of their potential and not so much through the lens of a specific currently valid conception of art. This might be a sign for a change in the current status of art and artists in society, working culture and in the economic system. The line between art, design and industry is ever more blurred, and looking back at the various ways that art and artists integrated their work into the markets of the time is an important task at this critical historical intersection.

Notes

1   Sense and purpose.
2   Kant (1790) describes the admirer of the artwork for aesthetic judgement with four moments: disinterestedness, universality, absence of a presupposed end or purpose, purposiveness/necessity.
3   Unmanned aerial vehicle (i.e., drones)

References

Barry, D. and Meisiek, S. (2010). Seeing more and seeing differently: Sensemaking, mindfulness, and the workarts, *Organization Studies*, 31(11):1505–1530.

Berthoin Antal, A. (2009). *Transforming Organizations with the Arts*. TILLT Europe Project: Research Report.

Berthoin Antal, A. and Strauß, A. (2014). Not only art's task—Narrating bridges between unusual experiences with art and organizational identity. *Scandinavian Journal of Management*, 30(1):114–123.

Busch, W. (1987a). Die Kunst und der Wandel ihrer Funktion—Zur Einführung in die Themenstellung, in: W. Busch and P. Schmoock (eds.). *Kunst. Die Geschichte ihrer Funktionen*, pp. 3–10. Weinheim, Berlin: Quadriga Beltz.

Busch, W. (1987b). Die Autonomie der Kunst, in: W. Busch and P. Schmoock (eds.). *Kunst. Die Geschichte ihrer Funktionen*, pp. 178–203. Weinheim, Berlin: Beltz Quadriga.

Chodzinski, A. (2007). *Kunst und Wirtschaft. Peter Behrens, Emil Rathenau und der dm-drogeriemarkt*. Berlin: Kadmos.

Friis Møller, S. (2012). *From Disinterestedness to Engagement: Towards Relational Leadership in the Cultural Sector*. Doctoral Dissertation, Copenhagen Business School, Frederiksberg. Retrieved from http://openarchive.cbs.dk/bitstream/handle/10398/8590/S%C3%B8ren_Friis_M%C3%B8ller.pdf?sequence=1

Gold, R. (1999). PAIR: The Xerox PARC Artist-in-Residence Program, in: C. Harris (ed.). *Art and Innovation: The Xerox PARC Artist-in-Residence Program*, pp. 12–20. Cambridge, MA: MIT Press.

Grau, O. (2007). Remember the Phantasmagoria! Illusion Politics of the Eighteenth Century and Its Multimedial Afterlife, in: O. Grau (ed.). *MediaArtHistories*, pp. 137–157. Cambridge, MA and London, England: MIT Press.

Groys, B. (1992). *Über das Neue: Versuch einer Kulturökonomie*. München: Hanser.

Haschek, H. (1986). Kunst, Kreativität und Wirtschaft. *Kunstforum International*, 87:230–233.

Heidenreich, S. (1998). *Was verspricht die Kunst?* Berlin: Berlin Verlag.

Kant, I. (1790). *Critik der Urteilskraft*. Berlin, Libau: Lagarde und Friedrich. (English Translation: *Critique of Judgment*. Oxford: Oxford University Press, 1952).

Lucas, R. S. (1961). Autonomous art and art-history. *British Journal of Aesthetics*, 1(2):86–99.

Meinhardt, J. (1994). Louise Lawler. Die Orte der Kunst—Kontext, Situation, Markt, in: P. Weibel (ed.). *Kontext Kunst. Kunst der 90er Jahre*, pp. 167–175. Köln: DuMont.

Paul, C. (2007). The Myth of Immateriality: Presenting and Preserving New Media, in: O. Grau (ed.). *MediaArtHistories*, pp. 251–274. Cambridge, MA and London, England: MIT Press.

Reichardt, J. (1968). *Cybernetic Serendipity. The Computer and the Arts: A Studio International Special Issue.* 2nd revised edition, London: Studio International.

Schiuma, G. (2011). *The Value of Arts for Business.* Cambridge, MA: Cambridge University Press.

Schnugg, C. A. (2014). The organisation as artist's palette: Arts-based interventions. *Journal of Business Strategy*, 35(5):31–37.

Schnugg, C. A. (2010). *Kunst in Organisationen. Analyse und Kritik des Wissenschaftsdiskurses zu Wirkung künstlerischer interventionen im organisationalen Kontext.* Doctoral dissertation, Johannes Kepler University Linz, Austria.

Scotese, P. G. (1978). Business and art: A creative, practical partnership. *Management Review*, 67(10):20–25.

Seifter, H., Luke, J. and Goldman, K. H. (2015). *Integrating Informal STEM and Arts-Based Learning to Foster Innovation.* Research Report.

Shanken, E. A. (2002). Art in the Information Age: Technology and Conceptual Art. *Leonardo*, 35(4): 433–438. Slater, H. (2000). The art of governance—On the Artist Placement Group 1966–1989. *Break/Flow*, Feb/Mar 2000.

Strati, A. (2009). Do you do beautiful things? 'Aesthetics and Art in Qualitative Methods of Organization Studies', in: D. Buchanan and A. Bryman (eds.). *The SAGE Handbook of Organizational Research Methods*, pp. 230–245. Thousand Oaks, London: Sage.

Taylor, S. S. and Ladkin, D. (2009). Understanding Arts-Based Methods in Managerial Development. *Academy of Management Learning & Education*, 8(1):55–69.

Ullrich, W. (2005). *Was war Kunst? Biographien eines Begriffs.* Frankfurt: Fischer.

White, H. and White, C. (1965). *Canvases and Careers: Institutional Change in the French Painting World.* New York, London, Sydney: John Wiley and Sons.

Wilcox, J. (1953). The Beginnings of l'Art Pour l'Art. *The Journal of Aesthetics and Art Criticism*, 11(4):360–377.

Section II

Organizing Collaboration

The second section of the book is about collaboration, which is at the very heart of the project undertaken by this volume. In particular, the three chapters included in this section offer a variety of contributions to the understanding of politics and practices of collaboration and raise a number of questions which more or less directly address even us as editors of this book.

The dialogue between artist **Kent Hansen** and business scholar **Anke Strauß** opens this section by focusing on the question of collaboration. Disguised by a beginning written in a traditional academic fashion, the collaboration between Kent Hansen and Anke Strauß takes the interesting and amusing form of a dialogue in a theatre piece where the voices of the two main characters, sometimes not clearly identifiable, discuss the issues of power, motivation, otherness and access in collaboration and widely reflect on the metaphor of the parasite and its role in collaboration. This text leads to the reading of the next two chapters as practical examples of collaborations.

The following two chapters are based on two cases. The text by marketing scholar **Tracy Harwood** and art scholar **Sophy Smith** discusses how storytelling is understood and used in business and the arts on the basis of a study of a performing art-based artistic intervention. The following text, by **Janina Panizza** and **David Stewart**, theorizes on sponsorship as a collaboration between different organizations, based on their study of different initiatives. Both chapters show the practical unfolding of issues such as power, motivation and interest, which have been raised by Kent Hansen and Anke Strauß in the previous chapter.

4 To the Manger! Collaboration in the Age of Access

Kent Hansen and Anke Strauß

"My friend, by enemy I call you out!"

(Dylan, 1946)

Collaboration seems to have become as rampant in management and organization studies and practice as it is in contemporary fine art. While scholars and practitioners of the former discipline are eager to promote collaboration as a way of organizing that succeeds competitive relationships (Markova and McArthur, 2015), collaborative practices have become an oeuvre-constituting element of contemporary art (Kester, 2004; Ruhsam, 2011). In management and organization research, this shift towards a collaborative notion of organizing is closely related to developments that are read as phenomena of a transforming business world. On the one hand, it is embedded in a narrative about business that has gone through fundamental processes of de-verticalization as to be "far more flexible and better suited to the volatile nature of the new global economy" (Rifkin, 2001:23). On the other hand, collaboration is considered to play a major role in what is often called knowledge-driven economies that are a "heterogeneous set of productive activities that revolves around the processing of information and to workers who focus on the creation, development and diffusion of knowledge" (Armano, 2014:246). With innovation and learning being regarded as major drivers of economic well-being, management and organization, researchers conceive collaboration an adequate organizational form for responding to the demands of knowledge-driven businesses (MacCormack et al., 2007). Used interchangeably with cooperation, collaboration is treated as rather neutral technique of organizing (Andrews and Mickahail, 2015). If scholars like Snow (2015) distinguish between cooperation and collaboration, they do so by means of a third notion—that of competition—conceptualizing cooperation as engagement with another party to accomplish a goal that cannot be reached alone. In cooperatives relationships, trust is an issue. Collaboration "is a process of shared decision making in which all the parties with a stake in the problem constructively explore their differences and develop a joint strategy for action" (Bengtsson and Kock, 2000:435). This notion of collaboration is embedded in assumptions of voluntary participation, care and commitment amongst the participating parties (Appley and Winder, 1977) that attribute to collaboration an undeniably positive connotation, closely connected to the democratic and humanistic values found in early organizational development approaches (Jamieson and Worley, 2008). This positive notion of collaboration tends to negate power issues that do not vanish into thin air by reducing hierarchies.

>>Have we already started? Who is speaking? Someone, something, made a head start on this very theatre of . . . business?<<

>>May I guess it was the voice of an organization scholar?<<

>>Could we—instead of someone, lingering in the role of narrator, or 'deus ex machina'—first of all gather as unspecified personas?<<

>>Agreed. As far as I can tell, we will eventually trace our different personas—artists, scholars, researchers, members of business organizations and others of various trades—on our different paths, perhaps as individual people in individual situations, perhaps as assemblages of multiple events that we have encountered . . . <<

>>Let's just get on with it!<<

>>Everyone! We need not to push something through. Let us for now accept that we are situated in a collaborative arrangement. Well, we all heard the . . . Anyhow! We heard from somewhere that we seek to extend the notion of 'collaboration'.<<

>>Before I turn into a mere footnote, I'd much like to continue . . . <<

Chorus (while entering): >>YES! For crying out loud, get on with it!<<

>>Ok . . . In art, collaborations between discourses, disciplines and communities have become a global phenomenon since the 1990s. Such collaborations take place outside the art institution and are often site-specific, that is, carried out in a specific local context.

In the 1960s, various artists' initiatives—such as Experiments in Art and Technology and the Artist Placement Group—foregrounded contemporary projects, experimenting with non-artists to "reposition art in the decision-making process of society" (Steveni 2002:172). These kinds of engagements have been theorized much later. Aiming at defining a new genre of artistic practice, theorists call it 'New Public Genre Art' (Lacy, 1994), 'Dialogic' or 'Littoral Art' (Kester, 2004), 'Discursive Art Process' (Gillick, 2009) or 'Participatory Art' (Bishop, 2012), with each one displaying slight differences regarding its discursive underpinnings.

Regardless of their individual differences, overall, attention is paid to "the creative rewards of participation as a politicised working process" (Bishop, 2012:1). This is often linked to "a mode of generating ideas and placing structures into the culture that emerges from collaborative, collective, or negotiated positions rather than as varied forms of 'pure' expression of super-subjectivity" (Gillick, 2009).

In contrast to most management and organization research, collaboration in art has developed with regard to questions of power structure within the art (institutional) system and in society as a whole.<<

>>Still, in art as well as management and organization research and practice, the dominant notion of collaboration has a positive connotation used in the sense of co-labour, meaning to participate, to be involved in, taking part in something.<<

>>Although this notion of collaboration dominates, there is a second one that is usually overlooked, especially by writers stemming from an Anglo-Saxonian language milieu. This second notion—prevalent in post-war France and Germany—has a completely different connotation. It means 'to consort with'—to associate with someone, typically with the disapproval of your usual peers. It's a secret pact with an agency that one is usually not considered to be connected with—a source of off-territorial movements that carries with itself the potential of power, agency—as well as shame and betrayal. This path leads us to a site of opportunists, Trojan horses, revolutionaries, traitors and enemies . . . <<

>>So, collaborations are constituted by a set of paradoxical relationships (Schneider, 2007:n.p.) that do not allow for an ultimate settlement judging it either 'positive' or 'negative'.

>>Hey, in this entire academic lingo, where is this so-called 'Other'?? All difference is vaporized and everyone is "forced to speak in languages that are not its own" (Mäki, 2014:n.p.)!<<

>>I am not your enemy! Here I am—wanting to work on collaboration, now caught up in discussions, unable to move. Power paralyzes us, but I insist; I am not your enemy.<<

>>Hm . . . Someone making the distinction of who is or who is not somebody else's enemy appears to me as immanently suppressive. Only I myself am to decide who is and who is not my enemy; you're not my enemy.<<

>>So this is friendly fire then? Do we simulate collaboration on 'collaboration'?<<

>>We do not simulate. We go through what can happen when working in a relationship that is not necessarily backed by a notion of commonness. As there are differences, there are interests. Collaboration doesn't need trust. Just the instinct that the other can bring you further in what you want.<<

>>It's a personal investment and it's concerning one's professional trade.<<

>>It's subjectivity that matters; it's part of social struggle.<<

>>. . . But up to now, collaboration had—for me—a connotation of closeness, against conventions, against all odds, because I find the other interesting, because I am addicted to this energy, this power that comes

into being, when we manage to shoot through the walls of what we already know to the maelstrom of creating something new. Expecting such kind of engagement, however, is not a personal tick.<<

>>Personal or not, what it comes down to is to deride "all the common sense objections and adulations and all the blah-blahs [. . .] which are totally irrelevant to what goes on that's exciting to do [in art production. . .] They all seem to know what they ought to do next because they have a medium [money] for how to exchange value. And it's flawed just the same as the verbal medium" (Latham, 2002:n.p.).<<

>>Ah come on! "Approaches [. . .] that imbue 'art' with sets of specific powers that constitute themselves around knowledge's blind spots.[??] Compared to this, it seems much better to engage proactively with knowledge-making processes on all levels" (Schwab, 2014:n.p.).<<

>>But "[h]ow can an initiative to invite authors for research reassure an egalitarian basis of collaboration, a frame of collectivity without central leadership?" (Cvejić, 2005:n.p.)<<

>>We could maybe start off by seeing ourselves as contributors among contributors; leaving habitual positions and a 'super-subjectivity'. The 'discursive artist' disengages from concepts of autonomy and the 'sovereign creative being' (Hansen, 2005:175), whilst 'the researcher' in collaborations leaves habits of objectifying subjects of scientific interest. Thus, we all team up as a temporal "cross-disciplinary conglomeration of amateur-specialists" (Hansen, 2005:181)!<<

>>Once I asked an artist about his motivation to collaborate with a company. "The reality of an organisation is so complex that I could never have invented this myself. It's so rich, it eludes artistic fiction", he replied. There seems to be a parasitical interest in this collaboration.<<

>>"I am only interested in what's not mine", writes Oswaldo de Andrade in his "Cannibal Manifesto" (de Andrade, 1928/2002:n.p.).<<

>>There is more to it than just retrieving the 'reality of life' beneficial for the production of work—be it a work of art or a work of academia. It's about the potential of developments of personas, potentials of becoming another. Not to confuse with becoming the Other. Here, next to parasitism, could 'anthropophagy' be another sensitizing concept when it comes to notions of collaboration?<<

>>"What matters is access", says Florian Schneider (2007:252), "not a generously granted accessibility but a direct, immediate and instant access. Rather than through the exertion of the alleged generosity of a group made up of individuals in the pursuit of solidarity, it often works as a brusque and even ungenerous practice, where individuals rely on one another the more they chase their own interests".<<

>>Whilst chasing one's own interests, a parasite is a master of flows. This means that he doesn't seek to establish property rights, but to create a vector where everything flows towards him. It's not about forcing one's way in, but being invited by a host.<<

>>But why do parasites get invited to meals? Parasitism appears to me a one-way relationship. The host serves and the parasite consumes without giving back until he is discovered and driven out—until hospitality becomes hostility.<<

>>I have an anecdote about a family-run business for agricultural technology whose management was interested in collaborating with two artists. Although the business was very successful, growing from a local player to an internationally operating organization, they felt that there were also downsides of their success. One issue that the management identified was its scant internal communication. "We really do care for our employees and therefore we feel like we have to do something special for them to address this issue instead of just inviting a consultant". They agreed that two artists would creatively engage the employees.

When the artists, interested in collaborative art practices, met the employees, the atmosphere was fierce. The employees had worked through weekends and extended nightshifts to satisfy the high demand for their products. Given that situation, they showed very little understanding for what the management had come up with. Engaging in a 'sidetracking' project meant losing time for fulfilling the contracts that were piling up in the full order books, and time was really the last thing they had. "So, on a scale from 1 to 10, with 1 being very keen on and 10 being not up for it at all, how much do you feel like taking part in this project?" asked the artists. Silence. And then someone shouts from the back row, "13". Everyone nods.<<

>>The management invites the artists to host them in their organization, they invite a parasite to parasitize on the employees. This points to the assumption that inviting a parasite can be beneficial for the host.<<

>>Yeah, in contrast to predators, parasites do not eat the whole prey but re-direct parts of the host's (re-)productive power. By re-directing the employee's time, attention and energy for engaging creatively with questions about themselves, their products and practices—questions that they have never asked themselves before—parasites can open up new flows of communication, new ways of engaging, new products, purposes, perspectives.<<

>>In such cases, the artists redirect flows of production by adding information, thereby creating art from the raw production of the organization that hosts them. "The parasite does make a contribution to the host whom it parasitizes. It provides information and novelty in exchange for energy and production"(Brown, 2013:90).<<

>>When it comes to participative notions of those art practices, the very site of decision-making is an interesting place to linger. Here one could also say that it is not the artists who claim the 'time' of the employee, it's the manager who does. It is the condition of a prefixed setup: managers push forward the artists to make a claim of (more)

time. The power of the powerless is to not participate, to say '13' to the ones who were invited to consume parts of their (re-)productive power—their time, their attention, their energy, their ways of getting things done. Of course, the possibilities of refusal within the power structures of the organization are limited. But they have the power to shift to a symbolic level, performing pseudo-participation, minimizing what there is ready to consume.<<

>>Again, this is a question about access. Parasites consume with friendly faces, exchanging meals for anecdotes that entertain the feast. The artists answered the hostility they met with humor, making the way they consume the employees' time, attention and energy a pleasant experience, thereby redirecting the energy of the pushback against the artists' project into an employees' engagement that carried their project much further than they had expected. With some of the employee even investing private time, the relation between the artists and the employees became amicable in character.

Yet, a change in position can immediately change such fruitful consumption. Serres (1982:107) says that the parasite "has but one enemy: the one who can replace him in his position of parasite". The only one missing in this equation between the parasite and her meal is the manager who invited her to the feast: "Please, be my guest! Become a parasite on my employees!"<<

>>Serres also points out that parasites always come back and that "a parasitize logic is in operation at the heart of organizing" (Brown, 2013:97). And there is the risk that the artist in such collaborative settings with business organization members will become a parasite by proxy, ready to nurture the one replacing her at the end of the food chain: the parasitic manager. There is a painful insight lingering in the depths of those relationships. "The organism reinforces its resistance and increases its adaptability [by parasitism]. It is moved a bit away from its equilibrium and it is then even more strongly at equilibrium. The generous hosts are therefore stronger than the bodies without visits", says Brown (2013:91).<<

>>Such forebodings can generate discomfort in the parasite's mind, and she might choose to leave, wiping away the friendly face.<<

>>Here is another anecdote: an artist group that for an extensive period of time had worked collaboratively with industrial workers in an organizational setting. Many lived experiences of working lives of the employees (and the artists) have been touched upon; future potential had been projected.

At the end, the project was made public in an exhibition at the regional fine art museum. The exhibition was meant to feed into the continuation of the ongoing collaborative processes, thereby being part of 'gaining access to the Other'. Suddenly, the artists announce, "We are now on our territory. We solely decide what, and what not, and how, to display the project". The workers: perplexed, lost. Potentialities of other modes of (art) production lost too.<<

>>Parasites are painfully aware of the spatio-temporal dependency of their existence. Crossing a threshold to another sphere, such as crossing over to the whiteness of an exhibition space can, too, instantly change roles. The parasite becomes the host and the ones he used to consume are ready for consumption now.<<

>>But not every parasite suits a host—as seen, the art institutional body may not become a space of hospitality. (Business) organization members parasitizing on the art institutional body might add information that constitutively questions power structures in arts organizations that favor precarious work conditions, exploit the labour and distributes wealth in an uneven way. Risking being exposed in this way, art institutions would have very little left to maintain a boundary that legitimizes their (rather traditional, see Chiapello, 2004) way of critique.<<

>>"It is the foreigner, or the stranger, who brings into question our capacity for hospitality and thus our self [. . .] [T]o offer hospitality is always [. . .] to risk [. . .] the hostility of the enemy, which is nicely indicated by the Latin word hostis meaning both enemy and guest", say Corris and Gere (2008:16).<<

>>Yes. But it is also very clear that such a reaction would immediately lead to searching for the scapegoat: "who has invited this parasite?" The artists' fear may be one of managerial concern—a fear of losing control in a collaborative relationship with members of what is often considered the hegemonic system. They fear that this way, their 'critical competence' and 'cultural capital' could be swept away.<<

>>Inviting the enemy who—without asking permission—has already occupied most territory around you into the intimacy of your own home would make you a traitor in the eyes of the ones who try to resist. Hence, tragically, the artists unwittingly became 'neo-managers', themselves instigating on their home turf exactly the regime what they so much feared. Here, artist and manager alike, "lack [. . .] the possibility of exposure to chance, mischance, error" (Connor, 2004:106).<<

>>Matthew Soules (2010a:20) criticizes the concept of the parasite as "shift[ing] too easily to a negotiated pragmatic that could ultimately end up foreclosing politics 'proper'". He suspects a "totalizing tendency that potentially denudes its operational modus in its enfolded proclivity, doesn't the parasitic shimmy too closely with some of the more unnerving logic of contemporary liberalism?" (Soules, 2010a:20).<<

>>Hm, I come to think of the Western colonization of the 'unknown world' and a different form of consumption holding transformative potential for the one who consumes. The notion of the cannibal,

originally used to segregate the 'wild' native from the civilized culture of the colonialists, has become a powerful means of constructing post-colonial identities.

In the 1920s, Brazilian artists successfully took on the task of artistic and social transformation. They commemorated 'the cannibal' through a cultural anthropophagist practice, subsuming the colonist cultures, expropriating the expropriator, re-territorializing lost territory.<<

>>So parallel to the notion of 'parasitism'—the sensitizing concept of a *cultural* or *ritual* anthropophagy—is a question of incorporating difference, thereby transforming and regaining power. The anthropophagist devours the other to become another. "Ritual anthropophagy is a branch of anthropophagy in which the cannibal eats his enemy not for greed or for anger but to inherit the qualities of his enemy" (Funkhouser, 2012:n.p.).<<

>>"There has to be a 'becoming-Other', taking a point of view as self-metamorphosis. [. . .] Re-definition of being by becoming [. . .] not based on the fixed and hierarchical nature of positions such as subject and object but one in which subjects interrelate and therefore may devour each other" (Sztutman, 2015:214). Further characteristics of this anthropophagist tradition are "plasticity in the contours of subjectivity (instead of identities) [. . .]; hybridization (instead of a truth-value assigned to a particular repertory); an agility of experimentation and improvisation to create territories and their respective cartographies (instead of fixed territories authorized by stable and predetermined languages)—all of this carried out with grace, joy and spontaneity" (Rolnik, 2011:32).<<

>>So, artist, manager and researcher should with delight devour one another in a feast of collaborative interaction? But how will we be able we drag these maybe-anthropophagists to the manger if they won't eat? They seem invested only in their own professional traits and curriculums. If those 'actors' of power do retreat from being 'contributors among contributors' and just let 'the others', the fellow participants, the employees, exchange something of interest, then it's unlikely that any transformation happens.<<

>>Hm, did any managers join the cast? If any did, they're disturbingly quiet.<<

>>Management needs to leave us alone! Otherwise the power executed on a daily basis prevails this experiment of a virtual 'free space' for collaborative actions.<<

>>Wouldn't it be better if we were directly confronted with management 'in the flesh' and, correspondingly, they were confronted with the blood and flesh of the collaborate group?<<

>>I think so too, otherwise, the results of such collaborative endeavours will merely be translated, transcribed, historized for the sole benefit

of the powerful. Our bodies would be sheer information available for management, art, research and thus (re)enforce formulas that might have otherwise been transformed.<<

>>And if these translations become common sense, they create stable relations (Strauß, 2013). So if transcription serve only the transcribers' enduring formulas, it's very likely that the perhaps collaborative embryonic attempts for 'change' are eradiated by 'business as usual'.<<

>>Yes . . . and the only way out would be—again—cultural anthropophagy: foreign values assimilated in an attempt to "destroy their hierarchy, escape their oppressive forces and transfigure their [. . .] energies" (Subirats, 2004 in Siewierski, 2007:507).<<

>>So, after also having ascribed parasitical tactics to employees—such well-rehearsed tactics of artists, researchers and managers—we introduce the notion of anthropophagny. But soon after, the odd triplets hold forth: "All are parasites! . . . but we are as well anthropophagists!" This proclamation 'all parasites unite!' is yet another soothing rhetoric that's evading inherent conflicts and the factuality of powers. And by the very same gesture, employees are segregated from the artists, managers and researchers.<<

>>Oh! But all contributors in a collaborative setting can potentially manifest the parasite or the anthropophagist. Which kind of 'phenotype'—and to what relative 'intensity' (here perhaps homologous with 'creativity')—may depend on the degree of concealment or re-encounter. All are potentially able to oscillate between various tactics and identities-not-yet-fixed, and in such a way crisscross the habitual boundaries between 'institutions', disciplines and practices. Such bewildered oscillations might be sanctioned in collaborative settings.<<

>>Hey collaborators! Do incorporate us extras, too.<<

>>Oh! A voice from the audience, a manager even!<<

>>By the way, where are the editors at? Backstage?<<

>>..? <<

>>So, bring artists, researchers, employees and managers to the manger! And invite the chorus, audience, readers and editors, too. All on the stage!<<

Pause

>>Wow, we have now walked a long way. From an exclusively positive notion of collaboration prevalent in management and organization studies that negates power issues to the shallows of collaborative relationships that are constitutively infused with power games. Some elements are addressed explicitly, whilst others are more implicit in character. Unusual as it might seem, this might owe to the fact that not scholars but practitioners of collaborations between the art and the business sphere have somewhat taken over the staging.<<

>>But my fellow collaborators! It's soon time for exodus!¹<<

>>Well then, scholar, do your thing!<<

>>Perhaps we could vote on this proposal?<<

(Several Are Giggling)

>>. . . We must admit this is a scholarly context. So scholar, do again your thing! We'd like to hear you out.<<

(Everyone Nods)

A scholar >>You want me to speak now that you have messed up the territories of management and organization studies and art theory by means of a detour into the shambles of art and business collaborations? Ha!

But, if you insist; conclusion: your idea to leave the dominant path determined by Anglo-Saxonian language that constructs collaboration as co-labor to explore a connotation of this term that has mainly developed in France and Germany since the Second World War grants collaboration a dark side. It immediately conjures up the enemy as partner—'both partner and adversary', as Foucault says (Foucault, 1997:28). Apart from making such relations much more complex, your notion of collaboration shifts attention to power. In order to engage with the questions, you have introduced anecdotes that involve the spheres that are usually perceived as antagonistic: the art and the business organization spheres. These anecdotes led you to explore dimensions of Michel Serre's concept of the parasite that point out why business leaders invite artists into parasitical relationships: artistic parasites re-directing resources and adding information have the potential to dope or excite the (capitalist) system—as exemplified by Boltanski and Chiapello (2007)—thereby bringing about changes that strengthen it. Yet, in boosting the immune system of business organizations, artists feel uncomfortable. It seems like being invited for a meal has turned their own territory into a colony of (creative) industries. Being part of an unequal relationship, however, does not lead to defencelessness when hospitality turns into hostility. Parasites that get expelled can always flee the scene and go back to the territory they came from: non-involvement as form of resistance whilst lamenting the loss of power of their artist critique. Yet, there is a second concept that involves another kind of consumption: that of anthropophagny. In contrast to the parasite that gets invited by a host to include an exteriority, colonialists (those uninvited guests) use the notion of the cannibal to exclude beings from a (new) social organization. At the same time, however, the notion of the anthropophagnist challenges clear-cut boundaries that determine inside and outside, friend and foe, subject and object. As you have pointed out, (cultural) anthropophagny can become a means of re-appropriation. It's the anthropophagnist who changes, who becomes another by subsuming enemy powers and qualities that weren't before sanctioned within 'the tribe'

(Sztutman, 2015:213). Both concepts are concepts of proximity without falling for a notion of collaboration based on commonness. It allows for thinking about the potential, risk and boundaries of intensive relationships that elude control but hold the chance for profound transformation.

(Chorus Enters, Seems Perplexed)

> *An artist*: >>Ok guys, the chorus is here. Let's join them. Come, my fellow protagonists.<<
> *Someone, anyone (whispering)*: >>Guess he means 'fellow antagonists'.<<
> *An artist*: >>Now, come on, we're back in business.<<

Note

1 'Exodus' concluded the story in the ancient theatrical tradition of Greek tragedy.

References

Andrews, K. and Mickahail, B. (2015). Business and Social Media: Collaboration for the Sixth Discipline, in: J. P. Sahlin (ed.). *Social Media and the Transformation of Interaction in Society*, pp. 158–172, New York: Wiley.

Appley, D. G. and Winder, A. E. (1977). An evolving definition of collaboration and some implications for the world of work. *Journal of Applied Behavioral Science* 13:279–291.

Armano, E. (2014). The relational network of knowledge production. *Ephemera* 14(2):245–262

Bengtsson, M. and Kock, S. (2000), "Co-opetition" in business networks—To cooperate and compete simultaneously. *Industrial Marketing Management* 29:411–426.

Bishop, C. (2012). *Artificial Hells: Participatory Art and the Politics of Spectatorship*. London and New York: Verso.

Boltanski, L. and Chiappello, E. (2007) The *New Spirit of Capitalism*. London and New York: Verso Books.

Brown, S. D. (2013). In praise of the parasite: The dark organizational theory of Michel Serres,. *INFORMÁTICA NA EDUCAÇÃO: teoria & prática* 16(1):83–100.

Chiapello, E. (2004). Evolution and co-optation. *Third Text* 18(6):585–594.

Connor, S. (2004). Topologies: Michel Serres and the shapes of thought, *Anglistik*, 15:105–117. Retrieved 30.12.2015 from <http://www.stevenconnor.com/topologies/>.

Corris, M. and Gere, C. (2008). *Non-Relational-Aesthetic*. London: Artwords Press.

Cvejić, B. (2005). Collectivity? You Mean Collaboration, *Republicart* 01. Retrieved 22.10.2015 from <http://republicart.net/disc/aap/cvejic01_en.pdf>.

de Andrade, O. (1928/2002). "Cannibal Manifesto", *Exquisite Corpse, cyber issue* 11. Retrieved 22.07.2015 from <http://www.corpse.org/archives/issue_11/manifestos/deandrade.html>.

Dylan, T. (1946/1997). To Others than You. in: W. Davies (ed.) *Everyman's Poetry*, p48. London: Dent.

Foucault, M. (1997). *The Politics of Truth*, trasl. by S. Lotringer and L. Hochroch. New York: Semiotext(e).

52   *Kent Hansen and Anke Strauß*

Funkhouser, C. (2012). *Augusto de Campos, Digital Poetry, and the Anthropophagic Imperative*. Retrieved 10.11.2015 from <http://www.lehman.cuny.edu/ciberletras/v17/funkhauser.html>.

Gillick, L. (2009). Maybe it would be Better if we Worked in Groups of Three? Part 1 of 2: The Discursive, e-flux journal 2(1). Retrieved 04.01.2016 from <http://www.e-flux.com/journal/maybe-it-would-be-better-if-we-worked-in-groups-of-three-part-1-of-2-the-discursive>/

Hansen, K. (2005). Positionists' Productions. The Scope of a Correlative Art Practice in Contexts of Organizing. in: Mari Brellochs & Schrat, Henrik (eds.). *Raffinierter Überleben. Strategien in Kunst und Wirtschaft. Product & Vision Reader*, pp. 170–181. Berlin: Kadmos.

Jamieson, D. W. and Worley, C. G. (2008). The Practice of Organization evelopment. in: T. G. Cummings (ed.) *Handbook of Organization Development*, pp. 99–121, Thousand Oaks: Sage.

Kester, G. H. (2004). *Conversation Pieces: Community + Communication in Modern Art*. Berkeley: University of California Press.

Lacy, S. (1994). *Mapping the Terrain: New Public Genre Art*. Seattle: Bay Press.

Latham, J. (2002). Countdown to Zero, Count up to Now—An Interview with the Artist Placement Group. Interview conducted by J. Berry & P. van Mourik Broekman, *Mute magazine* 25. Retrieved 10.10.2015 from <http://www.metamute.org/editorial/articles/countdown-to-zero-count-to-now-interview-artist-placement-group>.

MacCormack, A., Forbath, T., Brooks, P. and Kalaher, P. (2007). From Outsourcing to Global Collaboration: New Ways to Build Competitiveness. *HBS Working Paper* 07–080. Retrieved 22.11.2015 from <http://www.hbs.edu/faculty/Publication%20Files/07-080.pdf>.

Markova, D. and McArthur, A. (2015). *Collaborative Intelligence: Thinking With Pepole Who Think Differently*. New York: Spiegel & Grau.

Mäki, T. (2014). Art and Research Colliding, 10th version, *Research Catalogue, Society for Artistic Research*, Bern. Retrieved 03.01.2016 from <https://www.researchcatalogue.net/view/49919/49920>.

Rifkin, J. (2001). *The Age of Access: The New Culture of Hypercapitalism, Where all of Life is a Paid-For Experience*. New York: Tarcher.

Rolnik, S. (2011). The Geopolitics of Pimping. in: G. Raunig, G. Ray & U. Wuggenig (eds). *Critique of Creativity. Precarity, Subjectivity and Resistance in the 'Creative Industries'*, pp. 23–40. London: MayFlyBooks.

Ruhsam, M. (2011). *Kollaborative Praxis: Choreographie. Die Inszinierung der Zusammenarbeit und ihre Aufführung*. Berlin: Turia und Kant.

Schneider, F. (2007). Collaboration. Seven Notes on New Ways of Learning and Working Together. in: A. Nollert and I. Rogoff (eds.). *A.C.A.D.E.M.Y.*, pp. 249–254. Frankfurt: Revolver Verlag.

Schwab, M. (2014). Editorial. *Journal for Artistic Research*, 5. Retrieved 22.10.2015 from <http://www.jar-online.net/index.php/issues/editorial/487>.

Serres, M. (1982). *The Parasite*. Baltimore, MD: Johns Hopkins University Press.

Siewierski, H. (2007). Utopia and Anthropophagy, *Third Text* 21(5):499–508.

Snow, C. C. (2015). Organizing in the age of competition, cooperation, and collaboration, *Journal of Leadership and Organizational Studies* 22(4):1–15.

Soules, M. (2010). Response. in: M. Jahn (ed.). *Byproduct. On the excess of Embedded Art Practices*, pp.20–21. Toronto: YYZBOOKS.

Steveni, B. (2002). Reposition the Artist in the Decision-Making Processes of Society. in: L. Davis (ed.). Real Life/Beyond the Event, pp.171–194. Singapore: Focas, Forum On Contemporary Art & Society.

Strauß, A. (2013). *Researchers, Models and Dancing Witches: Tracing Dialogue between Art and Business*. Doctoral thesis, University of Essex, Essex

Subirats, E. (2004) Una Última Visión del Paraíso. Mexico City: Fundo de Cultura Económica.

Sztutman, R. (2015). The (Re)turn of the Anthropophagites: Reconnecting Oswald de Andrades's Proposal to Amerindian Art-Thought. in: L. Lagnado and P. Lafuente (eds.). *Cultural Anthropophagy, The 24th Bienal de Sao Paulo 1998*, pp.206–220. London: Afterall.

5 Embedding the Corporate Story Through Performance

Tracy Harwood and Sophy Smith

"To tell a story and to receive a story you have to be inside the story, to find your place in it. The storyteller leaves it to his audience to interpret events for themselves . . . The connections are for the audiences to make for themselves".

(Steinman, 1995:121–2)

Introduction

This chapter outlines the conceptual and practical perspectives of performative storytelling using a case study of a site-specific contemporary dance theatre performance at a medium-sized agri-business located in the east of England. Storytelling as a means to build authenticity in the corporate communication of brands has a relatively recent history in business research. Ever since Descartes's foundational proposition, leading to the separation of emotion and feeling from rational discourse, scientific and abstract dialogue has been the main premise of academic thought, but there has been a growing recognition over the last 30 years of the contribution of narrative to organizations, including works by Schank and Morson (1990), Weick (1995), Simmons (2000) and Gabriel (2001) highlighting its role in tacit and implicit knowledge transfer through organizational structures. By sharing stories, employees may contribute to the interpretations of organizational practices (Boyce, 1997; Fenton & Langley, 2011) that can have the power to silence other narratives in both positive and negative ways (Simpson & Lewis, 2005; Geiger & Antonacopoulou, 2009).

Whilst stories may be constructed through the interpretation of narratives, there is little research into the role of theatrical performance as a means of storytelling within a business environment, such as that highlighted in this chapter, and in the ways that the brand within the organization may be reinforced through cultural production and performance. Storytelling as a textual narrative has been used in practice to explore ritualized events, advertising and publications through official channels expressing desirable qualities in typically narrative form. Alongside these official formats, a breadth of stories often co-exist which challenge, ridicule or subvert official texts, exposing some of the emotional challenges experienced by employees in the service of the brand. These stories are typically unmanaged, where fantasy may overtake lived experience, and yet stories provide metaphors, mnemonics, images and acronyms that produce effective and memorable devices with power to motivate and enrich engagement with the brand (Denning, 2000; Simmons, 2002; Gabriel, 2004). Our chapter explores the nature of storytelling from both management and performance arts perspectives before presenting a case study that offers insight into the potential and role of performance as an embodied approach to storytelling. The impacts challenge the traditional dichotomy of creative versus organizational mindsets, highlighting the contributions to each discipline.

Literature Review

Management Perspective

The narrative approach of storytelling in organizations has long been recognized as a useful technique to transfer knowledge across departmental boundaries and between generations of workers to facilitate change within organizations and promote learning (e.g., Boje, 1991; Kahan, 2006; Lämsä and Sintonen, 2006). Barker and Gower (2010) highlight that the approach enables rapid communication to a diverse workforce with complex information needs, where the contextual environment has less time for relationship building among team members (Jarvenpaa and Leidner, 1999) because of increasing pressures to generate profits. Drawing on social exchange theory (Blau, 1964), the narrative paradigm provides both verbal and non-verbal cues embedded with values (Cragan and Shields, 1998) that communicate cognitive and emotional concepts to position a message quickly, often from the position of others (Lämsä and Sintonen, 2006). Being based on the innate human condition for social exchange, stories are enriching and engaging, resulting in symbiotic understanding (Barker and Gower, 2010) by providing contextual and timely information upon which others may act. As Boje (1995) suggests, the approach provides a collective memory of the firm.

Typically, storytelling within organizations has been recognized as having one or more of three core subjects:

1) about people, often with the aim to build trust and authenticity so that others develop an understanding of how to engage and interact with individuals (Guber, 2006);
2) about the nature of the work, in order to build mental models to facilitate knowledge sharing; and
3) about the organization itself, to provide a vehicle for sense-making on how the organization works, building on the social community within the environment.

Stories enable social bonding through ritualized exchanges of information and emotion ('phatic speech'). Stories can be interpreted as signals of the environment which may also be embedded within the architecture and physical configuration of space, indicating, for example, how people work or inhabit ('habitus', Bourdieu, 1977) the space. Stories tell about the past, conveying messages and learning about the firm's evolution as a form of retrospective sense-making (Weick, 1995) as well as the future, relating what the firm would like to be, for example, through vision statements. Stories also promote transformation and change, supporting modes of learning and unlearning within the environment, including about life and identity.

Stories typically comprise four elements: characters, message, plot and some conflict or disruption that interferes with 'normal' harmony (McKee, 2003; Fog et al., 2010). Characters may include, for example, a benefactor, a beneficiary, a supporter, a hero, an adversary. The stages of a story include an opening, introduction of the conflict, a point of no return, a climax and a fade out or closing position. The plot may encompass testimony (open to the interpretation of others), aesthetic expression or structured dialogue (Labonte, 2011). While there may be no right or wrong way to tell a story, Denning (2006) has suggested that a minimalistic approach enables the audience to develop their own interpretations of the material (Lämsä and Sintonen, 2006). This restates Boje's (1991) suggestion that the most effective stories are short because they leave interpretation to the receiver: "the terser the telling, the more shared the understanding of the social context, since insiders know what to leave to the imagination" (1991:115–116). There is, however, no consensus or overarching framework that summarizes the best methods for telling the most successful stories, primarily because of the idiosyncratic and co-evolving nature of knowledge in social exchange environments (Ochs and Capps, 1996). For example, storytellers may be individuals within firms whose aim is to interact and engage others, sometimes by eliciting stories through the process of interaction (Gabriel, 2004; Seely Brown et al., 2005). Storytellers may also, however, be the artifacts within the firm that communicate knowledge (through signs and signals) about the firm and employee behavior. Collectively, stories resonate and support resilience through the organization by capturing knowledge without 'killing it' (Seely Brown et al., 2005).

Narrative practices of storytelling focus on the specifics and impacts of stories told within organizations. The emphasis of research has been on the processes associated with transferring narrative, i.e., content, knowledge and sense-making, rather than the processes of telling the story. After White (1987), narrative is defined as 'a set of events, or actions, put together chronologically' whilst story is 'emplotted', with a focus on plot and events that have a point. The mode of performance is, however, also an important aspect of communication. This research extends prior research by focusing on the performative aspects of storytelling to develop an understanding of the impact of the approach in the firm context. While performance has been conceptualized for organization studies (see Czarniawska, 2011), this has referred to descriptive narrative relating to the theory of action rather than embodied and enacted as a performance. The next section explores a contemporary performance arts interpretation of storytelling, where performance and oration are long-established traditions in storytelling.

Performance Arts Perspective

Applied performance and community performance are both established approaches that use storytelling as part of a transformative process—each is now briefly described before we present an overview of the common creative process of 'devising'.

Applied performance practice is "intended to be socially or personally beneficial to participants", either to promote the well-being of a specific group or engagement in a particular issue (p. 241). Ackroyd (2000) suggests the term is used to describe a variety of educational and community-based theatres, each with different agendas, for example, theatre-in-education (creating performances that engage young people in key issues such as bullying and crime), reminiscence theatre (creating performances from oral history for a therapeutic effect), theatre for development (creating performances that empower communities) and theatre in hospitals (creating performances that develop patients' health and well-being). Applied performance does not have a particular performative style; rather, it is an approach to making work. Distinctions between creator/performer/audience are blurred as performers and participants engage in creative dialogue through interaction. Shaughnessy (2012) has developed a taxonomy of applied performance practice through which to define and evaluate work structured around seven key areas: pedagogy (engaging in the process of knowledge and identity production), process (the process of making the work is as important as the final piece), play (play-based practices to encourage social engagement), presence (engaging participants in a lived experience in the here and now), participation (spectators actively engaging with work produced through participation and interaction), performance (a dissemination or sharing) and pleasure (capacity to trigger liminal and embodied experiences).

Applied theatre practitioners inhabit an unusual position, working simultaneously from both within an institution or community setting and outside the community in which a performance is situated. Kershaw (1999) and Nicholson (2005) regard this as a creative space open to interventions. In performance disciplines such as dance, where the story or narrative is not communicated verbally, audience members may relate to the performance in different ways, each constructing a personalized narrative dependent on their ideologies and experiences. For Kershaw (1999), all performance is an 'ideological transaction' between the performers and audience in which the spectator is engaged in constructing the meaning of the performance. Esslin (1987) states that ". . . any attempts to predict what 'meaning' the performance as such contains, is bound to be doomed to failure, simply because that meaning must be different for each individual member of the audience" (1987:21). That said, Kershaw (1999) recognizes the possibility of a collective response based on shared readings: "Such collective responses, shaped by the ideological identity of the audience's communities, are the very foundation of performance efficacy. They are the first link in a chain that connects the individual experience of each audience member to the wider historical development of his or her society" (1999:91). Thus, a shared meaning may be derived through performative storytelling within a context where values are established among community members. This may be generated through the interpretation of key actions embodied by the performers rather than explicated through any dialogic content.

The practice of community performance work, where the performance takes place within a community environment, is built on the premise that "artistic practices can have an affect on the social world" (Kuppers and Robertson, 2007:2) and that social change relies on concepts of community and narrative (Govan et al., 2009). Boundaries between artist, audience and product become blurred with a "blending of creative process into the concerns of a community" (2007:2). Govan et al. (2009) assert that the efficacy of community-based theatre lies in the way that participants' personal stories are represented, reframed, rewritten and reinterpreted and describe how communities are developed "when people shape their autobiographical narratives in relation to the perceptions of the narratives of others" (2009:74). They cite phenomenologist Ricoeur (1992), proposing that narrative ". . . is both an instrument of self-understanding, a way of locating oneself in relation to others, and a mechanism for social change" (2009:74).

Within community performance practice, a linear plot is not always used: stories may be built through different components, such as bricolage, collage and montage. Steinman (1995) describes how these different parts are in 'fertile contact' with each other, combining to make some new 'performance' through combination and juxtaposition. Within performance practice, Broadhurst (1999) describes this kind of work as 'liminal performance', where audiences find meaning in the "free association of themes rather than a linear narrative" (1999:77). Liminal space between the past, present and future is explored through embodied action: "communication that takes place in the auratic moment is one between the present and the past as embodied in the object, but this past is itself dynamic, and accumulation of present moments, including the present in which the object is now observed" (Indyk, 2000, cited in Shaughnessy, 2012:232). Thus, a performance explores connections between stories to develop an empathic understanding 'in-between lives'. Through engaging with the process and watching the performance, the audience blends their personal memories with the collective memory. Such an approach within complex environments such as firms enables key events to be synthesized and presented, highlighting significant components that audiences may engage with, potentially reinvigorating the shared memory of the community.

The creative process of 'devising' emerged as a core feature of community arts practice within the 1960s (Heddon and Milling, 2006), characterized by a process where a work is made from scratch, without a script, and is "open, flexible and responsive to the conditions, cultures, spaces and places in which the work is produced" (Shaughnessy, 2012:27). There are a number of alternative devising frameworks, e.g., Govan, et al. (2009) list the process of devising as research, generating material, improvisation, scripting, editing and rehearsing. Heddon and Milling (2006) describe a purpose of devising with communities as forging a sense of community through community involvement. Devising methodologies create models of collaboration, build self-esteem and enable participants to experiment with alternative modes of thinking and behaving. Through collective action, devising has the potential to create a 'renewed sense of belonging' in participants. Like community performance practice per se, devised work is "typically compartmented or fragmented with multiple layers . . . whilst still retaining some sense of 'narrative'" (Heddon and Milling, 2006:221).

Within devised community performance practice, "[n]arrative makes experience knowable, enabling participants to recognize and relocate themselves in the context of their immediate audience and wider community" (Govan, et al., 2009:82). Involvement in the devising process encourages individuals to reflect on their personal experiences to reframe and reshape their personal stories. In discussing community storytelling within devised practice, Govan, et al. reflect: ". . . building communities is a creative endeavour and an imaginative process, in which the process of narration provides a sense of social coherence . . . and a way of representing events which makes them meaningful within a particular community and for a known audience" (2009:76). Thus, devising is a useful tool to develop stories that align with and through communities that have potential application to business contexts and further draws from business to add context to creative performance.

Drawing on management and performance arts perspectives provides an interesting approach to the embodiment of brands through storytelling. Storytelling in management research has primarily focused on narrative-based attempts to build a shared memory which has synergy with the applied and community performance arts practice, where narratives are used to situate individuals in relation to a broader context. A performance, however, is more fluid in that it is embodied and emplotted, giving a 'sense of action' that holds meaning for participants and audience. Thus, while the process of sense-making post-performance may be narrative based, the performance itself is enacted. The shared experience of performance events may therefore be a powerful way to instill community by reinforcing the shared history of the context on which it is derived. The next section describes a case study example of the development of performative storytelling.

Case Study

A deeper understanding of the role of storytelling across business and the arts can be gained through a specific case study—the creation of a new piece of site-specific contemporary dance theatre production, devised from the lived experiences of the employees of a medium-sized agri-business located in the rast of England. Through engaging with contemporary dance theatre practice, employees explored their roles and experiences of the brand as the business has developed over the years. This chapter draws on findings from units of analysis that comprise the managers and employees of the firm, contemporary dance theatre artists, performance commissioners and recordings of a performance (see Table 5.1 for a summary of the data collected). Data from interviews was analyzed thematically.

Case Background

The firm, Elsoms Seeds, has a long history, forming in 1844 originally as a small, family-owned business growing seeds for nursery and market garden plants and flowers and latterly cereal crops for its UK and international customers. The firm remains family owned, currently employing 95 staff members in administrative, warehouse, maintenance and production-related roles.[1] The performance was developed with and for Elsoms working with Assault Events. At the outset, the brief for the performance piece was open and emerged over a period of six weeks through creative engagement and devising with staff across the business. The result was a theatrical performance that drew on personal stories and associations with the brand through its history. The performance was enacted in a new state-of-the-art

Table 5.1 Summary of Data Collected

Description (codes—number of participants)	Data
Observations of day-to-day running of the factory, interactions between staff, corporate historical and promotional materials	Field notes (performance devising stage)
Preliminary interviews with staff about their roles within the firm, factory floor tours, informal discussions	Field notes (performance devising stage)
Artistic critical reflection of performance development (choreographer/composer)	Transcripts
Snapshot interviews with firm managers (FM-2) and colleagues (FC-6)	Video edits 00:44:36
Snapshot interviews with Assault performers (AP-3) and staff (AS-2)	Video edits 01:31:22 hrs:mins:secs
Recorded Performance (P)	Video 00:37:22 hrs:mins:secs
Interviews with firm staff 10 months post event	Audio 01:02:00 hrs:mins:secs

warehouse in front of the workforce, having been devised and rehearsed in the refectory area, allowing staff to have maximum access to the creative process. The devised piece that emerged comprised a story of the brand, reflecting the history, present and future of the business from different perspectives within the firm. This was formulated into a 30-minute professional performance structured around different themes that arose from discussions with the staff. The findings presented articulate the creative process in two key areas: emergent goals of the firm, artistic interpretation of the story and sense-making.

(i) Emergent Goals

The generative nature of the creative devising process over the period of weeks prior to the final performance was central to the development of the story. Themes emerged through dialogic and social interactions between staff and performers. Four performance themes were generated that constituted a 'layered experience' and 'thematic articulation of life' at the firm (AS-1). The story themes related to:

1) people—how the workforce has developed;
2) place—how the space has developed, the size of the site, e.g., the opening of a new state-of-the-art warehouse;
3) nature—the role of nature (growing, pollinating, etc) and how it is dealt with; and
4) technology—how it is incorporated, the juxtapositions between 'old' and 'new' machinery at the site.

These broadly reflect the management perspective, dealing with people, the nature of the work and the organization, but importantly reflect the work environment through time and space by connecting actions, activities, events and artifacts. What is interesting is the way in which these themes emerged through processes of social exchange, only some of which were led by the performers. Themes were interpreted at the firm in a range of ways, reflecting the staff's sense of comfort with the performance-based approach, whereas managers took a more holistic approach to describing the goal. Staff related the themes to discursive operational aspects of their roles, commenting on the ways in which the performers 'allowed' them to reflect on what they do everyday, how they interact with others in the work environment and how their work fits into the business model. Other themes identified communicative events that incorporated learning about others' roles, about what is 'done' on site, the history of the firm and 'happenings' from its early days as well as about the business of growing seeds, how old 'transforms' to new within the firm across generations of staff. Most related the site-specific performance as a 'culmination' and 'celebration' of the firm's history to the point of the launch of the new high-tech warehouse. As one member of staff put it: ". . . it's about handing over, generational change and progression . . ." (FC-2).

Thus, there is a sense of a 'mysterious contract' between performers, the performance, firm members and the place of work, with sense-making being a collective, emergent process. The mystery was borne out of a lack of prior experience with similar activities, both within the firm and the broader social contexts of firm members ("I don't know what to expect": FC-3) yet dialogic through "the right and opportunity to comment on what they are seeing" (AS-1). Similarly, albeit a familiar devising process to the performance company, members had no previous experience of firm-based site-specific performance and the type of material they were working with ("it's rare and unique, and that's what makes it an important project . . .": AS-1). Overall consensus within the firm identified that the focal performance, prior to its enactment, would provide staff with an opportunity to connect with the firm's history by exploring their own roles within the business and with the most recent firm developments. It thereby aimed to improve relationships across the firm ultimately to enhance workflow and customer experience. A further goal was to bring the employees together as well as influence their perception of the role of arts in a business context. The 'mysterious contract' can be understood through play-based methodologies evident in the applied theatre approach used by the company—a 'liminal inter-subjective space' recognized by play-workers as the 'Ludic 3rd': "This third space . . . is an in-between zone, occupied by practitioners and participants in the act of making participatory performance" (Shaughnessy, 2012:38).

(ii) Artistic Interpretation of the Story

In relation to the artistic work, story was dealt with in three stages:

1) elements of the story were discovered through conversation and interaction with staff, key elements of the story gradually unfolding throughout the first half of the devising process;
2) the story was retold, embodying narrative in physical performance; and
3) the story was reflected back to staff through a live performance at the end of the project.

Using this approach, the performance was devised with nine sections representing the accumulation and interpretation of datasets by the performers. The second stage was critical to the development of the performance: the process involved placing smaller stories within the four key themes (people, place, nature and technology). The structure of the performance, i.e., the storytelling process, was part thematic and part chronological, with past and present intertwining throughout. Performers vocalized the script and performed characterizations: the process resulted in simultaneous co-expressiveness of speech, gesture, image and sound (see Image 5.1). The

Image 5.1 Performance (performer, Eileen McClory).

Source: Gary Naylor Photography

involvement of staff added new insight into the devising process through a deep level of engagement and shared experiences to localized performance of actions, reminiscent of the goals of community performance arts. This enabled the professional performers to reinterpret tacit and implicit knowledge of the history of the firm and ways and means of interaction among staff directly through daily exchanges and indirectly through intergenerational knowledge transfer.

(iii) Story Performance and Sense-Making

Firm members evolved their own interpretations of components of the story from the ways in which they had interacted with the performers, particularly during the creative development and devising phase. Thus, sense-making comprised a repositioning of knowledge intertwined with emotional appreciation of the firm through its ages of evolution. Emotional engagement was evident in the connections made between the performance and work context. The performance itself was perceived to be largely abstract in nature and, whilst not intended to be minimalistic (as highlighted by Denning, 2006, as a means of developing breadth of interpretation), nonetheless allowed employees to connect with it in multitudinous ways.

The performance took place in a new space on site and served to connect staff with a new experience related to the site and the performance, effectively building into the storytelling process a sense of resilience to future development of the firm: "The setting was important, in our new warehouse. We used it as a launch of our warehouse to our teams. That was a useful springboard for that [it was the first time lots of people had been in the warehouse]" (FM-1). It also built external connections, developing community beyond the firm boundaries with a view to business continuity and establishing its contribution towards creating 'habitus' for the workforce, reflecting the 'ideological transaction' referred to by Kershaw (1999). From the management perspective, the challenge recognized was the nature of liminal performance: in a sense, this falls between business and arts practice, but connects both perspectives to each other (Ricoeur, 1992; Broadhurst, 1999; Indyk, 2000).

Conclusion

The case study highlights that through engagement with storytelling, both business and arts may collaboratively develop a co-created performance, effectively turning a community of location into a community of practice with multifaceted benefits. As well as knowledge transfer within the firm and between the firm and performers, the approaches described enabled artists to develop methods of best practice in storytelling reflecting community engagement. Engagement with storytelling through play and experimentation from the management perspective has the potential to build new and interesting relationships between people, the nature of work and the history of the firm through time and space. The combination of arts and business perspectives builds understanding in the liminal space between past, present and future (Broadhurst, 1999; Shaughnessey, 2012). Central to this is the reflexive interplay between accord and discord both between theoretical perspectives and applied practice. Through storytelling, each sector must acknowledge the necessary systems and processes of the other, yet animate and stimulate experimentation and growth through challenging the systems. Working with storytelling processes necessitates a cycle of reflection through practice that benefits those involved in the process through reflective, creative, performative, interactive and observational modes. As the firm's chairman commented, "We spend a lot of time looking forward, planning what we're doing in business and this is a good opportunity to reflect on who Elsoms are, what we are, some of our values and the people who work here" (FM-1). Similarly, the performance director remarked, "We have really had to think about the relationship between artist and audience/participant. Working with people's stories means we have to be much more responsive as artists, allowing meaning to develop naturally over time to produce a co-created experience that truly reflects the histories of participants" (AS-1). As such, benefits extend performance beyond firm brand and creative interpretation to a deeply relational, generative and emergent form of storytelling practice.

Bringing together performance arts storytelling with management practices highlights new frameworks relating to how companies and professional arts practitioners can work together in the creation of meaningful original art in the workplace. Importantly, the resultant cultural production has the potential to produce transferable knowledge through stories that interact and resonate with the work environment (Steinman, 1995), created through the narratives that take shape and play out in performance (Weick, 1995; Gabriel, 2001). Beyond narrative, this is a reimagination of the firm that through the 'stickiness of emotion' connects past, present and future through 'inter-textuality', i.e., the relationships of stories to other stories within the firm, which stimulates intrigue and relational investment. While the process inevitably involves relational investment, the embedded learning may become a core value that empowers and enriches all stakeholders engaged with the processes. This is not so much by reflecting the people, the nature of the work and the organization or aspects related to these, but through the processes of storytelling that become connective tissue that bind components together, more reflective of folklore. As Steinman (1995) highlights, narrative is not a linear thing, but is fragmented and reconstructed from individual stories into a coherent whole, providing a collective vision of the firm that incorporates the multiple perspectives.

The benefits of embedding corporate history through cultural production emanate from the embodied experiences of stakeholders (performers and firm members) over time through the creative processes. In our case study, the arts have been placed within the bounds of firms and vice versa through the devising process, resulting in new ways of thinking that transcend traditional disciplinary boundaries. The outcomes described are, however, not well understood within either arts or business. This chapter therefore provides the impetus for a rich stream of future research into the processes and contributions of devising as a mode of co-creation.

Note

1   The contemporary dance-theatre performance on which this chapter reports was commissioned by Transported, The Creative People and Places Programme for South Lincolnshire, funded by Arts Council England.

References

Ackroyd, H. (2000). *Literacy Alive: Drama Projects for Literacy Learning*. London: Hodder Education.

Barker, R. T. and Gower, K. (2010). Strategic application of storytelling in organizations. *Journal of Business Communication*, 47(3):295–312.

Blau, P. M. (1964). *Exchange and Power in Social Life*. New York: John Wiley & Sons.

Boje, D. M. (1995). Stories of the storytelling organization: A postmodern analysis of Disney as "Tamara-Land". *Academy of Management Journal*, 38:997–1035.

Boje, D. M. (1991). The storytelling organization: A study of story performance. *Administrative Science Quarterly*, 36:106–126.

Bourdieu, P. (1977). *Outline of a Theory of Practice* (translated Nice, R.). New York: Cambridge University Press.

Boyce, M. E. (1997). Organizational story and storytelling: A critical review, *Organizational Change Management*, 9(5):5–26.

Broadhurst, S. (1999). *Liminal acts: a critical overview of contemporary performance and theatre*. London: Bloomsbury Publishing.

Cragan, J. F., Shields, D. C. (1998). *Understanding Communication Theory: The Communicative Forces for Human Action*. Needham Heights, MA: Allyn & Bacon.

Czarniawska, B. (2011). Performativity in place of responsibility: *Journal of Organizational Change Management*, 24(6):823–29.

Denning, S. (2006). Effective storytelling: Strategic business narrative techniques. *Strategy & Leadership*, 34(1):42–48.

Denning, S. (2000). *The Springboard: How Storytelling Ignites Action in Knowledge-era Organizations*. London: Butterworth-Heinemann. Esslin, M. (1987). *The Field of Drama*. London: Verso.

Fenton, C., Langley, A. (2011). Strategy as practice and the narrative turn. *Organization Studies*, 32(9):1171–1196.

Fog, K., Budtz, C., Munch, P. and Blanchette, S. (2010). *Storytelling: Branding in Practice*. 2nd ed. Heidelberg, Germany: Springer.

Gabriel, Y. (2001). *Storytelling in Organizations: Facts, Fictions and Fantasies*. Oxford: Oxford University Press.

Gabriel, Y. (2004). *Myths, Stories and Organizations: Pre-modern Narratives for our Times*. Oxford: Oxford University Press.

Geiger, D. and Antonacopoulou, E. (2009). Narrative and organizational dynamics: Exploring blind spots and organizational inertia. *The Journal of Applied Behavioral Science*, 45(3):411–436.

Govan, E., Nicholson, H. and Normington, K. (2009). *Making a Performance: Devising Histories and Contemporary Practices*. London and New York: Routledge.

Guber, P. (2006). The four truths of the storyteller. *Harvard Business Review*, 85:52–59.

Heddon, D. and Milling, J. (2006). *Devising Performance: A Critical History*. Basingstoke: Palgrave Macmillan.

Indyk, I. (2000). The critic and the public culture: For example, Walter Benjamin. *Australian Humanities Review*, 18: http://www.australianhumanitiesreview.org/archive/Issue-June-2000/indyk2.html

Jarvenpaa, S. L. and Leidner, D. E. (1999). Communication and trust in global virtual teams, *Organization Science*, 10:791–815.

Kahan, S. (2006). The power of storytelling to jumpstart collaboration, *Journal for Quality and Participation*, 29:23–25.

Kershaw, B. (1999). *The radical in performance: between Brecht and Baudrillard*. London: Routledge.

Kuppers, P. and Robertson, G. (Eds.) (2007). *The Community Performance Reader*. London and New York: Routledge.

Labonte, R. (2011). Reflections on stories and a story/dialogue method in health research, *International Journal of Social Research Methodology*, 14(2):153–163.

Lämsä, A. M. and Sintonen, T. (2006). A narrative approach for organizational learning in a diverse organisation. *Journal of Workplace Learning*, 18:106–120.

McKee, R. (2003). Storytelling that moves people: A conversation with screenwriting coach, Robert McKee. *Harvard Business Review*, 80:51–55.

Nicholson, H. (2005). *Applied drama (theatre and performance practices)*. London: Palgrave Macmillan.

Ochs, E. and Capps, L. (1996). Narrating the self. *Annual Review of Anthropology*, 25:19–43.

Ricoeur, P. (1992). *Oneself as Author*, trans. K. Balmey, Chicago IL: University of Chicago Press.

Schank, R. C. and Morson, G. (1990). *Tell me a Story: A New Look at Real and Artificial Memory*. New York: Scribner.

Seely Brown, J., Denning, S., Groh, K. and Prusak, L. (2005). *Storytelling in organizations: Why storytelling is transforming 21st century organizations and management*. Oxford: Elsevier Butterworth Heinemann.

Shaughnessy, N. (2012). *Applying Performance: Live Art, Socially Engaged Theatre and Affective Practice*. London: Palgrave Macmillan.

Simmons, A. (2000). *The Story Factor*. Cambridge: Perseus.

Simmons, A. (2002). *The Story Factor: Inspiration, Influence, and Persuasion Through the Art of Storytelling*. London: Perseus.

Simpson, G. and Lewis, P. (2005). An investigation of silence and a scrutiny of transparency: Re-examining gender in organization literature through the concepts of voice and visibility, *Human Relations*, 58(10):1253–1275.

Steinman, L. (1995). *The Knowing Body: The Artist as Storyteller in Contemporary Performance*. Berkeley: North Atlantic Books.

Weick, K. E. (1995). *Sensemaking in Organizations*. Thousand Oaks: Sage Publications.

White, H. (1987). *The Content of the Form*. Baltimore,: The Johns Hopkins University Press.

6 Understanding Sponsorship Relationships

Janina Panizza and David Stewart

Introduction

Since the late 1980s, there has been a global trend for governments to reduce public funding in the cultural sector (Ryan and Fahy, 2003; Cooper, 2011; Lindqvist, 2013; Bennett, 2014;), resulting in the provision of economic incentives for arts organizations to seek commercial funding sources by way of sponsorship (Belfiore, 2003; O'Brien, 2010; Allan et al., 2013; Lindqvist, 2013). There is a substantial quantity of literature covering sponsor-linked marketing objectives (Rhonda, 1999; Kotler and Keller, 2012; Mazodier and Merunka, 2012; Wiedmann and Gross, 2013), which can be grouped into five general categories: corporate brand imaging, marketing promotion and sales objectives, media focused on reaching a target market, relationship building both internally and externally, and the personal objectives of the senior manager or CEO (Johnston and Paulsen, 2014:637). It is worth noting that these objectives may not be mutually exclusive.

However, when examing the literature regarding the interaction between sponsorship parties, the language used is one of 'sponsor' and 'property', reflecting a sense of ownership by the corporation that is strongly resisted by the performing arts literature, where fear of a power imbalance impinges upon the artistic integrity of the performing arts organization (PAO), thus creating a barrier to commercial funding (Preece, 2005; Cornwell, 2008; Dalakas, 2009; Thomas, Pervan and Nuthall, 2009; Lindqvist, 2013;). With PAOs adopting a stronger marketing orientation, there has been concern for the possible 'marginalisation of artistic goals and principles' (Thomas et al., 2009:737), and with regard to sponsorship in particular, there has been some concern raised in the arts marketing literature about the possible negative impact on artistic integrity (Dalakas, 2009; Thomas et al., 2009; Wishart et al., 2012; Lindqvist, 2013).

There is general agreement that a firm's capacity to effectively activate its sponsorship (whatever the objective) is largely dependent on the congruency of brands (sponsor with sponsee) and the internal resourcing of that sponsorship project (Cornwell et al., 2006; Cornwell, 2008; Walker and Gross, 2013). Congruency of sponsorship brands is seen as reducing cynicism, particularly in those more philanthropic sponsorships that fall into the corporate social responsibility area (Plewa and Quester, 2011; Deitz et al., 2012; O'Reilly and Horning, 2013; Johnston et al., 2014). While professionalism is a repeated theme in attracting the right sponsor, congruency of brand and assistance with activation also features (Ryan et al., 2003; Colbert et al., 2005; Clegg, 2008; Bower, 2010; Thomas et al., 2009; Rupp et al., 2014;). As Marc Sands, Director of Media and Audiences at the Tate Gallery, states, "Generally you look for a fit between the content you're dealing with and where or how the sponsor operates" (Cooper, 2011). In particular, the studies of Ryan and Fahy (2003), Lund (2010), Daellenbach (2012) and even the small business studies of Zinger et al. (2010) highlight the added value that can be created beyond the more traditional ticketing, hosting and backstage options.

Here we explore the corporate sponsorship relationship from the perspective of the corporate and the performing arts organization. While corporates view the relationship from the desire to fulfil marketing objectives, the performing arts organizations view the relationship as an economic necessity, with the fear that they may lose their artistic integrity. Using a phenomenological approach, responses from each participant's point of view were sought based on their experiences as expert informants. Data was primarily collected through a series of semi-structured interviews covering both sides of the sponsorship relationship.

Methodology

Given the scenario outlined above, this study explores the sponsorship relationship from both the sponsor's and the PAO's points of view. The perspectives of both parties are investigated to determine the common and opposing objectives when a sponsorship relationship has been created. Four PAOs and five corporate organizations were interviewed, with two of the corporate sponsors having more than one relationship with PAOs. The PAOs were long-running organizations (a minimum of ten years) covering classical and contemporary live performance, including theatre, music and dance.

The objective of the interviews was to capture the entire relationship of the sponsorship from the two different perspectives. From reviewing the respondents' transcripts, four themes were identified, namely the beginning of the relationship, the nature of the exchange, the nature of the relationship and reviewing the relationship.

Findings

The Beginning of the Relationship

On the one hand, direct approaches to a PAO from a business were rare, while on the other hand, one business reported receiving many applications for sponsorship. One corporate respondent reported receiving between three and five proposals per day. Even those PAOs whose compliance regulations require requests for proposal from a prospective sponsor still made the initial approach before going through the formal process. As one PAO respondent said, "You don't get approached for sponsorship, you go out and hunt for it".

While sponsors are increasingly choosing a partner for strategic purposes, the PAOs were equally strategic in their choices: "We have been quite targeted in our sponsorships." Research and demonstrating an understanding from a business perspective is critical for both parties. However, as one PAO noted, "[A] prospect list is a worthy goal but it doesn't happen that much as there are a very finite group of organisations in New Zealand who will sponsor, and they like to be exclusive in the sector as well". Therefore, their advice is to "look for who might have a gap in their portfolio, look for a contact, and make an approach".

Initially, PAOs provided as a standard offering information regarding the demographic and size of their audience, as well as the market reach. Additional information was provided to suit the specific sponsoring, or prospective client.

As many of the relationships explored in the interviews endured over an extensive period of time, it was not surprising to find several respondents who had inherited relationships. For most of the interviewees, there was little or no difference in the nature of the exchange as the personnel changed. This is because the sponsorship is a business decision by both parties, so it is viewed from an organizational perspective, but the individuals involved can influence the quality of the exchange. However, one particular inherited sponsorship changed the relationship significantly. This was largely a contra-based exchange where there was a change in the key PAO manager of the relationship. For the first three months, there was a period of learning about what had been set up and why it was not working for the sponsor. The parties sat down together and revisited the substance of the exchange by assessing the strengths and skills of each party in meeting their own goals (the dollar value remained the same). The willingness of both parties to honestly explore the most effective way to use the skills and talents of all those involved "set up the relationship for the next four years", a relationship that the initiator of the change described as "the most satisfying of my career".

The Nature of the Exchange

Much of the literature concentrates on what the PAO needs to provide for the corporate sponsor. The interviews gave a more balanced view of where the expectations of the exchange were to have mutual business benefits. Table 6.1 outlines the broader types of value exchanges and the benefits that are accrued by the sponsor and the PAO.

Sponsorship does not imply monogamy. Both PAOs and commercial firms hold a portfolio of sponsorship arrangements. All four of the PAOs

Table 6.1 Accrual of Sponsorship Benefits

	Benefits received by performing arts organization	Benefits received by sponsor
Categories of sponsorship benefits	Services and/or products from the sponsor ('in kind' or 'contra' sponsorship). In kind and cash. Funding for a specific event or program, such as a performance for schools or education material, a winter season or specific event. Fundraising or financial support for a specific artist. Increased marketing reach. Amplification of marketing presence. Increased attractiveness to other funding sources and sponsors.	Tickets for clients (of the sponsor) or staff. Direct association with event. Direct association with an artist. Hosting important clients. Exclusive 'backstage' experiences for staff and/or clients. Branded merchandise. Naming rights (exclusivity). Digital presence (brand awareness). Positive brand affiliation. Lower activation spend (1:1) compared to other advertising channels. (IEG 2012).

had a specific process and strategy for guiding their sponsoring partnership decisions. The sponsors, on the other hand, were mixed in their responses. Those with less formal strategies explained that their portfolio was largely influenced by an advocate (internal or external). However, the final decision to select or continue a contract was either values or brand-congruency based. As one respondendent commented, "[The PAO] mirrors everything we aspire to ourselves". In other words, the POA had values and a culture that the sponsoring corporate desired for their own organization.

There are a number of realities of business that create obstacles to either party setting up more novel modes of exchange. As one PAO noted, "A lot of what we hear is, 'We'd love to do more but we just don't have the time'". From a corporate perspective, the challenges of internal capacity centered on resourcing issues and core businesses' schedules that were not always conducive to radically new initiatives. Another sponsor expressed it as simply having reached their capacity to serve any new relationships. Resistance was also attributable to the position of sponsorship within the corporate sector. Only one corporate respondent noted that sponsorship was considered a shared service within their business' ". . . [that] goes far and wide . . . We integrate it into everything we do". This comment reflected that sponsorship for this organization was part of an overall strategic plan and not just part of the marketing plan. This indicates that without the perspective of other departments within a business, it is more difficult to identify broader opportunities. Also, in some cases, the sponsorship policy has been set at a global level, thereby limiting the local and national-level opportunities. "It's all down to the individuals involved and what they are empowered to do", reported one PAO respondent.

The greater the trust and understanding of each other's business (core operation, processes, systems, strategic direction), the broader the view, thereby increasing the likelihood of spotting an opportunity. This was particularly highlighted in one of the relationships, whose grasp of the other's business enabled the PAO to refine the offering to maximize the value added to both. As noted by the PAO respondent, "At the start the sponsor was very traditional and very protective of its traditional base. Anyone could have done the more traditional style of 'in kind' sponsorship. For the corporation to do what we had in our vision took bravery from the client's point of view and obviously it took time, because we couldn't do that in the first year—it took four years". This statement encapsulates one of the critical influences of trust and willingness to explore the relationship in new ways.

The Nature of the Relationship

"We both get it. Both parties understand each other and we both respect each others' values" (a sponsor). "The best relationships are a relationship" (PAO respondent). The term 'relationship' was used 37 times over the ten interviews. 'Communication' and 'understanding' were used 30 times. PAOs and sponsors gave equal emphasis to the importance of the partnership and relational behaviour elements such as communication, including style, frequency, honesty and openness, and understanding the sponsor's business. Greater depth of understanding seemed to be expected from the PAO about the values and general mechanics of the sponsoring organization's business as well as their specific marketing objectives. The sponsor's focus was a mixture of shared values of the brand and companies. Others focused primarily on their marketing objectives. The third group tended to be deeply involved in the business of the PAO and so had a more personal, business-to-business exchange beyond the tickets for services exchange.

Since the global financial crisis of 2008, there has been a stronger focus on return for investment rather than philanthropic giving. Spending is under greater scrutiny, and as one sponsor put it, "[you] can't be seen to be parting with company money on a whim, it's all got to be thought through a little more scientifically and clinically". Both PAOs and their partners emphasized the growing commercial aspect of their relationships.

The number of points of contact between organizations tended to add depth to the relationship and increase the delivery of appropriate value exchange. As one sponsor related, "It makes the relationship much stickier as well, it's harder to let go of it than if you have all those relationships running through just one person".

Reviewing the Relationship

Almost every respondent's first reaction to the question of measurement was to chuckle. As one sponsor explained, "The reality is that you can't get an accurate fix on the return . . . It is part of an overall annual marketing mix". The literature agrees with this assessment, as it is challenging to isolate the elements that contribute to a specific result (Thomas et al., 2009; Meenaghan et al., 2013). All PAOs used a mixture of formal and informal metrics to evaluate the state of the relationship. The PAOs tended to have the more comprehensive list of formal measures. This could partly be attributed to the processes and systems that are already in place for reporting to other funding bodies. By contrast, informal metrics dominated the sponsor's side of the relationship. Only one of the corporate partners used extensive metrics to form a 'Net Promotor Score'. This may be a reflection on the types of marketing and communication goals of this particular sponsor. For several of the in-kind sponsors, the value gains they were seeking related to the creation of a virtuous circle of business-to-business interaction where ". . . ultimately it is the relationship and how it positively or negatively informs the work".

The subjective nature of the measures for success is further reflected in the list of signs that it is time to move on. Even for the sponsor with the clearest set of metrics, poor return on benefits was last on the list. As one participant describes, ". . . it's just got to do with the relationship. It's more of a feeling, is this relationship going smoothly or not?"

There are several indicators that sponsorship in New Zealand has made its way into a 'partnership' space rather than purely transactional. The clearest of these indicators is in the dominant vocabulary of relationship rather than ownership and of the shared expectation of a collaborative approach to defining the substance of delivery on the specific objectives of a given arrangement.

Discussion

The need for PAOs to look toward the commercial sector for additional funding has been well established in the extant literature (Thomas et al., 2009; Allen et al., 2013; Lindqvist, 2013). Despite the dominance of relationship theory in the literature, most research only looks at one side of the equation. In this analysis, there has been an opportunity to examine the interaction of each perspective. While transactional sponsorship arrangements appear to dominate, they also have elements that create deeper, enduring, high-value engagements that strongly align with partnering relationship theory. How those relationships look varies according to the nature of the business of the sponsor, the nature of the interaction (in kind, cash or a combination) and the reasons for sponsoring a particular PAO.

It can be seen that the current balance of power between corporate organizations and PAOs is skewed toward the sponsoring companies, as they are the holders of the purse strings. Therefore, the PAO feels they need to go cap in hand, and the sponsor feels 'burdened' by the arrangement rather than benefited. Neither position provides futile ground for developing trust.

However, relationships based on mutual respect and shared values rather than desperation are more likely to produce strong returns on the investments made by both sides of the sponsor partnership.

All of the PAOs had spent time and energy learning about the business activities and interests of their sponsors. Those with the strongest relationships had proffered opportunities beyond the marketing goals of the sponsoring company. There was a strong correlation between expressed interest and involvement in the business of the sponsor and of the PAO, developing mutual trust and respect and a willingness to continue that relationship.

It appears from the experiences of the interview subjects that fully formed symbiotic relationships are still relatively new in New Zealand. The language used by the participants was also a mixture of 'asset', 'property' and 'partner'. However, there were also examples of added value offerings. The PAOs tended to be the initiator of many of these, but offers were also made by their partners. The onus is on the PAO to look for unique added values, which means the PAO needs to research and gain knowledge of the prospective partner. Table 6.1 outlines the benefits that each organization realizes from the sponsorship. The more benefits that are on offer, the greater the value of the sponsorship. For example, the corporate sponsor who benefits from brand association, entertainment opportunities for key clients, staff involvement and media exposure is able to accrue more value compared to a sponsor who realizes just one of the above benefits. PAOs, on the other hand, accrue the best value from gaining cash or a contra deal, but again, the more benefits realized, the better off a PAO will be.

One thing that is certainly agreed upon across the participants is that relationships are time and energy consuming. Therefore, taking the time and expending the resources on research and profiling reduces the risk and expense of making a poor choice. Research provides information that can reduce the risks of connecting with an unsuitable arrangement or partner. By starting with congruency of brand and shared cultural values, organizations can quickly provide a simple yes/no judgment of whether it is worth 'testing the waters'.

Being able to accurately target a market and present a business case to support the potential partnership reduces the risk of the endeavour (Bower, 2009; 2010). Using the language of business to present a tailored offering demonstrates the credibility of the offer and reduces risk perception (Daellenbach, 2012). The key factor each participant emphasized was showing an understanding of the drivers for their respective organizations and how each was going to be better off as a result of a collaborative effort.

This is the point at which the concept of social network theory and the role of a 'wing man' seems to fit most closely (Daellenbach et al., 2006; O'Reilly et al., 2013). Getting in front of the decision makers is challenging. Daellenbach's (2012) research examines the role of the advocate in detail. One starting point for finding these connections is internal networks, such as the board and employees, as well as external networks through business contacts, clients and suppliers. The advice from several participants on both sides of the relationship was that if an organization does not have those particular skills, then they should engage a professional.

The management of sponsorship partnerships requires a heavy time commitment. Clearly, it is important to be able to measure the return on the invested time, money and resources (Rentschler et al., 2001; Zinger et al., 2010; Meenaghan et al., 2013), as giving money for no expected return is philanthropy (Walker et al., 2013). All respondents cited the importance of regularly reviewing the sponsorship proposition. And yet, this research showed a belief that formal metrics are limited to largely transaction-based objectives.

The exchanges that had the greatest return for both parties occurred later in the relationship, as it takes time to build trust and understanding (Ryan et al., 2003; Lund, 2010). It takes courage to step outside the box and the support of those ultimately held responsible to their stakeholders. Some of the participants found that their value-added offers were less enthusiastically received by those outside the initial idea exchange. By contrast, in examples where more unusual arrangements were contracted, the sponsorship managers were able to convince their respective colleagues of its value.

The regular informal and formal reviews conducted by all of the participants confirms the belief that measuring intangibles is challenging but not impossible (Hubbard, 2007; Sullivan et al., 2009). Digital communication channels are providing greater opportunities to track exposure, purchasing behaviours and brand association. If we focus on the purpose of measurement, expanding it from a precise quantity to include an estimated understanding that reduces uncertainty, then it becomes easier to explore ways of monitoring the financial, material and relational aspects of a partnership, making it possible to evaluate the worth to the company of the sponsorship.

Each sponsor and sponsee set objectives for their particular engagement. For example, the sponsor whose prime objective was maximizing the regional engagement of their customers developed both commercial and brand metrics to generate a Net Promotor Score. These same metrics would also provide significant information for other sponsors; however, they may give those measures a different weighting, e.g., the sponsor whose objective is to reach the CEOs of another business would rate hosting opportunities highly. A PAO may prioritize other aspects of a sponsorship, focusing their resources on in-kind exchanges that the sponsor finds easy to say 'yes' to when it is time to renew the contract. While priorities differ, what is clear is that if partners are to avoid the problems caused by misaligned agendas or disappointed expectations, they will need to agree on what and how success is to be measured.

No matter how much a company is liked, sometimes the sponsorship just doesn't work as well as it should. The business environment can change, and the partners may start moving in different directions. Regular formal and informal conversations (not just information exchange) are an integral part of any relationship and are no less important in a business partnership. Emotional attachment to a company may not hold enough sway if it is not serving the objectives of both organizations. In business terms, when the objectives are being measured, the value targets are not being met and the brand congruency is no longer strong, it is time to re-assess the partnership (Mazodier et al., 2012; Greenhalbh et al., 2013; Meenaghan et al., 2013). Sometimes it is the human element that simply doesn't gel.

Upon reviewing the literature and the findings of this study, it became evident that the relationship between a sponsor and a sponsee resembled the stages of dating, namely, setting yourself up for success, putting yourself out there, having a successful date and building on the first date. The purpose of any framework is to use a new lens to look at an old problem in order to find a new solution. Using the dating analogy, we see that what applies to one partner may also apply to the other. Sponsorship is most effective when it forms a part of an overall business strategy for both. To realize the full potential of any business-to-business exchange, all those involved need to have a clear grasp of the purpose of the partnership and what success looks like (Bower, 2009).

References

Allan, C., Grimes, A. and Kerr, S. (2013). *Value and Culture: An Economic Framework*. Wellington, NZ: Manatū Taonga- Ministry for Culture and Heritage.

Belfiore, E. (2003). Measuring the "Economic Importance" of the Arts: Problematic Issues, *Arts Professional*, 43, 9–10.

Bennett, R. (2014). How small charities formulate marketing responses to major reductions in income: A study of nonprofit contemporary dance companies. *Qualitative Market Research: An International Journal*, 17(1):58–76.

Bower, G. (2010). *10 Steps to Sponsorship Success*. Retrieved from <http://www.swprn.com/blog/10-steps-to-sponsorship-success-by-gail-s-bower/>.

Bower, G. (2009). *How to Jump Start Your Sponsorship Strategy in Tough Times*. Philadelphia, USA: Bower & Co. Consulting LLC.

Clegg, A. (2008). *Evolving Art of Sponsorship*, FT.Com. Retrieved from <http://search.proquest.com/docview/229119279?accountid=14782>.

Colbert, F., d'Astous, A. and Parmentier, M. (2005). Consumer perceptions of sponsorship in the arts. *International Journal of Cultural Policy*, 11(2):215–228.

Cooper, L. (2011). Arts sponsorship: Culture club courting mass-market brands. *Marketing Week*, 34(21): 26–27. Cornwell, T. (2008). State of the art and science in sponsorship-linked marketing. *Journal of Advertising*, 37(3):41–55.

Cornwell, T., Humphreys, M., Maguire, A., Weeks, C. and Tellegen, C. (2006). Sponsorship linked marketing: The role of articulation in memory. *Journal of Consumer Research*, 33:312–321.

Daellenbach, K. (2012). Understanding the decision-making processes for arts sponsorship. *International Journal of Nonprofit and Voluntary Sector Marketing*, 17(4):363–374.

Daellenbach, K., Davies, J. and Ashill, N. J. (2006). Understanding sponsorship and sponsorship relationships—Multiple frames and multiple perspectives. *International Journal of Nonprofit and Voluntary Sector Marketing*, 11(1):73–87.

Dalakas, V. (2009). Consumer response to sponsorships of the arts. *Journal of Promotion Management*, 15:204–211.

Deitz, G. D., Myers, S. W. and Stafford, M. R. (2012). 'Understanding consumer response to sponsorship information: A resource matching approach. *Psychology Marketing*, 29:226–239.

Greenhalgh, G., and Greenwell, T. C. (2013). What's in it for me? An investigation of North American professional Niche sport sponsorship objectives. *Sport Marketing Quarterly*, 22(2):101–112.

Hubbard, Douglas W. (2007). *How to Measure Anything: Finding the Value of Intangibles in Business*. Hoboken, N.J: John Wiley & Sons.

IEG (2012, March 19) 12th Annual IEG Performance Research Sponsorship Decision-Makers Survey. Retrieved 16.03.2016 from: www.performanceresearch.com/2012-IEG-Study.pdf.

IEG (2012, March 19) 12th Annual IEG Performance Research Sponsorship Decision-Makers Survey. Retrieved from: www.performanceresearch.com/2012-IEG-Study.pdf.

Johnston, M. and Paulsen, N. (2014). Rules of engagement: A discrete choice analysis of sponsorship decision making. *Journal of Marketing Management*, 30(7–8):633–663.

Kotler, P. and Keller, K. (2012). *Marketing Management*. 14th ed. Harlow, England: Pearson Education Ltd

Lindqvist, K. (2013). Making sense of financial incentive as a policy tool of the independent arts sector. *Public Policy and Administration*, 28(4):404–422.

Lund, R. (2010). Co-creating value in sponsorship relations: The case of the royal Swedish opera. *International Journal of Quality and Service Sciences*, 2(1):113–127.

Mazodier, M., and Merunka, D. (2012). Achieving brand loyalty through sponsorship: The role of fit and self-congruity. *Academy of Marketing Science Journal*, 40(6):807–820.

Meenaghan, T., McLoughlin, D. and McCormack, A. (2013). New challenges in sponsorship evaluation actors, new media and the context of Praxis. *Psychology and Marketing*, 30(5):444–460.

O'Brien, D. (2010). *Measuring the Value of Culture: A Report to the Department of Culture, Media and Sport*. United Kingdom: Department of Culture, Media and Sport.

O'Reilly, N. and Horning, D. L. (2013). Leveraging sponsorship: The activation ratio. *Sport Management Review*, 16(4):424–437.

Plewa, C. and Quester, P. G. (2011). Sponsorship and CSR: Is there a link? A conceptual framework. *International Journal of Sports Marketing & Sponsorship*, 12(4):301.

Preece, S. (2005). The performing arts value chain. *International Journal of Arts Management*, 8(1):21–32.

Sullivan, P. and Wurzer, A. (2009). Ten Common Myths about Intangibles Value and Valuation. *Intellectual Asset Management*, May/June 2009: 313–4.

Rentschler, R., Radbourne, J., Carr, R., and Rickard, J. (2001). Relationship marketing, audience retention and performing arts organisation viability. *International Journal of Nonprofit and Voluntary Sector Marketing*, 7(2):118–130.

Rhonda, W. M. (1999). Event sponsorship: An exploratory study of small business objectives, practices, and perceptions. *Journal of Small Business Management*, 37(3):25–30.

Rupp, C., Kern, S. and Hemig, B. (2014). Segmenting nonprofit stakeholders to enable successful relationship marketing: A review. *International Journal of Nonprofit and Voluntary Sector Marketing*, 19:76–91.

Ryan, A. and Fahy, J. (2003). A relationship marketing perspective on the sponsorship of the arts in Ireland: A Galway arts festival-nortel networks case study. *Irish Marketing Review*, 16(1):31–42.

Thomas, S., Pervan, S. and Nuttall, P. (2009). Marketing orientation and arts organisations: The case for business sponsorship. *Marketing Intelligence & Planning*, 27(6):736–752.

Walker, M. and Kent, A. (2013). The roles of credibility and social consciousness in the corporate philanthropy-consumer behavior relationship. *Journal of Business Ethics*, 116(2):341–353.

Wiedmann, K. and Gross, P. (2013). Image transfer in a sponsorship alliance. *Marketing Review St.Gallen*, 30(1):22–35.

Wishart, T., Lee, S. and Cornwell, T. (2012). Exploring the relationship between sponsorship characteristics and sponsorship asking price. *Journal of Sport Management*, 26:335–349.

Zinger, J. T. and O'Reilly, N. J. (2010). An examination of sports sponsorship from a small business perspective. *International Journal of Sports Marketing & Sponsorship*. 11(4):283.

Section III

Performing and Agreeing on Values

The third section includes chapters dealing with the question of value in different ways. Surprisingly for us editors, the texts in this section present dialogues which all show the ambition of an intellectual 'reconciliation' between business and the arts. Rather than neatly opposing the voices from the two fields, these texts are written in a one-voice fashion in which the authors have united their thoughts.

In the first chapter, business scholar **Emilie Reinhold** and visual arts scholar **Kahena Sanaâ** tackle the currently highly debated question of performance focusing on management studies and visual arts. After having identified a strong relation between performance and effectiveness, efficiency and results in management studies and between performance and defined performance art as a particular kind of artistic action, they move to the so-called performative turn in social sciences for a sort of synthesis of the two views. Conceptualizing what they call the performing body, Emilie Reinhold and Kahena Sanaâ conclude their chapter by proposing a redefinition of performance as effective embodied action.

The second chapter of this section, co-authored by marketing scholar **Chloé Preece** and communication and culture scholar **Aleksandra Bida**, develops a discussion on value by taking the case of how art is valued and which values are being considered in the visual arts market with particular reference to the valuation of Da Vinci's *Mona Lisa*, Felix Gonzalez-Torres's *Pile of Candy* and Bansky's *Eat the Rich*.

The two following chapters deal with the issue of how value is performed in practice in between the world of business and the arts, and they can be read as implicit dialogue between one author and the voice of the Other echoed through the voice of the author. Organizational scholar **Ester Barinaga** reflects on her own collaboration with an artist in the specific context of a community art project that she had initiated. Through a vivid account of her experience, Ester Barinaga's text raises questions about different values or orders of worth, as she chooses to call her world of civism and the artist's world of inspiration. In the irreconcilable relationship between the two, issues such as otherness and transformation through collaboration, which Hansen and Strauss had raised in their chapter on collaboration, become more concrete.

The fourth chapter of the section, written by management and informa-tion systems scholar **Ravi Dar** and management and culture scholar **Pamela Schultz Nybacka,** fosters a discussion on the question of legitimacy and validation based on their study of a private art gallery owned by a family business. The BKH finds itself juggling being legitimate in the art world and at the same time needing to legitimize itself from a business perspective. Ravi Dar and Pamela Schultz Nybacka use this case to reflect on the role of criticality and critique, continuing the discussion initiated by Ericsson and Eriksson in their chapter, and make considerations on the performativity of evaluation, thus linking to Reinhold and Sanaâ's chapter opening this section.

7   A Short Dialogue on the Meaning of Performance

Emilie Reinhold and Kahena Sanaâ

Introduction

In a time when artists define themselves as entrepreneurs or aesthetic con-sultants, when museums, theatres and even artistic research have to stick to managerial standards, when art performances are bought as masterpieces by big institutions, it makes no sense to separate art and business. The art world and especially the specific market organizing actors around what is called contemporary art is closely linked to fashion, luxury and finance. It would surely be comfortable to think that business has to do with economi-cal value and individual performance, while art has to do with aesthetic value and shared creativity, typically linking the first to numbers and rigor and the second to ideas, images and gift economy. Art is a great business, and business can be done in many ways, including artistic ways. Besides, as shown by Boltanski and Chiapello (1999), artistic critique is easily swal-lowed by capitalism's never-ending hunger.

Notice that the word performance seems more natural in a business con-text, unless it is preceded by the word art. An art performance or hap-pening is a special kind of artistic action. Artists basically perform some peculiar action in a public context: slapping each other in the face until exhaustion like Abramovic and Ulay, being shot in the arm like Burden, masturbating under a gallery floor like Acconci or showing your breasts in a box like Export. Quite opposed to that, employees have a performance, broadly meaning the measurable value they bring to the organization they are part of. Indeed, the notion of performance intended as efficiency acts as a paradigm in management studies and in the business world. With its rule of 'publish or perish', academic knowledge generation itself is under the spell of the performativity paradigm. Therefore, the notion of performance in management studies could usefully be contrasted to its understanding in live arts. Overcoming a typically French cultural boundary between busi-ness studies and art studies, the first author convinced the second to conduct a somewhat difficult dialogue on the meaning of performance in arts and business.

The aim of this chapter is thus to bring a better understanding of the notion of performance through a cross-fertilization between management studies and visual arts. Our main contribution is to redefine performance as effective embodied action thanks to performance theories in arts. The goal is to understand how a public gesture can have a social and emotional effect.

A consultant or a lawyer performs a profession very much like an actor performs a role, showing that the meaning of performance could reasonably be linked to bodily action. The verb to perform has a broad meaning, referring both to action taking place and to the result of action. After a look at the word's etymology and semantic evolutions, we will explore its different understandings in the contexts of management studies and arts. We will then connect what has been called the 'performative turn' in social sciences with the practice of performance art and innovative methodologies in social science. Finally, we will focus on the performing body to better understand performativity's dynamism based on repetition and interruption, embodied presence and relation to an audience.

Clarifying the Different Meanings of the Word Performance

Performance is a complex word in which contradicting meanings seem to cohabit. It is thus useful to search for the word's etymology and use in different languages. Surprisingly, the word is not English, but stems from a word in ancient French that was later adapted to English. The word is *parformance*, stemming from *parformer* or *par-former*. Its meaning in the 16th century was to accomplish, to execute. It gives the idea of acting with an extra layer of perfectionism and surely intentionality. It usually implies an act for which a process or pattern of movement has already been established, especially one calling for skill or precision.

The English verb 'to perform' later took on other meanings: it is the expression of a deed, an extraordinary action or a return on investment. In the common language, the English word has often been associated with live arts and was extended in the 17th century to mean the interpretation of a text by an actor or a music score by a musician. Performance finally included all kinds of public representation, from politicians talking to pop stars singing. To perform thus means to act, to play, to present or represent, expressing something in order to produce an effect on an audience. In Goffman's perspective (1959), performances are activities that serve the purpose of creating an effect on others. Refusing to oppose sincere to false performance, he indicated that what counts as the 'solid world' in the performance is what is effected—and how well.

The French contemporary use of the word *performance* is linked to the execution of an action, the accomplishment of a task or the specific efficiency of a function or an operation. It is thus both the accomplishment of a task and the ideal qualities needed for a good result, be it in a machine, a human or an animal. Efficiency could seem a recent development of the word, but the Latin etymology of *performance* already gave us an idea of perfection, exceptional action and excellence. The ambiguity of the word performance thus resides in its reference both to action (accomplishment, execution, realization) and the result of action, in other words, both to the capacity to act and to action's efficiency or effectiveness.

Performance in Management Studies

The managerialization of society has contributed to the spreading of the concept of performance as seen by management to all sectors of society. "Management is taken as a given, and a desirable given at that, and is not interrogated except in so far as this will contribute to its improved effectiveness" (Fournier and Grey, 2000:17). Management has effectiveness at its core, and the argument is good enough to be adopted by all sectors of society. Critical management scholars have begun a dialogue with other social sciences to question the meaning of performance and performativity, and it is to this field that we want to contribute, but before that, we will have a look at more mainstream understandings of performance.

The notion of performance is central in the sports world. It is a competition's result expressed in numbers; it is at the core of sportsmen's activities. As numbers facilitate the comparison and classification between bodies, performance is often expressed in time, distance, weight, height etc. It can also be a simple ranking between individuals or teams. The word performance carries the idea of success (a failure is politely called poor performance). It pervades all types of games and activities, measuring and confronting human capacities. It gives the idea of a record to be broken, be it in competition with other bodies or with oneself. Indeed, it is hard to imagine the sports world without the measuring of various performances; it would be liquid and somewhat uncanny. As shown by smartphone applications and connected clothes, it has become a habit to measure the slightest personal exercise. The notion of performance easily invades our private lives, from sex to leisure activities.

The word performance is widely used in management contexts with a meaning that is close to the sports world. We should remember that the science of management is based on workers' physical performance measured in production pace. It builds mainly on one unit of analysis obviously linked to the body: the gesture. In a mechanistic conception of the human subject, scientific organization of work aims to identify, normalize, chronometer, evaluate and monitor working gestures (Clegg et al., 2006). The goal is to find the most efficient gesture that could easily be learned and repeated, the focus being on the result (production) rather than on the gesture itself (body).

Sports and management seem to walk hand in hand to define what a competitive body should be: goal oriented, fast and measurable. Performance is usually expressed in numbers and is used to classify individuals.

Management is embedded in the modern paradigm of progress and productivity and has thus focused on only one dimension of the concept of performance: efficiency. This has led to the development of various measuring instruments, with the underlying assumption that what cannot be measured does not have importance. Comparing output to input gives you the performance of a machine, a human being or a system. To perform well is to be efficient, to add value, to produce a return on investment, a benefit.

Individual and organizational performance has been increasingly formalized and made auditable, which has led to a situation where persons are not supposed to speak or affirm their presence, but merely to write and tick boxes (Power, 1999). We keep on producing records and traces of our activities, behaving as if we might one day be inspected. The audit society seems to produce disembodiment, making it more and more difficult to see performance's initial link to the body, physical capacities and the gesture.

HRM studies is perhaps one of the fields where the body could re-emerge: it's not only about designing individual and collective action, but more and more about preserving health or avoiding moral or physical sickness. It is crucial for a firm to make sure employees enhance their individual performance in order to contribute positively to the firm's productivity, but this cannot be done at the cost of individual well-being. The expression 'human resource' itself builds on the idea of efficiency and productivity; human beings are defined as measurable resources because they contribute to the overall performance of a system. Individuals are ranked in terms of economical performance, for example, sales or number of achieved contracts.

"Performance appraisal systems generally attempt to anchor the individual to some type of behaviourally or numerically anchored measuring system. Thus, for example, a performance dimension might be 'leadership' ability, which might be graded on a five-point scale, ranging from 'well above' to 'well below average'" (Townley, 1993:529).

There is a one-sided understanding of performance in HRM; we should reconsider the conceptualization and measurement of performance, bringing in dissenting voices into the consensus-oriented field of HRM (Janssens and Steyaert, 2009). This is precisely what performance as seen by live arts can help us to do. To perform is to have a specific embodied activity that produces an effect on others. Performance has a link to the body and its physical capacities; to perform well is not only to produce economical results, it is also to have an emotional effect in a given context, which is not limited to charismatic leaders.

Performance in Live Arts

Performance art was a way for artists to counter the art market's dominating mechanisms. Artists refused to produce goods meant for a market and decided to produce experiences instead, often shaped outside the art world's boundaries. Performance art pushed art out of institutional spaces and frames and produced new public reflexions about what art actually is. It includes different practices: live arts, action art, happenings, body art, ordeal art and performance art. All these practices have the body as a common ground; the body is both a medium for the artist and a means of participation for the public. A good performance clearly has an effect on an audience.

Performance art can't be defined once and for all; it depends widely on various cases emerging in different historical contexts. "By its very nature, performance defies precise or easy definition beyond the simple declaration that it is live art by artists. Any stricter definition would immediately negate the possibility of performance itself" (Goldberg, 1979:6). The first art performances took place in 1909, when the Italian futurists began to put declamations and gestures at the core of their practice. They allowed themselves to become artworks, with the intention to "instil doubt in a public full of self-righteousness". From the beginning, the body and its possibilities of movement and sound were central, acting as an antidote to the rigidities of the art world. The gesture and the embodied character of the event is a central ingredient of an art performance, as are also risk and sometimes danger.

Between the 50s and the 70s, new artistic practices emerged: they had the body as territory of intense experimentation and the interaction with the public as an important condition of success. Artists came from all different disciplines: dance, theatre, poetry, music, painting and sculpture. Important names from performance art's beginnings include Anna Halprin, John Cage, Allan Kaprow and Yoko Ono in the United States, Ben, Yves Klein and Michel Journiac in France, the Zaj group in Spain, Joseph Beuys in Germany, Viennese actionists in Austria and the Gutai group in Japan.

Goldberg (1979) distinguishes performance art from theatre: the performer is not a character but him- or herself, and the performance is not a narrative or a representation: it simply happens. Art performance is opposed to all routine, order and expectations in art.

On the contrary, Schechner (1988) does not make a clear distinction between theatre and performance. For him performance is a large field including theatre, script and drama and resulting from a mixture of dance, oral poetry, painting and theatre. What counts in his eyes is the process that leads to the encounter with the audience, what he calls the gather/perform/break-up sequence. Performances differ from material artworks because they don't have a clear intention. They are first and foremost experimental; they are spaces of play for the physical interaction between performers and spectators. The gathering of different people for a performance produces new relationships between individuals, questioning norms of embodiment and social conventions.

Performance art is experienced through the co-presence of the artist's body and the spectators' bodies. Phelan (1993) insists on the impossibility of repeating a performance and on the inter-subjectivity that is created between bodies during a performance. Performance is a blurring between art and life (Kaprow, 1993) that can't be defined precisely because of its great heterogeneity. Freedom and fragility, the body and inter-subjectivity seem to be the main ingredients in the practice of performance. Like the artist Esther Ferrer says, "performance is an ephemeral and homeless art that could establish itself anywhere". As it often has a clear political programme, it tends to penetrate spaces where power relations operate rather than museums.

Here are some famous art performances that can help the reader to understand its diversity. In 1985, Mona Hatoum, a Palestinian artist living in England, walked barefoot in the streets of Brixton in a black overall. She had black boots (Doc Martens) attached to her ankles and walked very slowly and heavily. In 1972, the American Vito Acconci performed *Seedbed*, a real marathon of masturbation in an art gallery in New York. Lying under the floor, he listened to the visitors' steps and words while masturbating three days a week from 10 am to 6 pm. In 1975, Esther Ferrer, a Spanish artist, measured her naked body in an empty apartment. Using a simple tape measure she gauged all parts of her body to confront them with the apartment's spaces. The action took 40 minutes and was registered on a video. Between 1967 and 1969, Bruce Nauman conducted a series of walking and standing experiences in his studio, questioning the body's balance and the repetition of gestures. His actions were registered and later became famous videos to which many artists refer. There are of course many other actions: Gina Pane cutting herself on a ladder, Chris Burden being shot in the arm, Michel Journiac making sausages out of his own blood, Yoko Ono asking spectators to cut up her dress, Joseph Beuys explaining art to a dead hare etc. Today artists refer to these emblematic performances as milestones, and some even re-activate them.

Be it in front of a camera, in the street or in an art gallery, the artists are putting their body at stake or even at risk in different experiments. They are interested in a kind of prowess, letting sensuality or crudeness step in. It's interesting to see that they are measuring their body in a social context; they either look for extreme situations or invert very banal facts into extraordinary events.

The Performative Turn in the Social Sciences

Theorizing the 'performative turn' in the social sciences Muniesa (2014) has only one small paragraph dedicated to art in his book. We suggest that the attention given to performativity lately can become a common ground for a discussion between arts and business. Building on Austin's (1962) important intuition that talking is sometimes equivalent to acting, organizational theorists are investigating the performativity of language but also behaviour, theories or artefacts like financial instruments or organisational charts.

"Performatives are statements that, in the uttering, also perform a certain action and exercise a binding power" (Butler, 1993:225). The best example is perhaps the priest pronouncing the well-known formula 'I declare you husband and wife'. The American philosopher Judith Butler has contributed widely to the development of the concept: "performativity must be understood not as a singular or deliberate 'act' but, rather, as the reiterative and citational practice by which discourse produces the effects that it names" (Butler, 1993:2). Gender norms, for example, are discursive and embodied practices that need to be repeated over and over again to be effective. But in the repetition of these everyday micro-performances, there is room for small perturbations and potential subversions; in fact, social norms may be reproduced awry or with a difference. Performativity has to do with the embodied way we repeat, cite and re-appropriate living norms.

In organizational and professional contexts, repetition is also a central dimension of performativity. Practitioners in the field of project management replay and recite norms in embodied rituals. "The repetition of identifiable performances enacts the 'professional' into being and simultaneously constrains the professional's conduct" (Hodgson, 2005:56). Take, for example, the way an academic presents a paper in front of an audience: there are norms to repeat to be identified as an academic—and not an artist—and these norms both help us and impede our becoming.

But through the process of repetition, a space of contestation, humor and subversion opens up; in this space, professionals can manage anxiety and ambivalence generated by a demanding work. To repeat or to imitate an action is very ambivalent: the professional gets disciplined in the process of professionalization, but at the same time, embodying the correct norms can help people to cultivate a distance. A professional can in fact play his/her part while cultivating irony, which brings in doubts about the reality of the situation.

There are in fact many occasions to practice performance art in business life: a consultant could, for example, dress in a slightly different way or alter the jargon a little to create confusion and interruptions in normality. Social movements and activists also use performance art when they design spectacular actions in public contexts. We should remember that there is no such thing as a real or false performance: the important aspect is what is effected and how well. Art performances in business life would perhaps reveal the artificiality of a situation that is otherwise taken for granted. Art can contribute to a redefinition of the situation.

Performance is about effectiveness in a public context, be it for an artist or for a manager. A visual study of large-scale management presentations such as annual general meetings, press conferences and analyst meetings shows how managers perform their profession. " 'Business is show business' and managers at large-scale events do not 'play' or 'act', but 'perform', they are performers, making use of genuine theatre techniques such as bright lighting and carefully designed settings, and creating an aesthetic experience" (Biehl-Missal, 2011:641). But their bodies appear rather constrained: their gestures, postures and voices indicate that they mainly stick to a prepared script and to the event's scenography. They express few emotions and conform to what organizations expect in such situations: rationality. Managers' bodies prefer to remain mute instead of risking a faux pas, for example, when gestures contradict the words that are uttered, which could be described as a-performative, when the body disturbs the performativity of talking. Unlike performance artists, who value chance and improvisation, managers want to be in control of a situation. In the context of a management-orchestrated show, the smallest deviant gesture might act as an art performance that could interrupt or even destroy the apparatus.

The American cultural environment in the 60s and 70s permitted both the development of performance art and experimental methods in the social sciences. In the 80s, the important field of 'performance studies' emerged in New York, examining theatre, dance and rituals and relating them to anthropology and psychology. What artists and sociologists actually did at that time in America had many things in common, especially regarding the study of collective action. When the sociologist Harold Garfinkel (1967) does a 'breaching experiment', for example, driving a car in an opposite direction or provoking chaos in a line, he transgresses established social norms in order to better understand how they work, both facilitating and constraining social interaction. It is research just as much as various art performances can be considered as social research. When the artist Joseph Beuys lives in a New York art gallery with a wild coyote for several days (*I love America and America loves me*), he enquires the human and animal condition through continuous interaction with the animal. It is both an art performance and an innovative research.

While artists and researchers seem to interrupt the social order, professionals repeat actions and pay a great respect to norms and rules defining each profession. At first glance, it could seem that artists stand for perturbations and chaos, while other professionals stand for repetition and order. Nevertheless, repetition generates a space for subversion in everyday working life, opening up spaces of experience and expression. Besides, there are surely routines, habits and norms in the practice of performance art.

The Performing Body

Confronting artists' dramatic gestures and embodied statements to performance measures and other managerial instruments result in a huge contrast: any kind of dialogue seems impossible. But if we see performance as embodied action made of repetition and expression, as some critical scholars have done, then a dialogue becomes possible. On the one side, performativity is linked to an outstanding gesture performed by a single individual in front of an audience; on the other side, it is linked to routines, habits and conformity with but also distance from a working context. Through the repetition or the interruption of embodied norms, any professional performs something thus contributing to the enactment of reality. It seems that professionals stand for repetition of norms at work, while artists take the risk of interruption of norms in different social contexts. Researchers stand somewhere in between, some very close to artists and others more dedicated to managers.

The practice of performance in arts does not clarify the concept of performance; rather, it brings in more complexity, which could be an adapted answer to the problem of its one-sided understanding in HRM. Artistic practice could help to enrich the dynamics of performativity. But how do artists reach effectiveness in their artistic action?

Effectiveness in the practice of art can be found mainly in the interaction between the artist and the public: the width of a gesture and the way it resonates in other bodies, the sharing of a sensation, the deviation of the public's expectations, the blurring between art and life but also the capacity of an action to produce new images or recall old images in the participants' minds. Effectiveness is when something happens in the interaction with the audience. A gesture has a certain scope and resonance with other bodies. Sensations are shared, and a common embodied understanding of the situation is produced. The artist often has a strong physical presence in the invested context; this is partly due to the injection of intimacy in a public or semi-private sphere, naked feet in the street, masturbation in public. Artistic gestures tend to expose the audience to constant doubts about what is actually happening, what is art and what is not and how they should react to the action going on. Somehow an audience should be challenged physically and feel that they have the power to interrupt or amplify the performance. Nevertheless, the artist works at always deviating what is expected from her/him. An art performance is thus an open-ended situation filled with physical tension. To perform is to have an effect, in other words, to affect participants.

Be it during annual meetings or face-to-face meetings, the world of business clearly has physicality and moments of performativity that could be compared to the previous description of art performance's functioning. There is seldom injection of intimacy or embodied subversion, but there could be smaller interruptions of embodied norms, leading to various forms of critique.

The notion of performance is problematic, be it in management or in arts. The way the term is used in management is perhaps closer to its original etymology; it relates to a deed, efficiency, achievement and result. In the art world, it refers to an experience having an inter-subjective effect in which the result is less important than the process, meaning the moment that has been shared between the performer(s) and the spectator(s). What is important is 'the doing and the showing' and not a pre-established result. It is the interaction between present bodies during the performance that counts. The circulation of feeling(s) is what creates an immediate effect (in terms of affects) but also a collective memory about the event. Performance art is precisely opposed to productivity and progress; it often shows slow, weak and deviant bodies. Performance art in the 50s was a way for artists to counter the manufactured object, break their links with the art market and invent new modalities of intervention in society. They refused to commercialize their performances, which is not the case of all performance artists today, like Tino Sehgal or Marina Abramovic working for the Guggenheim.

Today, many artists have a great interest for the aesthetic of ordinary life (Formis, 2010) and transpose ordinary gestures into the aesthetic sphere.

Dancers work with everyday gestures or micro-gestures, caught in a becoming-furniture or in the redefinition of their physical presence. They contribute to the reconsideration of banality while at the same time criticizing social life's artificiality. The gesturing body and its actions have an effect that could be called non-productive: the goal is to reach embodied presence, which cannot be done during regular productive work. The goal is to shake the established norms and the frames of our collective ordinary life.

We should also keep in mind artists' attempts to bring experimental art into corporations or public agencies, from the artist placement group in the 70s to the various programs of arts residencies today (Berthoin-Antal, 2012). Perhaps the best way to practice art performance today would be for artists to occupy or at least visit business contexts. This would mean that a critical reflection against capitalism and managerialism could physically take place, which is an alternative to the fictionalization of corporate life that also contributes to change.

References

Austin, J. L. (1962). *How to Do Things with Words*. Oxford: Clarendon Press.

Berthoin-Antal, A. (2012). Artistic intervention residencies and their intermediaries: A comparative analysis. *Organizational Aesthetics*, 1(1):44–67.

Biehl-Missal, B. (2011). Business is show business: Management presentations as performance. *Journal of Management Studies*, 48(3):619–645.

Boltanski, L. and Chiapello, E. (1999). *Le nouvel esprit du capitalisme*. Paris, France: Gallimard, NRF Essais.

Butler, J. (1993). *Bodies That Matter: On the Discursive Limits of Sex*. New York: Routledge.

Clegg, S. R., Courpasson, D. and Phillips, N. (2006). *Power and Organization*. London: Sage.

Formis, B. (2010). *L'esthétique de la vie ordinaire*. Paris, France: PUF.

Fournier, V. and Grey, C. (2000). At the critical moment: Conditions and prospects for critical management studies. *Human Relations*, 53(1):7–32.

Garfinkel, H. (1967). *Studies in Ethnometodology*. Englewood Cliffs, NJ: Prentice-Hall.

Goffman, E. (1959). *The Presentation of Self in Everyday Life*. Garden City: Anchor Books.

Goldberg, R. (1979). *Performance: Live Art 1909 to the Present*. New York: Harry N. Abrams, Inc., Publishers.

Hodgson, D. (2005). "Putting on a professional performance": Performativity, subversion and project management. *Organization*, 12(1):51–68.

Janssens, M. and Steyaert, C. (2009). HRM and performance: A plea for reflexivity in HRM studies. *Journal of Management Studies*, 46(1):143–155.

Kaprow, A. (1993). *Essays on the Blurring of Art and Life*. Berkeley: University of California Press.

Muniesa, F. (2014). *The Provoked Economy*. New York: Routledge.

Phelan, P. (1993). *Unmarked: The Politics of the Performance*. New York: Routledge.

Power, M. (1999). *The Audit Society*. Oxford: Oxford University Press.

Schechner, R. (1988). *Performance Theory*. New York and London: Routledge.

Townley, B. (1993). Foucault, power/knowledge, and its relevance for human resource management. *Academy of Management Review*, 18(3):518–546.

8 Evaluating Value
Stolen, Disappearing and Pseudonymous Art

Chloe Preece and Aleksandra Bida

Within both the arts and the business literature, there have been wide-ranging debates as to what constitutes value and how it can be defined or measured. In this chapter, we focus on the visual arts market, particularly since there has always been a significant lack of understanding as to how this market operates and how art is valued or indeed which values are being considered: aesthetic, social, cultural, critical and/or financial. Despite the art market being an increasingly valuable sector in the global economy—estimates indicate that auction and private sales amount to $50 billion annually, not including revenue made from public institutions (Horowitz, 2011)—it is the least transparent and least regulated major commercial activity in the world (Buck, 2004). The process through which art is valued therefore illuminates a market often considered impenetrable by outsiders to the field and thus can fruitfully provide insight into the question of value from the perspectives of both the arts and business (Robertson, 2005).

In line with Fitchett and Saren's (1998:333) suggestion that there is a need to reconsider the ways in which various "manifestations of value are constructed, produced and consumed", we consider the two key spheres within which artworks are produced and consumed: the art world and the art market. While they are inextricably linked and sometimes overlap, the former is occupied with aesthetic and socio-cultural value, while the latter focuses primarily on economic value. On one hand, the art world is "the network of people whose cooperative activity, organized via their joint knowledge of conventional means of doing things, produce(s) the kind of art works that art world is noted for" (Becker, 1982:p.x) and operates in the critical sphere. On the other hand, as Joy and Sherry (2003:177) note, "the market is one of many mechanisms by which we can evaluate the contributions of the art world. It is only one discourse in a universe of discourses that spans aesthetics, economics, politics and culture". While the art world and market overlap and influence each other, the art market constructs the discourse that is increasingly privileged in contemporary society, and Robertson and Chong (2008) note that it has recently gone through a period of unprecedented expansion. This art-creating versus commerce-generating divide is a fruitful context in which to consider value: how it is produced, delivered, consumed and perceived. Furthermore, an analysis of the divide provides a reconsideration of the very notion of value based on fixed criteria which can be objectively measured. We therefore argue that a multi-disciplinary macro-perspective, which can accommodate the tensions between and influences of socio-cultural as well as economic capital, is needed for a more nuanced and dynamic view of value creation.

After a brief examination of social capital and its role in the legitimation of artists and artworks, we take a closer look at three diverse examples of market value and its socio-cultural contexts in traditional, conceptual and street art. This perspective provides a different approach to value than that usually taken in the business literature, which focuses on economic value (see, e.g., Ramirez, 1999); by adopting sociological perspectives on the art market, we show the process through which economic value emerges out of the socio-cultural system. All our examples have nurtured a perception of exception as well as limited or endangered supply. Our analysis includes the role of media attention in making da Vinci's *Mona Lisa* an internationally recognizable work, of literally diminishing artwork in limited supply by Félix González-Torres and the dangers of erasure for street art by the nature of its location (or, more recently, disappearance from the location after being sold as a concrete canvas). These examples help us to demonstrate the ways in which historical processes, media attention and notoriety can work together in order to manufacture increasingly inflating market value that may or may not be perceived as inherently tied to art's intrinsic value as expressions of aesthetics, social commentary on human nature or many of the other socio-cultural functions of art that are highlighted or undermined through increasingly precipitous market prices. These prices can overshadow or distill the value of a work into a distinct, often seemingly disproportionate numerical form, while more broadly diminishing the perceived value of works that do not 'merit' such figures at auction houses or on insurance claims. An understanding of the perception of value in art requires a focus on the increasingly fluid, inter-related nature of the market price and social capital of any individual work and an artist's legitimation process.

Market Price: $-$$$, Social Capital: Priceless

The value systems of the art market are complex and the evaluation process through which works of art are recognized frequently have little to do with the materials or conventions used to construct them; their value is purely extrinsic. This is due to the fact that recognition of art is a social process that cannot be reduced to a reflection of artistic merit, and this recognition can wax or wane (Baumann, 2006). In order to access the market, art must first be legitimized and, thus, infused with value within the art world. According to Becker (1982) and Bourdieu (1993), art worlds and cultural fields are sites of collective action, and in order to understand the nature of cultural production and evaluation, we need to understand the social relations of the art world. Bourdieu explains, "Economic theory has allowed to be foisted upon it a definition of the economy of practices which is the historical invention of capitalism; and by reducing the universe of exchanges to mercantile exchange, which is objectively and subjectively oriented toward the maximization of profit, i.e., (economically) *self-interested,* it has implicitly defined the other forms of exchange as non-economic, and therefore *disinterested"* (2006:105–106). While exchange in the case of economic capital—as a means to an end—is transparent, self-interested and lacks intrinsic value; in the case of symbolic capital, such as cultural or social capital, this instrumentalization is suppressed through a sense of disinterestedness and intrinsic worth—the perceived intrinsic value of a work of art itself, for instance.

The perception of value in a work of art that has been commoditized through exchange in the art market clearly has both a self-interested, profit-seeking context (for any artists who seek to sell their work as well as buyers who seek to potentially re-sell them) as well as a more complex context of social and cultural forces or trends which serve to legitimate the intrinsic value of specific kinds of work by select artists, with no clear indicators or patterns in regards to aesthetic qualities, social meanings or historical nuances. Art collectors may cite philanthropic reasons such as the preservation of art as primary in their wish to personally accumulate notable artworks (Chen, 2009), but we suggest that this intention cannot be separated from the expectations of a profit motive through the fiscal value of a work— whether the potential increased monetary worth benefits the collector as an economic agent or serves to reinforce the perceived intrinsic worth of the piece as 'important' art and thus worthy of such a price.

Integral to an understanding of the creation and perception of value in art is the way in which an artist is legitimized, as the art and the artist are inextricably linked (see Preece and Kerrigan, 2015). The legitimization process comprises of a network of experts within both public and private sectors (artists, curators, academics, art teachers, critics, collectors and dealers) that negotiate the value of a work in order to decide whether it is worthy of a place in art history. Robertson (2005) demonstrates that the most likely route for the endorsement process to take starts at art school, with MFA degrees functioning as the first legitimator in an artist's career, followed by awards and residencies, representation by a primary dealer, reviews and features in art magazines, inclusion in prestigious private collections, museum validation in the form of group or solo shows, international exposure at well-attended biennials and art fairs and the appreciation signalled by strong resale interest at auction. This chain of events creates a socialization process which valorizes the artist (Galenson, 2005). Prices rise as art accumulates accolades from the endorsement chain, but price relates to the assurance of a work's quality rather than intrinsic qualities of the product. In this sense, the art is 'branded' (see Schroeder, 2005; Kerrigan et al., 2011;

Muñiz et al., 2014), whereby reputation, image and credibility are intangible assets, mobilizing forms of social attraction from followers and developing a sustained visibility contributing to brand equity. Indeed, focusing on the art world can provide broader perspectives for business approaches more generally, for example, in terms of the way value is collectively negotiated through a range of key stakeholders (Preece and Kerrigan, 2015) and how creativity can be managed to provide more flexible marketing approaches through practices such as risk taking or rule bending (Fillis, 2000).

This, however, does not tell us the actual criteria used in valuing artworks. Aesthetics alone are insufficient, and—particularly when contemporary art is concerned, whereby art can be made of anything or, indeed, nothing, as in performance and conceptual art—these criteria are shrouded in mystery. According to Danto's (1964) institutional theory of art, something commonplace may acquire art status through the embodied meanings interpreted through the lens of the art world, wherein art criticism, theory and history validate the work of the artist and imbue it with value. Therefore, "to see something as art requires something the eye cannot decry—an atmosphere of artistic theory, a knowledge of history of art: an art world" (Danto, 1964:580). In a somewhat circular process, then, 'art' is a sociological category and therefore anything art schools, museums and artists define as art is considered art; it could even be argued that the art world purposefully keeps the public in the dark in order to divorce itself from business and commerce (see Velthius, 2005) in order to appear 'authentic'. Artworks thus need to be 'framed' (explained, marketed, packaged) using the wider reasoning or values of the art world in order to be made comprehensible, valid, acceptable and desirable. Therefore, as Currid (2007) discusses, cultural value is not just an economic act, but instead part of an intense social process of legitimization and valorization.

The past twenty years or so have seen significant changes in the art market in terms of an increased shift towards art being described in financial and marketing terms and used as a financial investment due to an injection of wealth in the art market, primarily from new collectors from emerging economies (Robertson and Chong, 2008). This can be seen in a shift in popularity from art magazines such as *ArtForum*, where collectors used to form critical opinions on art, to a preference for *Bloomberg* and *ArtTactic*, where the emphasis is on monetary valuation as well as the growth of art investment funds (Joy and Sherry, 2003; Velthius, 2005). The proliferation of biennales, art fairs and media hype, not to mention gallerists, curators and celebrity collectors, predominates in a way that was inconceivable twenty-five years ago. The art industry thus impinges to an incredibly greater extent on how 'art' is viewed and thus valued. The scale is such that the art industry can now almost be compared to the music industry or the film industry, with branded galleries such as Gagosian and White Cube expanding around the world and branded auction houses such as Sotheby's and Christie's continuously setting record sales, much like the Hollywood box office. Indeed, recent decades witnessed a rapidly growing art market, which is widely reported in the media, particularly in terms of the steep prices achieved at auctions. A recent example is Christie's newest (May 2015) world record for the most expensive artwork, selling Picasso's *Women of Algiers* for $179 million in New York (up from $31.9 million when last sold in 1997) (Hickey, 2015). This comes at the expense of public museums; critic Jerry Saltz describes seeing the painting in Christie's: "I walked into Christie's in a state of strange pathos. Excited about seeing such great art; sad because it was displayed under these crowded conditions, and because I know almost everything I saw might not be seen again in public". Museums with limited funding cannot compete with private collectors; the art is often relegated to climate-controlled, tax-exempt warehouses. Saltz continues: "[u]nder the guise of so-called 'quality,' auction houses fabricate a pervasive psychic field that sees art in terms of price and profit. This seductive shallow field forces collections with similar work or similar-isms to rush the same artists and-isms to auction the following season to reap ever-higher prices" (Saltz, 2015). Exposing these market values as artificially high, Saltz highlights the fact that art is increasingly considered in terms of economic investment.

These changes imply a shift in how art is valued as the underlying framing discourse moves away from critical or aesthetic notions towards economics and marketing as impulsive collectors with little art history knowledge become more powerful than critics or curators. Indeed, art fairs are replacing quiet discussions held in the gallery with an experience akin to the shopping mall, blending art, fashion and parties in one place. Critic and curator Okwui Enwezor has argued that that art fairs have changed the critical context, making people pay more attention to the market than to artistic practices (Griffin, 2008). Unlike biennales, where some kind of relationship between the artworks exhibited is conceived by the curator, a fair comprises two or three thousand objects never intended to be seen together. For art, this means the supremacy of a culture of events and spectacle. Fairs also have an effect on the work sold, as Thompson (2008) points out: when a gallery sells at four fairs in three months, artists are required to churn out repetitive 'branded' work. It can be assumed that this will filter down in terms of what is bought, shown and therefore made, as well as affecting which artists' work is valued on the market. In this sense, concurrent with the "financialization" of the art world, arts enterprises are increasingly looking towards the business world to find new markets and building audiences rather than nurturing creative expression, social critique or other qualities.

To understand value in the art market, then, we argue that it is necessary to consider both how the work is legitimized and framed by the art market through an accumulation of social capital and also how the market prices the work, building on the art world's framework to 'monetize' the work. By examining the two discourses at work in three celebrated examples of art, we can see how economic and cultural values are being evaluated in the art and how deeply intertwined they are.

Enigmatic Smile: $$$, Mediatized Theft: Priceless

Our first example is the most celebrated and visited work of art in the world: La Gioconda, a.k.a. the *Mona Lisa*, by Leonardo da Vinci. An iconic painting, it has been stated that it is "the best known, the most visited, the most written about, the most sung about, the most parodied work of art in the world" (Lichfield, 2005). Its fame comes partly from the fact that it was painted by da Vinci, widely considered an artistic genius; partly from its atmospheric composition and the mystery of its subject matter, specifically the enigmatic expression of its subject; but also from the media attention it has received and, in particular, its theft in 1911. While the painting was quickly legitmized and valued within the elite of the art world, with a long history of provenance that traces back to the French monarchy, with Fran-cois I buying her from the artist himself, Louis XIV hanging her in Versailles and Napoleon moving her into his bedroom before she found her resting place in the Louvre (Chua-Eoan, 2007), general public interest in the work was relatively minimal. Indeed, at the time of its theft, the painting was not the most visited work in the museum, and the fact that the painting was not considered as valuable then as it is now is evidenced by the fact that it took 26 hours for museum staff to notice its absence (Zug, 2011). Yet, it was soon on the front page of every major newspaper, wanted posters for the painting appeared on Parisian walls, crowds amassed at police headquarters and a sudden boom in postcards bearing her image was noted (Lacayo, 2009). After word spread that this painting had been stolen, thousands of people queued to enter the Louvre in order to look at the empty wall where it had hung (Zug, 2011). Paradoxically, the absence of the work itself added to its value.

Here we see that the aura (to adopt Benjamin's term, 1968) of the piece extends well beyond the physical object, and examining only what is within the four corners of the canvas, or aesthetic value alone, is insufficient in explaining the value of a painting. Moreover, we see how the work was popularized thanks to the high-profile heist, leading to its now-iconic status worldwide and hefty price tag. Guinness World Records list the painting as having the highest insurance value of any painting in history, assessed as $100 million in 1962, equating to about $780 million now (Trowbridge, 2015). When the painting was found 28 months after the theft, it was returned to the Louvre, and more than 100,000 people viewed it in the first two days following its rehanging (Zug, 2011). Today, eight million people see the *Mona Lisa* every year and although most are unaware of the theft, they are also probably unaware of the unique innovation of Da Vinci's sfu-mato technique which gives her her enigmatic smile. Value, in this case, is thus neither singular nor solely attached to the product, but rather, we see a plurality of values (aesthetics, cultural significance, awareness, mediatiza-tion, financial) which come together through specific cultural trends, histori-cal circumstances and media-driven marketing practices.

Pile of Candy: $$, Consuming Art: Priceless

While we can easily understand how an original, figurative painting can be a highly prized object, it is more difficult to ascertain value when we are examining other types of works of art. For example, Félix González-Torres's (1957–1996) installation pieces are created in order to eventually reduce to nothing, most famously with piles of sweets that are meant to be taken by visitors. That his most valued works are his series of 'portraits' (see Image 8.1) created with these sweets is due to their symbolic meaning, which is intimately linked to the artist's private life. What collectors buy is the metaphorical representation of the person portrayed, in most cases the artist and/or his partner, who both died of AIDS-related illnesses. The weight of the candy represents their body weights before the illness; as visitors take the sweets, the diminishing amounts parallel their weight loss and suffering. This giving away of the art to the visitor who can then consume the work questions traditional capitalist concepts of ownership and value as taken for granted by most of the business literature. The transience of these pieces means that any collector or institution buying this work will get very little of a tangible nature, only advised weights and/or dimensions (complicating this further is the fact that the companies mass producing these

Image 8.1 Untitled (*USA Today*), Felix Gonzalez-Torres, 1990. The weight of the pile starts at 136 kg, the combined weight of Gonzalez-Torres and his lover, Ross Laycock.

sweets frequently change products and wrapping, meaning curators need to 'interpret' the work), as well as a certificate of authenticity signed by the artist. In theory, anyone could create the work, but yet those 'authentic pieces' are highly valued: one of them sold at auction for $4.6 million at Philips de Pury & Company in 2010 (Philips, 2010).

Here we see how the aura of the artist lives on and infuses the art to add value to the work and the significance of narrative in importing meaning (which often derives from the persona of the artist based on their perceived background or personality). This follows Brown and Patterson's (2010) work, which emphasizes the importance of building a brand narrative to enchant customers. In contemporary art, the concept of the work and the values it communicates are therefore crucial. Moreover, these artworks transform the audience from passive receivers into active participants in social action who can establish meaning in everyday objects. Building on the co-creation literature (Vargo and Lusch, 2008:7), we would agree that "value is idiosyncratic, experiential, contextual and meaning laden". However, in line with the socio-cultural marketing literature (see, for example, Peñaloza and Venkatesh, 2006; Brown, 2007), we do not think the service-dominant logic goes far enough, as the product is not necessarily created for a market. As Hirschman (1983) points out, the mainstream marketing concept is not always applicable to artists because they do not bring forth products in response to the desires or interests of consumers, but due to self-fulfilment of the creative process. Furthermore, there are other possible audiences: the general public, for example, in the form of museum/gallery visitors (rather than owners). González-Torres himself believed that "without the public these works are nothing. I need the public to complete the work. I ask the public to help me, to take responsibility, to become part of my work, to join in" (SFMoMA, 2015). While the history of portraiture is a record of the features of a sitter, depicting the look and character of the person shown (as in our first example), with conceptual art, we can see how an idea can take precedence over the work's physical form. By eliminating almost all references to the actual appearance of the sitter, González-Torres resists permanent records and permanent value, acknowledges the flux of time and presents an inherently dynamic piece.

Street Art: $0, Mysterious Mastermind: Priceless

Our final example shows just how fluid value can be and the importance of the positioning and framing of work in establishing any economic value. Street artist Banksy is famed for his tongue-in-cheek style, which heavily features irony and sarcasm as well as the political undertones which are also common characteristics of his work (see Image 8.2). This image, for example, appeared in London at the height of the recession, providing a strong socio-political critique. Furthermore, Banksy is an interesting example to consider, as his concealed identity illustrates the difference between

Image 8.2 Eat the Rich: with our new 2 for 1 offer including a choice of wine, Banksy, London, 2009.

the artist's persona and the actual person. In fact, the mystery surrounding the artist's identity fuels interest and attention, while the recognizable style of the work itself as well as its controversial content (often involving stunts, such as deploying a Guantanamo Bay detainee blow-up doll in Disneyland) has ensured tremendous brand awareness, making him one of the few street artists whose work now regularly sells at auction, a practice usually reserved for 'high' art rather than street art. This is of note, as street art is traditionally perceived as a democratization of art, an inherently political (usually illegal) form of communication which is for the general public and by nature ephemeral. When this art is preserved, transferred onto canvas and sold in gallery or auction (often against the artist's wishes, BBC, 2014) to celebrities and millionaires, the work's content is neutralized.

Banksy himself has stated that he created art for the street because "when you go to an art gallery you are simply a tourist looking at the trophy cabinet of a few millionaires" (Banksy, 2006:150); yet, ironically, his own work has sold at Sotheby's for over $1.8 million (Sotheby's 2008). His film *Exit Through the Giftshop* (see Preece, 2012 for an in-depth review) provides a critique of the art market by demonstrating how it can be manipulated for financial gain. Again, we have to consider the variety of values that are at work in any object and how these may work against each other—so while economic value goes up in this case, the political and social values are in some ways diminished. In order to better understand the relation between economic forces and the social capital involved in legitimizing and valorizing traditional as well as more innovative art (such as Banksy's), there is a need to consider the wider macro-context in which value is evaluated. The reasons behind the creation of the work as well as its perceived meanings as it is contexualized and interepreted and ultimately commodified need to be considered.

Conclusion

As the art market has grown, so has the chasm between the two discourses which artists need to negotiate. On the one hand, they must appear 'authentic' and 'innovative' to the art world (which often requires the appearance of a non-commercial existence) and yet be 'branded' in order to achieve easy recognition at the high-end auctions and art fairs on which the market operates. This tension between art and commerce is a long-standing one and has been explored in cultural studies (e.g., Hesmondhalgh, 2002) and in the arts marketing literature in some detail (e.g., Bradshaw et al., 2005; Fillis, 2006). In line with this recent work, this chapter suggests that, while there is still an underlying struggle between art and commerce, this struggle is complex as well as ambivalent and requires a reconsideration of the very notion of value based on fixed criteria in the art market. Furthermore, we argue, this distinction between art and commerce is a rather artificial one. While the notion of art for art's sake is generally assumed when discussing the work artists produce, this chapter demonstrates that a consideration of the artwork cannot be separated from the macro-level context in which it is produced, distributed and consumed. This has implications for other products that are valued predominantly for their symbolic properties. A more fluid approach can consider how work is legitimized, valorized and commoditized through expert opinions, pricing practices, insurance claims, media attention etc. in a dynamic way. Moreover, because it shifts in accordance to the context within which it is produced and consumed, as we show with our three examples, value must be framed, positioned and negotiated within these socio-economic contexts, taking into account historical nuances and legitimizing networks and necessitating a conversation between the arts and business spheres.

We therefore warn of the consequences of focusing purely on financial value, as much of the business literature does. For example, one of the results of the recent art industry boom has been to make new art too expensive for institutions, and coupled with the recession and public cuts, these have been forced to adopt aggressive commercial measures, leading to a "commercialization and depolitization of the cultural field" (Mouffe, 2013:70), which raises important questions in terms of how art is valued and in particular, which art is being legitimized as a result of such a shift in valuation structures. While traditionally, this process has been the domain of the museum and sheltered from the commercial, the branded auction houses and mega-galleries now have more power, implying that museums must relinquish such status with far-ranging effects on the art market, as noted by Chong (2008). We thus argue that there is a need to further consider the social, political and cultural values that underpin the works which are valued by the market, that is, their ideological role, as value is never fixed or neutral, it is socially constructed in a system of power relations that remains a part of the political economy.

References

Banksy (2006). *Wall and Piece*. Century: London.

Baumann, S. (2006). A general theory of artistic legitimation: How art worlds are like social movements. *Poetics*, 35:47–65.

BBC (2014). *Banksy Street Works to Be Auctioned in London*. Retrieved 15.07.2015 from <http://www.bbc.co.uk/news/uk-england-london-27136549>.

Becker, H. S. (1982). *Art Worlds*. Berkley, CA: University of California Press.

Benjamin, W. (1968 [1936]). *Illuminations: Essays and Reflections*. Berlin: Schocken Books.

Bourdieu, P. (2006). The Forms of Capital, in: H. Lauder, P. Brown, J-A. Dillabough and A. H. Halsey (eds.). *Education, Globalisation and Social Change*, pp: 105–118. Oxford: Oxford University Press.

Bourdieu, P. (1993). *The Field of Cultural Production*. Oxford: Blackwell. Bradshaw, A., McDonagh, P., Marshall, D. and Bradshaw, H. (2005). Exiled music herself, pushed to the edge of existence: The experience of musicians who perform background music. *Consumption, Markets and Culture*, 8(3):219–239.

Brown, S. (2007). Are we nearly there yet? On the retro-dominant logic of marketing. *Marketing Theory*, 7(3):291–300.

Brown, S. and Patterson, A. (2010). Selling stories: Harry Potter and the marketing plot. *Psychology and Marketing*, 27(6):541–556.

Buck, L. (2004). *Market Matters: The Dynamics of the Contemporary Art Market*. London: Arts Council England.

Chen, Y. (2009). Possession and access: Consumer desires and value perceptions regarding contemporary art collection and exhibit visits. *Journal of Consumer Research*, 35:925–940.

Chong, D. (2008). Marketing in Art Business: Exchange Relationships by Commercial Galleries and Public Art Museums, in: I. Robertson and D. Chong (eds.). *The Art Business*, pp. 115–138. Abingdon: Routledge.

Chua-Eoan, H. (2007). Stealing the Mona Lisa, 2011. *Time*. Retrieved 15.07.2015 from <http://content.time.com/time/specials/packages/article/0,28804,1937349_1937350_1937357,00.html>.

Currid, E. (2007). The economics of a good party: Social mechanics and the legitimization of art/culture. *Journal of Economics and Finance*, 31(3):386–394.

Danto, A. C. (1964). The Artworld. *The Journal of Philosophy*, 61(19):571–584.

Fillis, I. (2006). Art for art's sake or art for business sake: An exploration of artistic product orientation. *The Marketing Review*, 6(1):29–40.

Fillis, I. (2000). Being creative at the marketing/entrepreneurship interface: Lessons from the art industry. *Journal of Research in Marketing and Entrepreneurship*, 2(2):125–137.

Fitchett, J. A. and Saren, M. (1998). Baudrillard in the museum: The value of Dasein. *Consumption, Markets & Culture*, 2(3):311–335.

Galenson, D. W. (2005). *Artistic Capital*. London: Routledge.

Griffin, T. (2008, April). The Art of the Fair. *Artforum*. Retrieved 21.12.2009 from <http://findarticles.com/p/articles/mi_m0268/is_8_46/ai_31487382/>.

Hesmondhalgh, D. (2002). *The Cultural Industries*. London: Sage.

Hickey, S. (2015). Picasso Painting Breaks Record for Most Expensive Artwork Sold at Auction. *The Guardian*. Retrieved 29.07.2015 from <http://www.the guardian.com/artanddesign/2015/may/12/pablo-picasso-work-sets-record-for-most-expensive-artwork-sold-at-auction>.

Hirschman, E. C. (1983). Aesthetics, ideologies and the limits of the marketing concept. *Journal of Marketing*, 47:45–55.

Horowitz, N. (2011). *Art of the Deal: Contemporary Art in a Global Financial Market*. Princeton, NJ: Princeton University Press.

Joy, A. and Sherry, J. F. Jr. (2003). Disentangling the paradoxical alliances between art market and art world. *Consumption, Markets and Culture*, 6(30):155–181.

Kerrigan, F., Brownlie, D., Hewer, P. and Daza-LeTouze, C. (2011). 'Spinning' Warhol: Celebrity brand theoretics and the logic of the celebrity brand. *Journal of Marketing Management*, 27(13–14):1504–1524.

Lacayo, R. (2009). Art's Great Whodunit: The Mona Lisa Theft of 1911. *Time*. Retrieved 15.07.2015 from <http://content.time.com/time/arts/article/0,8599, 1894006,00.html>.

Lichfield, J. (2005). The Moving of the Mona Lisa. *The Independent*. Retrieved 15.07.2015 from <http://www.independent.co.uk/news/world/europe/the-moving-of-the-mona-lisa-6149165.html>.

Mouffe, C. (2013). Institutions as Sites of Agonistic Intervention, in: P. Gielen, (ed.). *Institutional Attitudes: Instituting Art in a Flat World*. Antennae Series (n. 8), pp. 64–74. Valiz: Amsterdam.

Muñiz, A. M., Jr., Norris, T. and Fine, G. A. (2014). Marketing artistic careers: Pablo Picasso as brand manager. *European Journal of Marketing*, 48(1/2):68–88.

Peñaloza, L. and Venkatesh, A. (2006). Further evolving the new dominant logic of marketing: Form services to the social construction of markets, *Marketing Theory*, 6(3):299–316.

Philips (2010). Félix González-Torres. *"Untitled" (Portrait of Marcel Brient)* (1992) Carte Blanche Philippe Segalot, Phillips de Pury & Company, New York. Retrieved 15.07.2015 from <http://www.phillips.com/auctions/lot-detail/FELIX-GONZALEZ-TORRES/NY010710/4/1/1/12/detail.aspx>.

Preece, C. (2012). Media review: A Bansky film: Exit through the gift shop. *Journal of Macromarketing*, 32(4):436–439.

Preece, C. and Kerrigan, F. (2015). Multi-stakeholder brand narratives: An analysis of the construction of artistic brands. *Journal of Marketing Management*, 31(11–12):1207–1230.

Ramirez, R. (1999). Value co-production: Intellectual origins and implications for practice and research. *Strategic Management Journal*, 20(1):49–65.

Robertson, I. (2005). *Understanding International Art Markets and Management*. New York, NY: Routledge.

Robertson, I. and Chong, D. (eds.) (2008). *The Art Business*. Abingdon: Routledge.

Saltz, J. (2015). Say Good-bye Forever to Picasso's Women of Algiers, Disappearing Tonight for $140 Million. *New York Magazine*. Retrieved 29.07.2015 from <http://www.vulture.com/2015/05/good-bye-forever-to-picassos-women-of-algiers.html>.

Schroeder, J. E. (2005). The artist and the brand. *European Journal of Marketing*, 39(11/12):1291–1305.

SFMoMA (2015). Felix Gonzalez-Torres. *San Francisco Museum of Modern Art*. Retrieved 05.07.2015 from <http://www.sfmoma.org/explore/collection/artists/2667#ixzz3gS2lpoNl%20San%20Francisco%20Museum%20of%20Modern%20Art>.

Sotheby's (2008). *Banksy (defaced Hirst): Keep It Spotless.* Retrieved 05.07.2015 from <http://www.sothebys.com/en/auctions/ecatalogue/2008/auction-red-n08421/lot.34.html>.

Thompson, D. (2008). *The $12 Million Stuffed Sharks: The Curious Economics of Contemporary Art and Auction Houses.* London: Aurum Press.

Trowbridge, C. (2015). *Mona Lisa—Fact or Fiction?* Retrieved 15.07.2015 from <http://www.teachkidsart.net/mona-lisa-fact-or-fiction-50-fantastic-things-to-know/>.

Vargo, S. L. and Lusch, R. F. (2008). Service-Dominant logic: Continuing the evolution. *Journal of the Academy of Marketing Science*, 36(1):1–10.

Velthius, O. (2005). *Talking Prices: Symbolic Meaning of Prices on the Market for Contemporary Art.* Princeton, NJ: Princeton University Press.

Zug, J. (2011). Stolen: How the Mona Lisa Became the World's Most Famous Painting. *Smithsonian.* Retrieved 15.07.2015 from < http://www.smithsonianmag.com/arts-culture/stolen-how-the-mona-lisa-became-the-worlds-most-famous-painting-16406234/?no-ist=>.

Illustrations

1 Photo by Russeth, A. Taken 21st Jan 2010, "Untitled (USA Today)," at WIELS, Brussels 'Felix Gonzalez-Torres: Specific Object without Specific Form," available http://www.flickr.com (accessed 01/09/13).

2 Banksy, London 2009, "Eat the Rich," available http://www.banksy.co.uk/outdoors/index3.html (accessed 01/09/13).

9 Community Arts

On the Precarious Compromise Between the Inspired and the Civic Worlds

Ester Barinaga

"This sketch is not based on us. These are your sketches. Where are our voices?!" These were some of the cries residents in Seved, Malmö, screamed at the artist during a community information meeting held in early October 2012. The meeting was part of a longer community-based mural process that aimed at empowering Seved's residents. The cries condense the different understandings of 'art' and 'community participation' held by the artist and by the residents. They are also an expression of a more fundamental disagreement within Voices of the Suburbs (VoS),[1] the social entrepreneurial initiative organizing the community process.

VoS is a nonprofit organization that I had founded in Stockholm two years earlier. Through the collective production of murals in public spaces, the organization engages in community-building efforts in order to nuance the prevalent image of stigmatized suburbs and their residents. By visualizing residents' own stories of their suburb in major outdoor walls, VoS aims to counter what Loïc Wacquant (2007) calls territorial stigmatization. The production of large murals in public spaces becomes the means to, one, organize residents in marginalized and vulnerable areas, and two, resist the dominant and derogatory image of the neighborhood. The public wall is turned into a space on which residents can cast their coordinated/collective voice, a platform from which to re-tell their neighborhood from their own experiences of it. In this way, art and community are, indeed, quintessential to VoS's work.

Since 2010 and up to that date in 2012, VoS had successfully organized eight community-based murals in the Swedish capital alone. Expansion to Sweden's southern city of Malmö was proving more difficult, though. Initially hopeful because of Seved's residents' welcoming reception, VoS did not realize the consequences for community[2] of the conflict between the artist's and the founder's (me) understanding of art, of community participation and of social change processes. This conflict was, as it were, only the most graspable manifestation of a more profound disagreement between two orders of worth co-existing within the organisation: the inspired order of worth (pertaining the artistic sensibility), and the civic order of worth (pertaining the world of the community organiser).

In looking at the incidents, compromises, open disputes, adjustments and justifications that took place during 2012 within the Malmö office of VoS, the chapter focuses on the way the involved actors qualified the events, things and humans that were the object of controversy. That is, the essay takes as its object of study the *disagreement in qualifications* between the various actors implicated in the particular situations. In qualifying art or the neighbourhood, in assessing the wall or specific residents, in justifying the mural's motif or community involvement, the artist and the founder invoked different orders of worth. That is, we built our judgments on unrelated, at times incommensurable, repertoires of evaluation. To illustrate: where the artist saw a piece expressing the individual experience of its producer—a qualification of the artwork along a principle of inspiration— the founder perceived an act of egocentrism that ignored those that were going to live with the mural—a qualification of artwork that followed the civic order of worth. And conversely: the founder saw democratic involvement where the artist saw sterilizing adjustment to a limited community.

Building heavily on Boltanski and Thévenot's influential book on the plurality of forms of worth (2006), the chapter focuses on the tension between the world of art (with an inspired order of worth) and the community organizer's world (guided by a civic principle of worth). After introducing the conceptual territory and building on VoS's experiences in Malmö during 2012, the chapter follows the sequence of events, criticisms and accommodations that characterized work relations in VoS, as this will shed light on how the tension between the two orders is managed in complex organizations, organizations whose operations obey demands originating in different orders of worth. In this sense, the chapter is a study of the grammar of action (and worth) in complex organizations.

Orders of Worth, or Moral Grammars of Action

It's been referred to as the sociology of critique,[3] pragmatic sociology, a sociology of critical capacity and the sociology of justification. All these terms emphasize a focus on the *arguments* actors use in particular *situations* to justify their *practical* interventions as well as to assess those of others. Indeed, these three characteristics may help sketch the kernel of Boltanski and Thévenot's ideas, but they will only do so if we remain mindful that at the centre of their sociology is a concern with the coordination of human action, with how people reach agreement and how, most crucially, they manage disagreement. It is this focus on agreement, or rather, disagreement, that makes their framework particularly interesting to understand conflict in a community arts organization.

But first, to the most salient trait of their framework: a focus on actors' justifications, the arguments actors give to identify and qualify their actions as well as those of others in the advent of dispute.[4] Justifications proceed by relating the particular case assessed to a general category. By associating the things and humans present in the particular event to a common principle of evaluation, justifications conjure up a form of generality. A study visit to the community murals in a social housing project guided by the lead community artist may serve as example.[5] The artist explains the way the particular mural expresses the experiences of the residents in the neighbourhood, the extent to which participation in the mural process guarantees residents keep away from vandalizing the painting. The motif, the well-kept painting, the pride residents take in the mural, the number of persons involved in its making—everything the community artist points to is qualified as pertaining to the general category of participatory community processes. Justificatory arguments are sustained by things (in the example, the motif, participants, the neatness of the wall, residents' pride), and things are associated with forms of generality (in the example, participatory community process). Agreeing on the form of generality, on the higher common good invoked by the community artist, visitors do not question the qualification of the situation. It is in this way that justifications summon the principles that make the things and humans involved hold together (Boltanski and Thévenot, 2006). The actions, humans and things that are part of the situation are identified as pertaining to a particular order of worth and qualified within that order (in the example, the civic order of the community artist).

Now, most real-life situations differ from this delightful agreement, either because the actors involved in the particular situation disagree on whether the accepted criteria of justification has been infringed, or, in a more fundamental type of disagreement, because actors apply criteria from different orders of worth in their evaluation of the situation. In the first sort of discord, actors agree on the standpoint from which to assess the things, humans, arrangements and events in the controversial situation. That is, while there is certainty on the criteria to use to judge the situation, there is, however, disagreement on how the objects in the situation stand up to those criteria. To continue with the example above, one of the visitors may remark that the painting peeling off the wall is a sign of indifference from the residents, or point to a graffiti tag on the corner of the mural as questioning the quality of residents' collective engagement. Such arguments cast doubt upon the qualification made by the community artist, but that doubt comes from within the very order of worth the artist used to justify their artwork. The community artist could answer to these concerns with recourse to their shared order. For example, that the community process behind the particular mural happened more than 15 years ago, today's residents being others than those originally involved in the mural, or that new families with a burdening social baggage recently moved to the neighborhood. Although disagreeing in the evaluation of the community mural, the visitor and the artist agree on the repertoire of evaluation applied to the situation. In the example, both critique and justification build on a community-based principle of justice (order of worth or grammar of action). Standing on the same evaluative criteria, the artist and the visitor have the possibility to agree on their judgment of the mural. That is, when there is agreement on the order of worth from which to evaluate, there is also the possibility of reasoned consensus over what is being judged.

If we follow Boltanski and Thévenot, consensus is, however, not possible in the second type of disagreement, when actors invoke different orders of worth, when they engage in the situation and with each other from a different metaphysics (Wagner, 1999). The visitor could denounce the painting as being too jazzy,[6] he could reason that the mural process is so formalized by the need to mobilize, coordinate and build community that all individual forms of expression disappear, or he could argue that the inspiration of the artist is stifled through the structure of the community process. Here, the possibility of agreement is nought. Not because either the visitor or the community artist is completely right and the other totally wrong. But because the criteria they use to judge the painting are incommensurable. The community artist and the visitor mobilize two distant registers of justification and evaluation. And so, when the community artist refers to the empowerment of a community, the artistic visitor refers to the individual creativity of the artist; when the first invokes the common good of a collective—the people living in the neighborhood—the second appeals to grace and singularity of the artwork; when the first alludes to general will, the later calls for the will of everyone (Boltanski and Thévenot, 2006:110). Agreement is not within reach. At best, there is the possibility of negotiated compromise, compromises that are, however, bound to be precarious, temporary and uneasy for those involved. To stress the instability and anxiety characterizing such blended situations, Boltanski and Thévenot describe them as monstrous, 'the monstrosity of composite setups' (2006:225).

Monstrous as they may be, composite setups are an inherent part of much organizational life. Indeed, the six orders of worth that Boltanski and Thévenot identify in *On Justification*—market, industrial, civic, domestic, inspired, fame—are seldom found in isolation. Examples abound: when state officials justify state activities in terms of markets, or when they use the criteria of the industrialist to argue for an efficient use of tax money (Nash, 2014); when the industrialist relates to his employees as family members, or when the recognition and fame of its author enters the evaluation of a piece of art. In such situations, actors allude to orders of worth that do not align with the way their environments (and themselves) are categorized. Or, as we will see in the case presented in this chapter, actors may attribute value to the things, persons, arrangements and events in the situation they are implicated in from the standpoint of different orders of worth.

An important clarification is due here. Taking distance from sociological theories that locate values, or some sort of guidance system, within persons, Boltanski and Thévenot are clear that the same person may adhere to different orders of worth in different situations.[7] They abandon the idea of associating worlds to individuals or even groups. As they write, "[a]ctors whose professional universe is deeply embedded in an industrial world [. . .] are nevertheless not stuck fast once and for all in the world of industry. Even at work they have to be able to shift into situations in which objects and worths from a different world are deployed" (Boltanski and Thévenot, 2006:216). Instead, their framework emphasizes that worlds can be attached only to the arrangements of beings (things and humans) that make up the situations in which actors act when they justify and assign value.[8] In this way, although a person's room for action and justification may be limited by the way the particular situation is arranged, a theoretical framework that acknowledges several worlds 'preserves uncertainty about people's actions' (Boltanski and Thévenot, 2006:216). It opens the possibility to study the indeterminacy of life.

With the conceptual terrain mapped, let me now turn our attention to the events that occurred in the Malmö office of VoS during the early fall of 2012.

VoS, Malmö Office

Founded in Stockholm in 2010 with the explicit mission of raising the voices of residents in the stigmatized suburbs of Stockholm—"to let those that are talked about in the public debate take power over their own story"—VoS had gained funding from the Swedish Inheritance Fund to expand to southern Sweden, the city of Malmö. Two persons were to be key in coordinating the first collective mural process in the city: Carl Malmkvist, an artist trained in a renowned academy of arts with a preference for the production of art in the public space, and Ramak Farini, a young woman resident of Seved, the particular neighborhood where VoS was to start its operations in Malmö. Carl was to lead the community art process; drawing on her local network, Ramak was to mobilize residents and strengthen relations with local associations and resident groups.[9]

To support the team and make sure that the nascent Malmö office aligned its work with the goal of the organization, I met the team at the beginning of every week, participated regularly in the community mural workshops held twice a week and met the head of VoS's Malmö office at the end of every week. The events here described come from the notes from these meetings, as well as from my fieldwork notes from participating in them. Guided by a focus on disputes and disagreement in qualifications, in what follows, I present two particular incidents that called forth divergent orders of worth in the actors implicated, and that instigated adjustments, compromises and justifications within the community arts organization. Each of these incidents highlight the extent to which the conflict in orders of worth affected the understanding of elements key to VoS's work; namely, there seemed to be divergent understandings of what art was, of how to relate to residents and of what it means to raise subordinate voices.

Workshops in Seved: Conflicting Modes of Engagement

Looking at the choices Carl made and the practices he engaged in when designing and leading VoS's community art workshops gives us further hints as to the system of worth he brought into his work with Seved's residents.

Two venues were found for VoS's community art workshops: 'Garaget', Seved's municipal library, and 'The Flying Carpet', a community center located at the very heart of Seved. Being midway between one of the local schools and the residential area, the workshops at Garaget had attracted a small group of three to four schoolgirls and two schoolboys. Aged between eight and 15, the children participated in the activities led by Carl. A small group of three to five gypsy women in their early 20's with their children participated in the workshops at The Flying Carpet.

At these workshops, Carl focused on instilling in individual participants a desire to create by developing their drawing skills, as well as on eliciting their imaginary and passionate dimensions by discussing their personal life experiences and dreams for the future. He asked those attending the workshops to think about questions such as, "Who am I, 'Seved resident'?" and "Who am I now? Who do I want to be? How do I get there?" Carl asked workshop participants to paint their answers to questions ranging from everyday routines—"What do I have for breakfast?"—to more existential anxieties—"What are my dreams?" As an artist disposed to the inspired world, Carl designed the workshops to encourage each person to look for one's inner voice, to develop one's very own form of expression, to get in touch with one's feelings and passions. He brought this focus on each person's uniqueness into his art workshops and conceived these exercises as tools to develop a person's relationship with oneself. It is in this sense that, in the inspired world of the artist, "the objects and arrangements that equip worth are not detached from persons" (Boltanski and Thévenot, 2006:160).

All the same, I was concerned about the lack of an explicit plan for a longer community dialogue in which individual residents and groups/associations were invited to discuss a particular matter of concern for the neighborhood. In an effort to bring questions that could conjure up a collectivity, I suggested to Carl topics that I had observed and that Ramak had repeatedly insisted were distressing to those who lived in Seved. These ranged from the low standard of the rental apartments in which families lived, the intrusive yet necessary presence of the police, residents' ambivalence towards the young men dealing drugs on the street corner and their irritation over the one-sided image of Seved in the media, to their indecisive relation to their neighbourhood, as they proudly proclaimed to love Seved, yet concealed where they lived whenever they applied for a job or were out in town to meet new friends or partners. Yet, whether due to a lack of experience, or to difficulty in identifying with the communities that VoS addressed or because of a belief in starting at the personal as opposed to the collective level, Carl felt uneasy about engaging with residents from those starting points. It is probably on this aspect that our difference in the orders of worth from which we operated at VoS was most obvious, as they shaped the form of our engagement (agency) with those VoS was to work with. While in the inspired world epitomized by the artist, one relates to others by asserting, or helping to assert, their own uniqueness, in the civic world of the community organizer, one engages with others by bringing about what they all have in common, by contributing to enact and represent the collective voice (Boltanski and Thévenot, 2006:161).

A conflict on operative worths for engagement manifested itself also in a tense relation between the parties: Carl experienced my suggestions as intrusive and opprobrious. He had worked with rough male convicts in the Malmö prison before and knew how to use art to develop trusting relations with social outsiders. Furthermore, the artistic skills of the convicts had improved tremendously. Thus, his answer to my concern for the lack of a clearly defined topic that could start the work of organizing a collective voice to portray on the community mural in Seved: "Have trust in me. I'll make sure that all these discussions end up in a clear mural motif"—an allusion to the criteria of efficiency proper of the industrial order that effectively extended the possibility of disagreement.

Further, in answer to my demand to relate the workshops to the Seved neighbourhood, he either acknowledged his own constraints—"I have never met gypsy women before. I don't know how to relate to them"—or challenged me to admit the special nature of individual residents in Seved— "Have you ever worked with gypsy women before?!" Carl then brought in attenuating circumstances: He had no previous experience working with persons like those making up the situation under dispute. With this argument, Carl thus suggested the unfairness of assessing the workshops too early. He needed some time to learn how to relate to these women, an effort that pointed to him wanting to do what was necessary to adjust himself according to the requirements of a civic world. He was ready to go beyond his own interests, passions and limitations to reach out to what is valued by a civic order of worth, the unity of a collective, the common will, the general. This adjustment, or rather, this will to adjust, facilitated a compromise that delayed open dispute between two worlds.

The inspired world's critique of the civic world refers not only to how one is to engage with others. It also refers to how one is to engage with art itself. This is beautifully described by Oscar Wilde. In "The Soul of Man Under Socialism", Oscar Wilde clearly articulates a value of art for its connection with the world of inspiration. Particularly interesting for the argument in this chapter is to observe the extent to which such a principle of evaluation condescends an approach that values an engagement with art for what it can serve to others.

> An individual who has to make things for the use of others, and with reference to their wants and their wishes, does not work with interest, and consequently cannot put into his work what is best in him. Upon the other hand, whenever a community or a powerful section of a community, or a government of any kind, attempts to dictate to the artist what he is to do, Art either entirely vanishes, or becomes stereotyped, or *degenerates into a low and ignoble form of craft*. A work of art is

the unique result of a unique temperament. Its beauty comes from the fact that the author is what he is. It has nothing to do with the fact that other people want what they want. Indeed, the moment that an artist takes notice of what other people want, and tries to supply the demand, he ceases to be an artist, and becomes a dull or an amusing craftsman, an honest or a dishonest tradesman. He has no further claim to be considered as an artist. Art is the most intense mode of Individualism that the world has known. *I am inclined to say that it is the only real mode of Individualism that the world has known.* [. . .] But alone, without any reference to his neighbours, without any interference, the artist can fashion a beautiful thing; and if he does not do it solely for his own pleasure, he is not an artist at all.

(Oscar Wilde, 1891, "The Soul of Man Under Socialism", emphasis is mine)

This passage condenses the specificity of the engagement with art and community that is guided by the inspired principle of worth. Those inhabiting that world, it seems, disapprove of relying on instruments or relating to art as a tool because theirs is an engagement that presupposes a direct relation between the individual and the higher good of inspiration (Boltanski and Thévenot, 2006:154). For those inhabiting the civic world, however, worth relies on the capacity of each person to leave her own cares, interests and passions aside to focus on a common, collective good that includes and transcends them (Boltanski and Thévenot, 2006:185). When the first value, everybody's wills, is equally relevant, the second value, a collective conscience, subordinates individual wills to the general will. Whereas the first respects individual talent, the second appreciates collective virtue. While the first relates to art for art's sake, the second relates to art for its potential to enact, mobilize and serve the collective will.

A Loud Community Meeting: A Precarious Compromise Falls Apart

The fragility of the agreement that had characterized relations between VoS's members and that had shaped the organization's workshops and engagement with Seved's residents was put to the test in a community meeting held at The Flying Carpet on October 4, 2012. Community meetings are occasions to convene residents into a dialogue that informs them of the status of the mural process as well as further informing the community artist of the representativity of the residents' sentiments he has managed to imprint in the artwork. In this sense, a community meeting enacts the collective person and allows it to express itself. Well, that is how the civic sensibility qualifies and justifies such meetings. The inspired world assesses them instead as meetings in which to present the motif of the coming mural to individual residents. A frail compromise between the two worlds may defend such meetings, as we did, as an occasion to secure that residents recognized their individual stories in the motif. In this line of justification, the motif presented is the artist's interpretation and condensation of the many dialogues and workshops he has had with residents. Whatever the qualification of such an arrangement, this is an important moment in every community mural process because residents are given yet another chance to engage in trimming the mural's motif and to give feedback on the painting which is both to decorate their neighbourhood and to raise (visualize) their voices.

Only fourteen residents turned up at the community meeting in Seved. The rest of attendees, also fourteen, were the VoS Malmö team, the property owner offering the wall to be painted, a local newspaper and city representatives. Presenting his work as 'an effort to capture the spirit of Seved', Carl showed three drawings made by children of what they wanted to become ('an artist', 'a hairdresser' and 'a combined taxi-police car') followed by paintings by Niki de Saint Phalle, 'an artist who inspires much of my work'. Carl ended his presentation with a projection of the mural's motif. It visualized a series of shadows of individual characters known to Seved's residents: Michelle, a young graffiti artist; Ariana, an outspoken teenage girl; Baashi, a calm old man of Eritrean background; two police officers checking up on two young men; and an older woman with a shopping trolley. The title of the work was to be "This is me. This is what I've seen". Carl presented it as a summary of the individual stories he had heard during the time he had worked in Seved.

FASAD MOT ÖSTER SKALA 1:100

FÖRKLARINGAR

F1 FASAD GRUDMÅLAS I MAGNOLIAVITT VARPÅ MURALMÅLNING SKER INOM ANGIVET OMRÅDE

The residents' reaction was swift. And loud. To Carl's invocation of individuality, the residents answered with collectivity. "This sketch is not based on us. These are your sketches. Where are our voices?!" Or, "Why do the police have to be there? Who identifies with the police around here?" Such a critique opposes a collective grounding of mural art against the expression of the individual artist, the concern for the issues preoccupying residents against the initial drawings of a detached artist. Although with these accusations, the residents present at the meeting challenged the validity of the arrangement—the mural's motif, the artist's involvement, the relation to Seved's residents—their denouncement took a personal form that accused Carl of being engaged in that meeting without having disengaged himself from a world of a different nature (the inspired world). Residents' criticisms aimed to reveal the presence of this alien world, not to challenge the importance of the community meeting or a community dialogue, but to show the shortcomings of the arrangement and to demand that it be purified (see Boltanski and Thévenot, 2006:221).

The property owner also had an opinion. "I have no problem with the sketch, as long as it has the full support of the residents". He ended with an observation that, when contrasted with his previous one, succinctly articulates the distinction between a general will of the collective (civic world) and the will of everyone call forth by the inspired order: "By the way, I don't see myself among the shadows".

Carl remained engaged in a world of a nature different to the world of those present at the meeting. His inclination to work with the individual and de-politicize/de-instrumentalize art starkly clashed with the demands for community and political engagement in Seved. As a resident, Ramak embodied such demands and expressed them in her disposition to focus VoS's work on the young female residents in Seved as well as in her insistence to relate the art workshops to matters of concern to Seved's residents. Ramak being responsible for mobilizing Seved's residents into VoS's community processes, it was no accident that those attending the community meeting on October 4th were furious that the sketch lacked relation to those living in the neighbourhood. Whereas cries such as, "Why do the police have to be there? Who identifies with the police here?" placed the emphasis on Seved as a community with its own particular concerns, exhortations like, "Wasn't this project about engaging women? " or "I thought this was going to be about immigrants, but I see nothing of that there" appeal to instrumentalize art for the formulation of political demands.

After the meeting, a group of women both young and older, of Swedish and immigrant backgrounds, took me to the side and doubted Carl's ability to convey their voices. Aiza, a young woman of immigrant background, summed up the group's anxiety:

> It's going to be mainly immigrant women painting. It is our stories that
> have to be painted. He is Swedish and a man, and he's the one who's

to interpret our stories. It won't work, him interpreting us immigrant women. I mean, it would be better with someone who is like us.

Alva, an older woman of Swedish background, formulated a similar sentiment:

This has to be for the youth, and not many have participated. It was his ideas, his sketches, his interpretation. It wasn't us. [. . .] I think only a woman, not a man, can capture our stories.

Residents' condemnations took a personal form. They blamed Carl for his inability to relate to them. However, the events that occurred a few months later point out that the critique was not to the person of the artist per se, but rather addressed to the overall arrangement of the situation; that is, to the particular connection of objects, individuals and groups that had been put together throughout the mural process. In the spring of 2013, merely four months after the loud community meeting, in the same neighborhood and on the same street where the initial mural was to be painted, a mural was painted by two local artists. No community dialogue had been carried out, nor had residents been invited to shape the mural's motif. Similarly, in 2014, a group of graffiti artists did a piece on the very wall that was thought for the first mural. These artists did not live in the neighbourhood. Nor, once more, had there been any efforts/intention to put together residents, collective voices and a mural in a single arrangement. And yet, residents were pleased with the painting of all these walls. The huge painting that came about in Seved only a couple of months after the controversial meeting, ordered by a major real state owner and carried out by a locally renown graffiti artist, was also very much appreciated. None of these murals represented residents, none portrayed the stories of women or immigrant or any other resident. And yet, residents valued the paintings. Such difference in the assignment of worth to the various murals painted in the neighbourhood is indicative of their qualifications and accusations thrown during the loud community meeting being addressed to the composite situation, to the mix of incommensurable worlds into a single arrangement. Their cries identified the male artist as a being that did not hold together with the rest of the situation. Other elements in the situation—such as allusion to raising a collective voice and the community workshops—activated in participants a mental disposition to apply a civic principle of worth. It is this disposition that helped them to identify those beings that belonged to a world foreign to the civic one. A composite situation thus fell apart.

Community Arts: A Tense Compromise Between Two Conflicting Orders of Worth

Throughout the chapter, we have seen the uneasy compromise between the world of art and the civic world within a community arts organization. We were able to observe decisions made on the design of activities, actors' disagreement on the benefits of specific actions, adjusting argumentations and modifications of work arrangements. Looking back at the friction between divergent qualifications of events, things and humans, as well as at the justifications those involved used for their actions, may help us sort out at least two degrees of conflict between the two worlds. Boltanski and Thévenot refer to these two types of disagreement as maladjustment vs. dysfunctionality (2006:41).

Maladjustment is brought up by critiques to one (or several) element(s) within a larger situation without, for that matter, questioning the framing of the situation. In a sense, the accusation unmasks the foreign element in a world that is otherwise shared across the parties. It has to do with the value assigned to some of the beings present (or absent), but never doubts the world exhibited in the situation. This was the case for the disagreements about the workshops in Seved. Certain elements were seen lacking—a longer plan for a community dialogue—but neither Carl nor I nor Ramak questioned the situation as belonging to the civic world. Maladjustments then call for a clarification of the foreign element—a way of working based on experience, not plans. They also call for a better adjustment between the extant elements—a demand to relate the workshops more closely to the concerns of residents in Seved. And because the world that makes up the situation is never doubted, there is the possibility of reasoned compromise.

Dysfunctionality stems from disagreement of a much deeper nature. The dispute is not merely one about qualifications of elements in the situation, but rather, about the very identification of the elements that matter and not (Boltanksi and Thévento, 2006:224). Disagreements that denounce the situation as being of a different nature than what it was purported to be are thus the expression of a clash between worlds. The girls and women participating in the loud community meeting pointed to the artist's gender and ethnicity as dysfunctional for the situation, an element from another world that could not possibly adjust to theirs. With these argumentations, they identified the dividing lines of gender and ethnicity as two elements that were relevant in a civic world that seeks community and unity. Either out of practical reasons— no female artist had applied to the job when VoS advertised it—or because of an inclination to listen more closely to the demands of the inspired world, these two boundaries had not been present in how we at VoS had thought about the artist's engagement in Seved. When Boltanski and Thévenot write about composite settings, they maintain that "tensions inherent in a universe embracing multiple natures [. . .] constrain judgement while allowing it a certain latitude" (2006:42). But, as we saw in the case, that latitude comes with a risk: The arrangement falls apart and the possibility of compromise is small (if ever there). There is, that is, a confrontation between different orders of worth each identifying different elements to which to assign value.

The events that occurred on October 4th are not for me, as an academic author, to evaluate. In this chapter, I strive to avoid passing a judgment on right or wrong, on whether the order of worth endorsed by the artist is more or less worthy that that of the community organizer or the residents. The event serves me however to highlight the co-existence in one and the same arrangement of a plurality of worlds. It also helps me to stress the extent to which, although reaching a compromise across the inspired and civic worlds as we at VoS had done, such agreements are to remain uneasy, fragile and ridden with stark emotions. The forms of generality endorsed by the inspired world and the civic world seem to be largely incommensurable. Both principles of worth may be equally valid. Yet, they have a difficult time speaking to each other so that what is worthy in one world is unworthy in the other. In composite settings such as hybrid community arts organizations, this results in an uncertainty of judgment that permeates much organizational life. In organizations that are to engage external groups, this lack of clarity affects the strength of the relations developed between the organization and those groups.

The conflict of worlds in community arts organizations, the clash between the inspired and the civic order of worths, cannot simply be wished away, or designed off their work with residents or ignored in a hope that it won't matter. On the contrary: It demands actors that are aware of the co-existence of multiple worlds, persons who are reflective of the way in which tension between worlds informs work practices. Competing worlds highlight the need to take into account the different competences needed, competences to act according to each world but also to keep a harmonic grounding on the presence of distress. Persons working in complex organizations and mixed situations need to be skilled in the design of composite arrangements that are able to hold together; they need to have an ability to manage the continuous threat of falling apart. They need to be able to live and flourish in situations that are undecided, not clearly determined as belonging to a pure world. And they need to be able to work with people that will value art, community and engagement in a different way than they themselves do.

Notes

1   In this chapter, I have baptized the community arts organization with the name 'Voices of the Suburbs'. The translation, however, loses a rich set of meanings implicit in the Swedish name *Förorten i Centrum*, the Margins at the Centre. Yet, since those meanings are not the object of this chapter, I have opted for a name that is friendlier to non-Swedish speakers.

2   Inspired by Cheryl L. Walter (2005), I want to make a distinction between 'community' and 'the community'. Whereas the second points towards an already existing social unit with which practitioners (artists, community organizers or others) interact, 'community', without the article, "becomes a milieu in which we practitioners interact with people and organizations and of which we are an integral part" (p.72).

3   Beware the distinction between Bourdieu's critical sociology, a sociology that focuses on the reproduction of inequality and thus makes groups (of people) its object of analysis, and Boltanski's and Thévenot's sociology of critique, which focuses on the ways actors justify actions and thus puts particular situations at the centre of attention (Boltanski and Thévenot, 2006, pp.16–18).

4   This precludes the study of all those occasions in which actors resolve disputes by resorting to violence. Violence presupposes inequality and suspends the human imperative to justify (Boltanski and Thévenot, 2006:37–40).
5   This example is taken from fieldwork in Lyon in May 2015, where the founders of CitéCréation showed us some of the community murals they had accomplished.
6   This example comes from a different guided tour, this time in Stockholm during the fall of 2012.
7   This is an element through which Luc Boltanski takes clear distance from his master's, Pierre Bourdieu's, notion of habitus.
8   Boltanski and Thévenot build this theoretical move—associating worlds with arrangements of objects and persons—clearly on the lessons taught by Actor–Network Theory.
9   To respect the confidentiality of the persons involved in the events here described, their names have been anonymized.

References

Boltanski, L. and Thévenot, L. (2006). *On Justification: Economies of Worth*. Translated by Catherine Porter. Princeton, US and Oxford, UK: Princeton University Press.
Nash, K. (2014). The Promise of Pragmatic Sociology, Human Rights and the State, in: S. Susen, and B. S. Turner (eds.). *The Spirit of Luc Boltanski: Essays on the Pragmatic Sociology of Critique*, pp. 351–368. London, UK and New York, US: Anthem Press.
Wacquant, L. (2007). Territorial Stigmatization in the Age of Advanced Marginality. *Thesis Eleven*, 91:66–77.
Wagner, P. (1999). "After Justification: Repertoires of evaluation and the sociology of Modernity." *European Journal of Social Theory*, 2(3):341–357.
Walter, C. L. (2005). Community Building Practice, in: M. Minkler (ed.). *Community Organizing and Community Building for Health*, pp.66–78. 2nd edition. New Brunswick, New Jersey, US & London, UK: Rutgers.
Wilde, O. (1891). *The Soul of Man Under Socialism*. Retrieved 28.02.2016 from https://www.marxists.org/reference/archive/wilde-oscar/soul-man/

10 Re-Casting Legitimacy

Validation and Criticality as Contemporary Art Joins Cultural Business

Ravi Dar and Pamela Schultz Nybacka

Introduction

On the way to the elevators of a twenty-story building in the Stockholm city center, we[1] paused at an odd sculpture in the lobby. A woman in bronze is lying flat on her back on the stone floor. She is well dressed in high-heeled shoes, blouse and a skirt ever so slightly creased in her odd position. Her head is raised and slanting, holding something in her hands. The pose is uncomfortable, foot slightly in the air, and she cannot remain still for long.

Photo: Pamela Schultz Nybacka

We snapped a photo and up we went, away from the lobby and more significantly leaving behind and below us the adjacent three-story building: the

arness 041ilet

whereabouts of Bonniers Konsthall (hereafter BKH), one of the many art venues in the Stockholm area, of which several are privately owned. We were in an office building of the media group Bonnier AB to interview the upper echelons of the corporate management. Bonnier AB is fully owned by the Bonnier family and has for 200 years been making business out of bookselling, publishing, journalism, broadcasting and digital business. BKH was set up in 2005 as a venue for exhibiting contemporary art.

By 2012, BKH's managing of art exhibitions had gained a reputation of high quality, particularly in the Nordic region. The year 2012 saw also a nearing the end of their second visionary cycle which helped hold together their strategic and their operative work. At this same time, the corporate media group experienced major financial uncertainty due both to the ongoing global recession as well as changes in the media sector. The consequences were the slashing of corporate costs and the selling of business units as well as a reassessment of direction within the whole corporation.

We were also aware of an ongoing transition of the art world, where exhibition work was diverging between on one side galleries and museums attaining flagship works of art at extremely high market prices, and on the other, an emphasis less on appropriating art in ownership and standing exhibition, and more on sharing, interacting and the using and re-using of forms (Bourriaud, 2005). Gielen (2013:2) has expressed this transition as a destabilizing of institutional structures, an increased importance of networks and "a globalized, 'flattened' world [where] numbers and capital have gained power, and art institutions struggle for survival".

The BKH management team was placed at the very center of the conflated relationship between the media group's corporate structure and the art world. From our point of view, we saw at this time and in this place an extraordinary situation of turbulence and transition. We had come to BKH to find out more about the ways in which quality in art exhibition could be expressed and how the management of art exhibition could be validated. We saw an opportunity to study the intricate workings of different orders of value and different methods used for the validation of quality in performance.

But as we entered the corporate high floors with our questions of how private business finds space in vision and the budget to establish and carry an art institution, we were not engulfed in a world of black and red numbers and investment returns, but literally surrounded by contemporary art. We met owners, managing the business of Bonniers in its own tradition, working with artistic and creative industries as its base, managing in the interests both of corporate vision and the cultural ambition of giving voice in society. Our challenge became to make sense of how these different contexts with possibly conflicting perceptions of legitimacy achieved some degree of alignment. We asked ourselves *how art management joins with business* and used the theoretical guidance of process-oriented ideas of valuation and validation in our attempt to find answers.

Evaluating performance from a management control perspective tends to rely on an atomistic perception of value-in-exchange and value-in-use. Capturing the value added (or destroyed) by management practices, though, cannot be equated with financial results or art reviews. A 'valuation process' approach considers instead that legitimacy through measures of performance does not come through a division of 'values' of what is sought and 'value' as something that can be measured (Helgesson and Muniesa, 2013), but rather as an ongoing process. Financial or artistic values do not precede financial or artistic value, or vice versa, but rather are 'co-created' in complex networks (Helgesson and Kjellberg, 2013).

We have sought terms that reflect legitimacy as a similarly constitutive and complex process that in an argumentative way offers structure and support to narrative progression and theoretical exploration. *Acclaim*, *trust* and *validation* are aspects of valuation processes, particularly in combination with a set of performative terms from art theory: *criticism*, *critique* and *criticality* (Rogoff, 2003). Pairing them together has provided a structure with which to explore the dynamics of the valuation process in the art world.

Acclaim and *criticism*, *trust* and *critique* and lastly, *validation* and *criticality* all add perspective on the development that from the direct patronage and commissioning that declined at the end of the 18th century (Rosler, 2013), attaining legitimacy in the art world has gone through critique. Increasingly, though, there are studies of validation processes in the art market that consider success within contemporary art as the result of efficient machinery for both symbolic and financial validation (Rodner and Thomson, 2013). The value of specific art is suggested to arise and increase through the mutual management between different actors within the art world (Becker, 1982). Rodner and Thomson (2013) suggest the term 'art machine' to illustrate this working of various 'cogs' at different stages of critique in a validation process.

After our interviews, returning to the ground floor, we took a closer look at the bronze woman and saw that her hands held two round objects. What was she balancing? With the mix of corporation and art exhibition in our minds, were we seeing a juggling act of the respective validity of good contemporary art and good cultural business? As we left the building, we carried with us this sculptured image, which came to symbolize BKH, and has become a central node in our construction of this chapter.

Managing Criticisms

Over their nine years of existence, the cultural impact of BKH has been considerable in terms of reviews and media coverage, including national newspapers, repeatedly given the status of exhibitions that should not be missed. BKH have filled their halls with a series of video installations and workshops as well as the exhibitions with themes such as space and architecture, the young artist, art and storytelling, and diverse sculpting materials. The building itself was used to project a video installation that commented on the Stockholm winter. They issued publications in co-operation with Albert Bonnier förlag (highly profiled among Bonnier publishing companies) and reaching out to the Jewish museum, the city library, the Strindberg museum, and the neighboring music and theatre library (Treijs, 2013).

As BKH exhibitions treaded new paths by bridging art to other cultural fields such as literature, theatre and film, they positioned themselves as the experimental and edgy among the private art institutions: "Here the avant-garde assumes its (rightful) place and the degree of abstraction is high" (ibid).

With BKH's target audiences being of two types, the general public and the national and international contemporary art scene, seeking acclaim from both groups was a challenge and skill at which the BKH management team had managed to excel.

There had been published criticisms in the early stages of the BKH project directed against the planning permission (at the cost of public space), against the architecture (a four-story metal and glass apparition that was criticized by the city architect), against the choice of exhibition (the inauguration[2] was with paintings by artists previously rewarded by a scholarship foundation for young artists formed, funded and chaired by Jeanette Bonnier, the chairman of the BKH board as well as the single largest owner in the Bonnier corporation).

One perspective of legitimacy thus positioned art and business as so different ideas in essence that the logics and values of either would negate legitimacy in the other. The issue of justification has been described in Cloutier and Langley (2013), drawing on the concepts of Boltanski and Thévenot, as a struggle of 'worlds of worth' in which a particular set of values gains top order in a particular situation. In this terminology, the 'inspired world' is where creativity and *art* give legitimacy. In being successful through acclaim, BKH's position as a valid part of the art world was justified.

Criticism, or 'finding faults' (Rogoff, 2003), came from the suspicion that the Bonnier AB pursued other worlds of worth and a different kind of legitimacy: the 'industrial world' (optimization and progress) and the 'market world' (taking advantage and reaping rewards). This ranged from the direct accusation that the Bonniers were planning to extend their office space (Knutsson, 2006) to the indirect suspicions of the investment in the Konsthall being in fact an investment in (what Pierre Bourdieu called) 'cultural capital' (Madestrand, 2006). In the same mode, the new, fresh, innovative glass and metal architecture that signaled contemporariness contrasted with the adjacent yellow brick Bonniers offices with its 1949 architecture, something picked up by Swedish public radio on the eve of the BKH opening in November 2006 (ibid).

The idea of 'worlds of worth' is particularly suited for justification as a consequence of face-to-face struggles (Cloutier and Langley, 2013), and the open expression of criticisms and acclaim can be seen as such a struggle between BKH as an unjustified reward to a media corporation or as a legitimate venue for the benefit of society. It was a struggle with a winner: BKH management. The acclaim received provided legitimacy within the art world and silenced the doubt on whether the corporate context of the Bonniers would trump artistic values.

Exhibition as a Business

From the beginnings of BKH, two members of the Bonnier family have had prominent roles: Jeanette Bonnier, as chairman of the BKH board as well as the single largest owner in the Bonnier corporation, and Pontus Bonnier, as executive manager of BKH as well as being on the top-level corporate board (the Bonnier Holding Company). Jeanette Bonnier initiated and drove the project forwards, expressing at an early stage that it was not to be a museum or a gallery, but an art space (Österholm, 1997)

Sara Arrhenius was hired as the first (and as of yet only) director of BKH. Strategies were developed in the form of 'visions' with very few preconditions. The first vision sought to combine the engagement from the scholarship foundation for young artists with Arrhenius's background as a critic and facilitator within the international contemporary art scene:

> We have decided to work with young, new, contemporary art and that is a challenge in itself. It can be difficult to invite people to something unexpected, something they do not recognize—and at the same time make it accessible and open and mediate the new to a large audience.
>
> (Ayata, 2007:282)

Both Jeanette Bonnier and Pontus Bonnier are avid art collectors (as are other members of the family and previous Bonnier generations) and had established both an active role in the Swedish art scene and working relationships with other venues in Stockholm. The philanthropic mindset has been apparent from the start. "[W]e [the family/owners] are proud and happy about this", Pontus Bonnier remarked at the time of opening of the Konsthall (Ayata, 2007:276).

When we asked Jeannette Bonnier about whether the corporate board had had any objectives for BKH, she found the question strange and foolish, as BKH was not set up by the corporation, and certainly not as a business venture (JB, 2012). According to Arrhenius in 2007, this was a vital aspect:

> That is why we did not need to define or argue for the artistic freedom. That part has been so self-evident that the creative freedom was granted from the beginning [. . .] Today many art institutions struggle: to draw a massive audience, to get revenue from ticket sales, with projects with limited means. Here I hope that there will be opportunities to create something to meet with the artists' conditions.
>
> (Ayata, 2007:282)

In those beginnings, though, there was no obvious benchmark for what the cost of their ambitions for quality would be. Bonniers had attempted to counteract this through personal relations and a shared focus on contemporary art with the publicly funded Moderna Muséet and the privately owned Magasin III. Knowledgeable representatives from these institutions formed the first constellation on the BKH board.[3]

The first set budget was overrun, but the experience gained from building the Konsthall (literally and figuratively) has meant an accumulation of knowledge. Although corporate management expected budget constraints to be respected, they were also well aware and accepting of the learning process of how to run an art hall. In a clarification of how the corporate holding board works, Pontus Bonnier explained to us in 2013 that "it is not only square blocks pointing, like arrows, downwards" and emphasized that informal structures are especially important in family-owned corporation structures where a relatively small group of owners are active.

This was similar to his words in 2007 of an absence of an overriding economic strategy:

> [W]e have no expectations or demands on the art hall like we have on the other companies in the corporation—no other than the art hall gives a positive image of Bonnier. Our objective for the art hall is to do a good project. We have consulted with the management of the art hall as concerns the question of what cost frame is reasonable for running it.
>
> (Ayata, 2007:276)

By 2012–13, there had evolved a stable relationship between the Konsthall activities, costs and corporate contributions. They had built validity in exhibitions of a high 'inspired world' quality, both of soaring visitor numbers and positive reviews. Moving on from the standoff between *acclaim* and *criticism*, what could validity from a corporate perspective mean?

Seeking Validation

The repercussions of financial uncertainty were not dramatic, but it was a reminder of a certain context and conditions, of being owned, managed and financed within corporate operations. Returning to the sculpture, while it was tempting to consider the sculpture's horizontal position as flattened by the blow of corporate realities and demands, searching for a way to get up, we came to consider that she instead was optimally positioned to balance and reflect in between the corporation and the art world. The situation within the Bonniers group, which Pontus Bonnier phrased as 'a complicated economy', meant there was an urgency to handle issues of cost and accountability. BKH had previously experienced the need to cancel minor exhibitions in order to cut costs, but were at this stage in a very ordered mode of business and could undertake a thorough analysis of the possibilities to cut costs and increase revenue.[4] Arrhenius could acknowledge both the room for manoeuvre and the challenges of a corporate context:

> Of course I could go to my board and say that if we want to do this it will cost this or that, and one could be positive to that in a situation if there is a lot of revenue in the corporation as a whole, but not if there isn't.
>
> (SA, 2013)

From an internal viewpoint, Bonniers was operating a decentralized management style which allows for the discretion of unit managers to design their own ways of dealing with the corporate structure. Within corporate ownership and top management, there was knowledge and respect for the challenges for the BKH management. As in the traditions within publications and newspapers, unit managers have always had the freedom to develop that respective business according to their respective ideas but within budgets. This was particularly the case for BKH, operating in a haven of trusting patronages yet not exempt from either corporate necessities or the mechanisms of legitimacy processed in art critique.

Art has been described as an organized and purposeful set of actions emerging in a subtle play of the artist's production, audience and critique, with aesthetical, technological, commercial, political, temporal and spatial contingencies (Guillet de Monthoux, 2004). Being part of the art world is being in an intricate web of interrelated practices and people that brings art to form and renders its meaning and value (Becker, 1982), thus severing the immediate connection between the individual artist and the appreciation of creativity and value. Dealing with these contingencies and intricacies meant more than administrative organizing, as art management takes place in the reflective process that rendered meaning and value.

The balancing act was done in a position of being entrusted as legitimate to make independent decisions, but also with the continuous expectations to validate the quality of their performances. The BKH management sought validation as they tried to figure out what ways they could cover and convey the non-quantified qualities and success of their work to others. Arrhenius explains the situation within the cultural sector:

> If one is attempting to describe vague ideas of quality, or culture is important, it feels like one would need a much better tool in order to narrate and account for when one is successful. Putting up stronger objectives for that sort of thing. Often it is just a lot of opinions. One is often caught in a quagmire both in the team and on the [BKH] board when one is trying to explain what is good and what is not. I find it very unsatisfactory to use media attention and audience numbers [as the only critierias], especially when one is running an operation that has other goals as well. Is it possible to find other models? All my colleagues everywhere are struggling with the same thing, how is it done?
>
> (SA, 2013)

The exhibition work and art management had to follow both business requirements and artistic ambitions, dealing with networks and a complexity of interests and stakes at the same time as the organizational order evolves. The experience of management requiring meaningful ways of communicating quality is part of ongoing societal trends of accountability and audit that place emphasis on overall performance as measurability (Power, 1999), having an impact on cultural organizations being increasingly vulnerable as public sector funding has turned to validation through auditing and performance measurement (Belfiore, 2004). This has also been described in a study of the validating of cultural activities in the Swedish public sector (Styhre, 2013). Despite the differences in ownership between public and private and in management control between commission and budget, there are similar experiences: a vagueness of objectives, an absence of an adequate vocabulary for evaluation and the positioning of management in the intersections between interests. For BKH, the corporate structure and private interests allow for legitimacy that transgresses a simple hierarchical order, allowing for different perspectives and professional competency, yet it still lacks desired methods that could take account of the quality of their work.

Our involvement was initiated to serve these aspects: interviews with project manager Björn Norberg often included discussions on the potentials of different instruments of validation, as he often was involved in the economic communication with the board. Although organizational legitimacy can often be based on numbers, it has been suggested that such requirements are a measure of distrust. (Porter, 1992) In contrast, Pontus Bonnier explains his role in being a 'link' within the organizational structure:

> I think it is very [important], and that we have discussed also, that the art hall itself must come up with suggestions on what types of target figures one could set up for it, and then it is up to the board and management up here to follow up . . .
>
> (PB, 2013)

So while Norberg expressed his perception of his work role as extending into management control, with an increased consciousness of costs, revenue and performance, he recognized it not as a matter of communication, but as a *pedagogical* problem:

> And then one quickly starts to grapple with, kind of . . . how can we explain this, are there economic concepts for this. We understand [now] that we cannot explain this in numbers any more, but we must . . . explain this in images, rather.
>
> (BN, 2013)

One such effort had been a joint EU grant application in 2012 with art institutes in a spread of European countries to share experiences with a stated ambition to develop 'methods for measuring success and quality'. Although the application was turned down, the questions asked remained a matter of concern for BKH:

> How can we measure spread knowledge? How can we prove that the society develops in a more positive way as a result of the activities of art institutions? How can we measure democratic values in society that connects to our activities?
>
> (BN, 2012)

Bonnier AB trusts the direction and activities of BKH rather than justifying resource allocation through calculative practices. The artistic freedom that has existed from the beginning is exercised in financing exhibitions ideas based on extending trust to a particular artist to perform an unrealized idea rather than a quantified return on investment. In terms of 'worlds', it seems that the *industrial* world merges in this example with the *inspired* world: their separate values and measures of value were balanced within trust and critique. Pontus Bonnier reacted to our questions about validating the performance of BKH through traditional accounting practices:

> Look, I understand that you terribly much want to squeeze this and make it become like . . . various templates and frames, but we are not running it quite that way . . . But from up here . . . As long as we have accepted to run this art hall et cetera within the given economic frame, we want it to be run as efficiently as possible; it sounds contradictory, but anyway . . .
>
> (PB, 2013)

Exhibition as Art

How art management joins business could be a struggle won by acclaim. It could also be settled in a critique of respective contexts in a realm of trust. Yet if acclaim and trust were absolute and unconditional, what would the challenges be? Cloutier and Langley (2013) point to the need for a process that builds a capacity for agency where possible balances of different worlds of worth mobilize collective action.

Whether it is innovative business or contemporary art, there is a need to be critically aware of the world in which one acts. Martha Rosler (2013:55) considers the market-centric art world though tending to seek "validation only within the commodity-driven system of galleries, museums, foundations and magazines, and in effect competing across borders". In response, contemporary artists push towards societal ambitions, defining contemporary art as markedly international, aiming at social critique through investigations, explorations and research into issues of concern (Vilks, 2011). Grayson Perry (2013) considered that 'we are at the end state of art', referring to a pluralistic art world that transgresses art as an exclusive/inclusive category.

These critical analyses are part of a shifting away from a stable role in an existing division of labor to artists becoming reflective activists, as every work of art not only contends with the societal, the pluralistic and the esoteric, but pushes forth the dialogue on art and society. Irit Rogoff's concept of *criticality* contrasts with *critique* and emphasizes 'the present', "actualising some of its potential rather than revealing its faults" (Rogoff, 2003).

The sense that art is something new, something different, and without any securities or guarantees of general appreciation or increase in value was expressed by Jeanette Bonnier when commenting in 2012 that the period designated by the second vision of BKH was nearing its end. Bonniers Konsthall had become an institution, yet Jeannette Bonnier warned of the dangers of regarding oneself as part of a big corporation, seeking validation in it and from it. In her perception, corporate people have different tasks than the artist, whose work springs from the mind and is quite difficult to understand. While stressing both a legitimacy of business models and corporate responsibility, she also expressed a disinterest in the numbers, even going as far as criticizing the role of the accountant as not being able to lift perspectives and envision where future business will come from, as she put it: "it has nothing to do with strategy, this is about philosophy" (JB, 2012).

The roles of art and art exhibition become not only a subject of critique as a study of particular contexts, but as a place for contesting existing conventions of order. In 1939, critic Clement Greenberg theorized about the avant-garde as a complicated relationship with one foot (the statue's hand) in a bohemian striving to do art for art's sake, yet with the other foot (hand) attached to bourgeois society through the necessity of resources. Yet conflated is the overriding function to keep cultural expression 'moving', as aesthetic validity lies in the exploration of that cultural medium. The values and measures of value are not pre-set, but are the result of the process.

The role of art management in this art world in transition attracts and deals with criticisms and critique but also has a very active part in creating meaning and value; it also cannot rest in a comfort zone of achievement. Pascal Gielen's idea of a flatter networked art world is expressed both as a vision and a fear. The risk is that money will kill the creativity and only mediocrity will remain. He asks, "Will they [art institutions] be able to create profundity and height again? Is this desirable? And if so, what would these new vertical ways look like? Or is it better to develop horizontal strategies in order to react more advantageously to the flat world?" Perhaps the bronze sculpture was not only positioned to balance, but also was uncomfortably trying out more adequate positions to deal with a flatter world?

BKH sought, developed and maintained contacts with many cultural institutions, both public and private, within Sweden and on an EU and international level: networking through participating in seminars and conferences, attending exhibitions and fairs, but also through defining common interests. For BKH, the contingencies of the societal, the pluralistic and the esoteric were accompanied by the corporate, all of which were and are in some form of transition as changing roles and responsibilities contend with new challenges. Internal networking too was sought: for example, an "Art Hack Day project" was held at BKH and resonated with Bonnier AB's increasing interests in cutting-edge digital talent.

BKH combine their own strong position in an institutional order with active participation in a networked art world; being less reliant on a single patronage but rather seeking validation as a 'cog' among other 'cogs' (art schools, dealers and galleries and critics etc.) of the 'art machine' (Rodner and Thomson, 2013), or in another analogy, by participating in the 'validation chorus' perceived as a 'cast of characters', "artists, teachers, dealers, collectors, critics, curators, the media, even the public maybe" (Perry, 2013). BKH play several roles, networked in several cogs, transgressing character definitions. The well-dressed sculpture may have found a space that accommodated a 'flat'-worlded 'new economy of art' where new practices and ways of thinking emerge, balancing the institutional order and the networked order. She doesn't look bohemian, yet seems uncomfortable in her position, reflecting on the balance she controls.

Re-Casting Legitimacy

In 2014, Norberg defined the process we had followed as a 'learning process'. The BKH management team had evaluated their previous success and was challenged in the development of a new vision. In further retrospect, he described it as perceptions of alternatives, which meant mapping out different paths as a reflective process on what they had built and what their core values were. Being able to communicate these values to the corporate structure and to uphold them in their relations to their patrons was a form of self-validation which entailed internal enquiries, increased documentation and developing stronger and more persuasive arguments for internal and external stakeholders (BN, 2015).

The BKH management team engaged an internal critical dialogue, bringing perceived dichotomies together; reflecting on the question 'where did we come from?' and pressing further to communicate the visions they had had from the start of being part of a public arena debate on society and culture. In 2013, Jeanette Bonnier had expressed this as:

> I think one must sit down and think about it, what is we will do in the future, because art is not just for, how should I express it, it's not just for pleasure, enjoyment, comfort for the moment, it's not . . . art is . . . in my opinion a support for people to think, to see things they have never seen before, make them ponder . . .
>
> (JB, 2013)

Self-validating thus included both the returning to core values on art, reflecting on their own position in between institutions and structures, as well as the need to move further outside safe havens. BKH pursued a continuous building of networks and exploration of new forms of cooperation and financing. Was the sculpture balancing not only perspectives of criticisms and acclaim, internal trust and external validation, but also of time frames, balancing the contingencies of the present with the ambitions and the possibilities of the future? Validation depended on the capacity to engage.

A particular case connects illustratively with Irit Rogoff's use of criticality: "the operations of recognising the limitations of one's thought [connecting] with risk, with a cultural inhabitation that performatively acknowledges what it is risking without yet fully being able to articulate it". (Rogoff, 2003). In 2013, Arrhenius mentions an ambition:

> I would really like longer opening hours and free entrance; that is one thing we have discussed in the board, many times [but the board] wants the revenue. They find it important that there is a measure of . . . that there is a value when coming here and paying.
>
> (SA, 2013)

In 2015, that ambition was achieved when Arrhenius expressed the desire to conduct an open and 'vibrant discussion on art' with visitors with little experience of contemporary art finding their way into the venue (Nordström, 2015). The strategic decision to remove the fees was made with a provision that it would indirectly lead to increased external financing. BKH was again balancing, re-emphasizing the importance of the institution as a driver of societal development and debate, phrased on their webpage as "generating a dialogue on art serves as the driving force" with an "active pedagogical approach" (bonnierkonsthall.se).

We return one last time to the bronze sculpture on the marble floor. She was made by Dan Wolgers and is called *Sagesman (Liggande kvinna)* (2007), *The One Who Tells (Laying woman)*. She is made in the cire perdue molding method where the sculpture is cast molded. Looking closely, we see that the round objects she holds are her own cast molds: she carries the structure from where she became (DW, 2015). The critic Mårten Arndtzén commented on how cire perdue means 'lost' or 'forgotten' form; the bronze sculpture thus raises the questions of how to understand the conditions that formed an existence and how to see oneself from the outside (Arndtzén, 2007). She sees herself from the outside and the inside, from external validation to internal processes, as part of different orders, keeping the outgrown cast mold rather than discarding it, always ready to re-cast herself anew. However, where the critic saw a melancholic, even nostalgic mode of self-reflection, we discern the conditions of criticality that was about extending its horizon and opening up a neighboring space for the unexpected, a frame for creating the unimaginable within arm's reach.

For us, in the end, the bronze sculpture centered our continuous re-interpretations of how art joins business and how legitimacy is attained—not singularly or univocally, but with a difference in every movement. The sculpture is both spoken of and speaking to us, shifting in a validation process in balances of acclaim and criticism, trust and critique, contending with institutional order and networked flatness.

Notes

1   We were three academic researchers at the time. Gabriella Wennblom, PhD, was involved in the early stages of the project. In total, we held six interviews over a period of two and a half years, a number of informal conversations and some email and message interactions, as well as had access to certain documentation on BKH activities.
2   The exhibition was *20 år* (*20 Years of the Maria Bonnier Dahlin Foundation*) and ran for the first four months of BKH's existence.
3   Lars Nittve and David Neuman, respectively. Artist Dan Wolgers also sat on the board.
4   According to Norberg (2013), income was 28% of the turnover, mainly from tickets, events and the gallery shop.

References

Arndtzén, M. (2007). Dan Wolgers/Cire perdue. *Expressen*.
Ayata, B. (2007). *Kulturekonomi: konsten att fånga osynliga värden*. Lund: Studentlitteratur.
Becker, H. S. (1982). *Art Worlds*. Berkeley: University of California Press.
Belfiore, E. (2004). Auditing culture: The subsidised cultural sector in the new public management. *International Journal of Cultural Policy*, 10(2):183–202.
Bourriaud, N. (2005). *Postproduction: Culture as Screenplay: How Art Reprograms the World*. Berlin: Lukas & Sternberg.
Cloutier, C. and Langley, A. (2013). The Logic of Institutional Logics: Insights from French Pragmatist Sociology. *Journal of Management Inquiry*, 22(4):360–380.
Gielen, P. (2013). *Institutional Attitudes: Instituting Art in a Flat World*. Amsterdam: Valiz.
Guillet de Monthoux, P. (2004). *The Art Firm: Aesthetic Management and Metaphysical Marketing*. Stanford, CA and London: Stanford University Press.
Helgesson, C.-F. and Kjellberg, H. (2013). Introduction: Values and valuations in market practice. *Journal of Cultural Economy*, 6(4):361–369.
Helgesson, C.-F. and Muniesa, F. (2013). For what it's worth: An introduction to valuation studies. *Valuations Studies*, 1(1):1–10.
Knutsson, U. (2006). Glashuset kan öppna. *Expressen*.
Madestrand, B. (2006). Bonniers Konsthall skapar debatt. *Dagens Nyheter*.
Nordström, A. (2015). Bonniers Konsthall inför fri entré. *Dagens Nyheter*.
Perry, G. (2013). Reith Lectures. *BBC Radio 4*.
Porter, T. M. (1992). Quantification and the accounting ideal in science. *Social Studies of Science*, 22(4):633–651.
Power, M. (1999). *The Audit Society: Rituals of Verification*. Oxford: Oxford University Press.
Rodner, V. L. and Thomson, E. (2013). The art machine: Dynamics of a value generating mechanism for contemporary art. *Arts Marketing: An International Journal*, 3(1):58–72.

Rogoff, I. (2003). Criticism, critique and criticality. *EIPCP Journal*. Retrieved on 28.02.2016 from http://eipcp.net/transversal/0806/rogoff1/en.

Rosler, M. (2013). *Culture Class: Art, Creativity, Urbanism, Part I*. Berlin: Sternberg Press.

Styhre, A. (2013). The economic valuation and commensuration of cultural resources: financing and monitoring the Swedish culture sector. *Valuations Studies*, 1(1):51–81.

Treijs, E. (2013). Avantgardet lyfts fram på konsthallarna *Svenska Dagbladet*.

Vilks, L. (2011). *Art: den institutionella konstteorin, konstnärlig kvalitet, den internationella samtidskonsten*. Nora: Nya Doxa.

Österholm, P. (1997). Bonniers vill bygga konsthall. *Svenska Dagbladet*. Retrieved 11.02.2016 from Bonniers Konsthall <http://www.bonnierskonsthall.se/en/about-us/>.

Retrieved Interviews

Björn Norberg 5 October 2012; 20 December 2013; 4 March 2015
Sara Arrhenius 5 June 2013
Jeanette Bonnier 14 August 2013
Pontus Bonnier 14 August 2013

E-mail Correspondence

Dan Wolgers 14 December 2015

Section IV

Leadership and Power

The fourth section of the book deals with concepts such as leadership and power. It includes four chapters, three of which are conceptual dialogues, and one is based on the authors' experience of founding and participating in an artists' collective.

The management scholar **Katja Lindqvist** takes the reader on a historical journey, focused this time on leadership, a central and highly debated issue in organization and management studies. She addresses how leadership has been understood and practiced in the arts and in business. First, she reviews what leadership is in Art History and comes to the remark that leadership might be called style in the arts. Then, she reviews the literature from business administration and points at a shift from focusing on personal traits to focusing on mundane tasks of the leaders. She then turns to the fields of Sociology of Art and Entrepreneurship in order to discover some common discourses on leadership between the two fields.

The second chapter by the arts scholar **Kerry McCall** and the organization scholar **Maeve Houlihan** continues the discussion of Lindqvist by focusing on the issue of entrepreneurship. Departing from the observation of the arts and business being separate, yet increasingly blending worlds (see also Schnugg and Vesna in this volume), they raise the question of the artist as cultural entrepreneur. Building on the history of entrepreneurship as a field, they problematize the invasion of the entrepreneurial language into the cultural spheres with respect to issues such as values (see also the section on performing values), creativity, innovation and risk.

The third chapter by business scholar **Yuliya Shymko** and arts and business scholar **Alison Minkus** focuses on the question of power in organizations and thus continues a discussion raised in several previous chapters (see Lindqvist in this section, but also the chapters in collaboration in section 2). Like in Lindqvist's and Schnugg and Vesna's chapters, the historical journey of Yuliya Shymko and Alison Minkus bring them to highlight common roots of their view rather than to distance their perspectives. Giving voice to wise old men, such as Max Weber, George Simmel and Anthony Giddens, the two female authors engage in an open discussion around bureaucracy, business organizations and the arts.

The third chapter is written by organizational scholar **Elen Riot**, in dialogue with cultural manager **Pauline Quantin**, and is based on Riot's experience as an artist-in-residence at the artistic wasteland La Fileuse, founded by Pauline in Reims, France. Riot's journey is about tracing the memories of the ex-textile factory La Fileuse and its recent development with the artists' occupation. This journey raises a number of issues common to other chapters in this book, like the valuation of the organizing practices (see Reinhold and Sanaâ), the establishment of a balance between individual and collective in the collaboration (see Hansen and Strauss), the relationship between art and society (see Barinaga). We have, however, chosen to lift up here the question of leadership and relate it to both Lindqvist's and McCall and Houlihan's reflections on leadership and entrepreneurship. In this somewhat intimate dialogue, the leader Pauline Quantin and the follower Elen Riot, who both happen to cross the worlds of art and business fluidly, reflect on the very process of building an artists' collective.

11 Leadership in Art and Business

Katja Lindqvist

Introduction

Leadership is prized both in the world of art and the world of business. But does leadership really refer to the same notion in the two contexts? Is it at all possible to discuss leadership in art and business and find a common ground? This question will be explored in this chapter through a closer look at how leadership is perceived in Art History and Business Studies (Business Administration), but also in Sociology of Art and the growing research area of Entrepreneurship. The specialization of disciplines significantly conditions the framework of research undertaken in diverse disciplines and has a substantial impact on the understanding of leadership in art and business. When discussing leadership in art and business, it is therefore important to recognize the differences in norms and practice in these practice fields as well as in the respective academic fields. Leadership can in general term be described as the function of organizing joint efforts for a specified purpose. In this sense, leadership refers to the function of combining resources and coordinating action towards specific goals, achieving compliance for decisions among contributors to the organized efforts. This chapter will not discuss the possible benefits of artistic expressions for management or leadership practice, nor will it discuss the practice of leadership in the art world, as these are beyond the scope of the chapter.

Leadership in the History of Art:[1] Style and Innovation

Leadership in art, at least from an Art History perspective, is defined in terms of style. Art History [2] as academic discipline consists to a large extent of analyses of changes in the style of artworks and artistic forms of expression. Leadership as a topic enters Art History through artist biographies. Vasari (1991) set the tone with his *Lives of the Artists*, where the context in which particular artworks were created gives relief to studies of the artworks themselves and also binds different artworks together in a chronological and stylistic development of the artist's *oevre*.

Art History developed as discipline parallel to the formation of History as discipline and strived for scholarly rigour, although with differences between individual researchers (Karlholm, 1996). In this process, leading researchers, in particular Wölfflin, aimed to distinguish Art History from Cultural History, its mother discipline. It is at this point in time, at the end of the 19th century, that style becomes the basis for much of modern art history as discipline, and scholars develop the theoretical basis of Art History. As a result, other aspects of artistic practice became of less interest. Art theory has continued to be an important part of Art History as a discipline, in particular referring to aesthetics and philosophy, together with frameworks borrowed from Psychology in later decades (Danto, 1981; Pointon, 1994).

The orientation of Art History towards style has implications for how artistic leadership is understood. Regardless of the development of the role of the professional artist, style becomes the foremost element around which to construct the history of art. Due to the development of Art History as a discipline, leadership in art is largely defined as technical mastery and innovation driving the field (market). In other words, leadership in art, at least from an Art History perspective, is defined as originality of style (of artworks), in the sense of being ahead of others in developing new styles of expression. This idea is expressed by the term 'the avant-garde' as coined by 20th-century art critics (Krauss, 1985; Calinescu, 1987). This in turn was a development that was a result of the decline of the art academy system, which had offered the art audience a minimum of a common ground for the interpretation and judgement of artworks (Goldstein, 1996). The idea of the avant-garde comprises some artists being 'ahead' of other people, expressing new sensibilities before they are recognized in other areas of society through style innovations expressed by one or a few artists later spreading to others, and has shaped the idea of artistic (stylistic) leadership.

In Art History, artistic mastery generates authority, since this is what renders influence and reputation. This means that masters in visual art are visionaries with a strong stylistic talent and the ability to materialize visions and ideas. Due to this mastery, they tend to become leaders of artistic ventures where other contributors (assistants as well as external parties) are involved due to demand from an audience with educated tastes. In order to realize the artistic vision, the master needs to control and coordinate the realization of the artistic vision. In general, the recognition of the mastery (skill) of the individual artist is the reason for invitations to commissioned work or collaborations, and therefore, this skill is also the basis for negotiations of terms of work. This is in particular illustrated by the description of the rapid and radical development in art during the second half of the 19th century and the turn of the century 1800/1900, with painters such as Cézanne, Monet, Picasso and others who were defined increasingly as leading artists due to their stylistic innovation.

The Artist as a Leader: A Changing Role

The nature of artistic work has developed substantially over the last centuries. A significant aspect of the development of artists as leaders is the organizational downscaling of the artist enterprise from workshop master to individual entrepreneur. There are historical studies of this development, but most descriptions of it have been undertaken in Sociology of Art rather than in Art History (Alpers, 1988; Jensen, 1994; Bourdieu, 1996). Even contemporary developments in the organization of the art world tend to be left to sociologists to describe. The artist role changed when the workshop system with masters and apprentices disappeared and was replaced by art academies controlling the quality of artist training and of the art produced. This development took place first in Italy and later in France in the mid-17th century and then later in other northern European countries. Academies taught what was considered the best of artistic style (Denis and Trodd, 2000). This generated opposition among artists in the 19th century, when more artists started to question the need to paint within a tradition and especially the idealism of academic art. This development coincided with reactions to Enlightenment that had emphasized rationality and resulted in Romanticism, with its emphasis on emotions and with a distinct individualistic approach. Nature, perceived as untamed and original, took on a role as the antidote to historical and idealistic painting. Artistic work should be based on natural forces rather than formed by antiquated norms. This led to an increasing individualism among artists, who at this point increasingly sought an individual style, and the broadening of the art market and the lesser influence of academies of art led to a greater emphasis on style as the individual trademark of artists. This was the point in time where the artist as a genius myth was formed (Wittkower and Wittkower, 1963; Emison, 2004).

With the deterioration of 'general' rules for painting through the decreasing role of art academies, art viewers could no longer rely on their general knowledge of classical styles and motives, and a large part of the audience could no longer interpret new styles based on a general canon. This is where the role of the art critic becomes increasingly important in the art field. By the mid-19th century, style was already a distinguishing mark for different groups of artists, such as the Realists, the Impressionists et cetera. At this point in time, art galleries had taken on the role of managers of artistic production, leaving the artist to focus on stylistic innovation and refinement. After the disastrous experiments in the early 20th century with governments dictating acceptable styles for art (in Russia, Germany and Italy), the political and societal support of art took on a more distanced role, with artists being able to receive public support regardless of artistic style. This made artists into state-funded professionals outside most other spheres of society than the art world. With innovation at the core of artistic value, artists tested the limits for public support, something leading to discussions of artist ethics and the purpose of public support of art. This development has led to what Bourdieu (1985) has described as the division of the art field in two, the field of restricted production and the field of large-scale production. The first more or less corresponds with publicly supported art production and display, whereas the second corresponds with the commercial market for art.

With the changing character of artistic work at the end of the 20th century, some artists have developed new kinds of organizations, where leadership can once again be said to be a relevant aspect of artistic work. With the increasing relational orientation of (some) art practice, aspects of leadership have become more prevalent in the art field, both in terms of organizational aspects of the artist's relation to her or his public, but also in relation to contributors to the realization of artworks. The studio of Olafur Eliasson is an example of this new development of the artist's workshop, not dissimilar to that of former times, but with a new theoretical framework (Jacob and Grabner, 2010; Coles, 2012). The artist role has also developed towards that of a researcher, both metaphorically and literally, with the development of reproductive techniques, where the artist can become more of a project leader for different kinds of investigations or productions even performed by others (Lacy, 1995; Sullivan, 2005). In this sense, the artist is today a leader in a more intellectual sense, resembling a modern designer more than an artisan. Leadership in this context can therefore mean rather different things depending on the type of activity artists are engaged in. What has remained is the reluctance of artists to discuss strategies and management, something which is in line with Bourdieu's description of the restricted field of the production of symbolic goods. Speaking of leadership and management, at least in Europe, is still downplayed in the art field, unless explicitly linked to artistic goals and purposes. Leadership in art is a practice, but not a practice that is discussed professionally. In this sense, it contrasts with practice in business, where leadership practice is of central concern.

Leadership in Business Studies: From Personal Aptness to a Mundane Task

In business practice, the issue of leadership has been central since the rapid development of industrial markets and capitalism in the last two centuries (Chandler, 1984). The birth of the limited company emphasized this focus, as businesses stepped out of families, and the manager became a specific and central position in business organizations (Barnard, 1938). It's not possible to summarize the development of leadership research, but what can in this context be emphasized is that leadership research has historically focused on personal traits and skills of successful leaders of businesses, but increasingly the context of leaders, and the situation and environment, as well as the function of leaders, have become more central in leadership research. Leadership today is largely perceived as relational today within research.

Barnard (1938), author of one of the classical texts on leadership and management, pointed out that a central role of the executive is to ensure cooperation. Decisions on cooperation need to be authoritative in order to be effective, and therefore the issue of authority is central to leadership and management. Authority of decision-making has been investigated by organizational sociologists, in particular Weber and Fayol. Weber described three ideal types of authority in society: legal, traditional and charismatic

(Weber, 1968a). But Weber's three ideal types of authority do not really leave space for the market and business leaders when it comes to authority. Legal authority is what characterizes bureaucracies, traditional authority characterized premodern societies and organizations and finally, charismatic authority is based on devotion and the norms conveyed by an individual. If the bureaucratic organization functions well as such, there is hardly any space for leaders, as actions are based on efficiency and value-rationality. In business studies as well as in business practice, there has, however, been an apparent demand for an understanding of the role of leaders and managers in organizations, to judge by the amount of publications in the area of leadership. An interest in individually based authority given the limiting framework for leadership given by the other two Weberian ideal types of authority is perhaps not surprising. In fact, descriptions of business leadership as an art abound (Grint, 2001; Ibbotson, 2008; Taylor, 2012). Perhaps due to bourgeois education, business leaders in the last century have to a certain extent been acquainted with cultural classics and sometimes even with newer developments in art. This might be the reason for the analogies made between artists as leaders and business leaders as creating metaphorical artworks and leadership as artistry in the Romantic sense of talent. This understanding of the notion of art corresponds with a view of the artist as a genius (Wittkower and Wittkower, 1963; Emison, 2004). In recent years, leadership studies have been undertaken in collective artistic contexts such as music, film and performing arts (Gyllenpalm, 1995; Ropo and Sauer, 2008; Koivunen and Wennes, 2011). These studies and analogies focus on the necessity of cooperation between leader and led, based on separate functions and skills. This change in interest from the individual, visionary artist to the collectively related conductor seems to have taken place more or less simultaneously as a general interest in the relational contexts and situations of leaders and managers, sometimes termed post-heroic leadership.

In the 1980s, after decades of leadership research focused on rational and effective decision-making, leadership enabling change and innovation in organizations was called for by researchers and business managers (Conger, 1993). This is when Weber's notion of charisma as authority raised interest and generated a wave of leadership research on charismatic leadership. The notion of charismatic leadership later gave way to increasing interest in transformative leadership, perhaps due to the inherent vagueness in Weber's definition of charisma in a management context. Weber (1968b) describes charisma as an emerging social relationship, and his understanding of it comes close to artistic practice as described by artists themselves in the 20th and 21st centuries, although not explicitly linked to artists, as disruptive and informal forces, not rational but personal and emotional. Weber's ideal type of the charismatic leadership divided social organizations into three general types according to the basis of authority and is a macro-level theory rather than a micro-level one, as it was formulated as a sociological theory. Rather similar to Schumpeter's understanding of the entrepreneur in an economic system (Backhaus, 2003; Swedberg, 2006),

Weber saw the charismatic leader as someone innovating social organization by building a community based not purely on rationality or tradition. According to Conger (1993), leadership research interest in the notion of charisma increased due to a perceived bureaucratization of companies in the United States in the 1980s. Nevertheless, many of the aspects that leadership research in business studies focused on neglected aspects of charisma that distances it from much of the conditions of large, established organizations.

The notion of charismatic leadership was initially focused on the positive initial energy and commitment distinguishable in organizations based on charisma. Later on, however, also the negative sides of charisma became more evident in leadership research, something already indicated by Weber. Shifting focus from leadership for change to leadership as an everyday practice, leadership research today increasingly emphasizes leadership as a managerial function, even talking of the triumph of emptiness and leadership as mundane activities (Cunliffe and Eriksen, 2011; Alvesson, 2013). Weber's ideas on shared strong norms rather than rational division of labor in organizations based on a leader's charisma has led to research on differences between such organizations, in other words, on how compliance and thereby leadership on an organizational level differ between organizations with different rationales. Parsons discussed the roles of leaders and managers of non-profit organizations as compared to business firms and discovered that the rationale of this position was substantially different due to the functions of the respective types of organization.

Etzioni developed the idea of norms of different types of organizations impacting on compliance and thereby leadership. These ideas have later developed into research on organizational identity and institutional logics, among other subareas within management studies. According to Etzioni (1975), organizations based on norms substantially differ in their organizational structure and motivation for compliance from utilitarian organizations. This means that leadership is undertaken differently in different types of organizations. Again, as the formal position of a leader derives its basis of compliance of subordinates not due to personal but due to formal position and mandate, the personal and informal basis of power and compliance ensures greater importance to the individual character of a leader. Leadership research has been interested in exploring this individual side of the social-structural construction which is the organization, as compared to structural aspects generally referred to as management and administration research. Normative organizations rely on normative compliance rather than coercive compliance, according to Etzioni, which in turn is based on high commitment among members and contributors and on high internalization of norms. According to Etzioni, leaders are actors whose normative power is based on the personal characteristics of the individual, and this basis of power is separated from power based on the organizational position of the actor. Etzioni further differentiates between formal leaders and informal leaders. This separation of the basis of compliance between personal and positional power has been a persistent dimension of leadership research since Etzioni's days. How far this separation can be explanatory in individual cases, however, remains to be specified.

In recent years, the context of leadership and leaders rather than leaders as individuals has been in focus for progressive leadership and management research. This research has emphasized relations and mundaneness of leadership (in fact, often the term management rather than leadership is used) practice, by some described as post-heroic leadership (Alvesson and Sveningsson, 2003; Tengblad, 2012; Parush and Koivunen, 2014). An interesting aspect of this development is that the leader is less and less seen as a hero, or at least this idea of the leader has been questioned by a number of other perceptions of leaders and leadership. The postmodern artist, as well as the contemporary leader, is a relational leader acknowledging the important contribution of co-workers and collaborators (Barling, 2014; cf. Costas and Taheri, 2012). Tengblad (2006) describes the development of leadership discourse both in research and practice in the 1980s as shifting from a focus on managers as efficient administrators to visionary leaders more oriented towards communication, much in line with concepts such as charismatic and later transformational leadership. In a study in Sweden in the 2000s, Tengblad (2006) did indeed indicate that managers spend more time today on communication and information than previously, and in particular see their role as inspirational and exemplifying company culture rather than as administrators of decisions.

If leadership in management studies has gone from being described as a task demanding heroic personal traits of individuals in this role to a task that is achieved by several actors in interaction and mutual dependence, the same can in fact be said about the entrepreneur as a leader in entrepreneurship research. Entrepreneurship research, expanding rapidly since the 1980s, today recognizes entrepreneurial leadership in many contexts and also the contextual impact on entrepreneurial action (Carlsson et al., 2013). As the individual is of interest in entrepreneurship research, and as the activities of artists have come to be recognized as entrepreneurial by researchers as well as politicians, the views on artistic leadership practice from the point of view of research where it is actually studied as such, Entrepreneurship and Sociology of Art, will be explored next.

Leadership Practices in Art: Sociology of Art and Entrepreneurship Studies

Leadership in Business Studies, in particular in the area of management, is of interest mainly in the context of large(r) organizations. Much of leadership training is also focused on the segment of managers in such organizations. As pointed out in the previous section, different organizational contexts might demand other leadership skills, and new venture establishment is such an example. Entrepreneurs are defined as individuals acting on opportunities and pursue these in contexts of uncertainty,[3] and therefore skills dissimilar to those of good managers tend to be to allocated entrepreneurs in research. Charismatic leadership has, as described in the previous section, from a management perspective been perceived as potentially beneficial as well as negative for the leadership of organizations. This is because charismatic leaders are linked to organizational change, and charismatic leadership has been described as difficult to sustain over longer periods of time in established organizational contexts. The characteristics of artists as leaders often come close to characterizations of charismatic leadership in Business Studies: personal, based on a context, transitory (project based) and based on commitment to the person. In this context, charisma can be seen as the lack of professional leadership skills (Chell, 2013; Coget et al., 2014). Informal creativity, personal commitment and a relationship focus are what are needed for new ideas, whereas structures and routines are demanded for standardized production.

Artistic practice has over recent centuries developed towards self-employed artists, with the superstar artist often described as a charismatic, iconic figure. This development, together with the increasing political interest in cultural and creative industries, has generated increasing interest in art entrepreneurship from researchers. Whereas art entrepreneurship is a rather new research area (Chang and Wyszomirski, 2015), the Sociology of Art has explored artistic practice, including entrepreneurial action, for several decades. The Sociology of Art is also the academic discipline where leadership has been mostly discussed, as part of the organization of artistic work in a market (Menger, 2003; Tanner, 2003). Whereas the Sociology of Art has had as its focus the dynamics of the art field, including strategic considerations of individual artists, Entrepreneurship research has been interested in factors and conditions related to entrepreneurial action, whether in art or business. Originating in Economics, research interest in entrepreneurial action has over time increased in Business Studies. In the new subfield of Entrepreneurship, however, leadership is discussed from an entrepreneurial perspective rather than from a management perspective. Chang and Wyszomirski (2015) state that published arts entrepreneurship research defines leadership as a way of working strategically (leadership vision) and tactically (leadership tools).

Whereas Art History (including Art Theory) researchers have been focused on the stylistic development of artistic practice as expressed in singular works and *oeuvres* of artists, sociologists have shown interest in the production of artworks from a practice perspective, including the organization and management of this work, and relationships with other actors involved in the realization of artworks (Wolff, 1981). So in order to discuss artistic practice from a leadership, management or organizational perspective, we need to go to Sociology of Art rather than to Art History or Art Theory. Topics related to the organization of artistic work (and its consumption) have been researched in the area of Sociology of Art, focusing on relationships between individuals, groups and institutions in the art field.

Bourdieu has, perhaps more than any other sociologist, explored the art field(s) as ground(s) for strategies of individual actors, including artists and other professional groups engaged with art. One vital element of Bourdieu's theory of the field is that strategies are based on what is at stake. In the field of restricted production, according to Bourdieu, what is at stake is the acceptance and legitimation of peers, or other producers, professionals of art, and an audience with educated taste, in contrast to the field of the large-scale production of art (Bourdieu, 1985), where production is for the acceptance of a public with non-educated taste. This in turn means that in order to be accepted in the field of restricted production, an individual artist needs to act strategically to achieve the same values as other actors in this field. Those values comprise foremost artistic innovation and stylistic development, rather than the appreciation of a larger audience. This has as a consequence that dimensions of work organization, efficiency and other aspects relating to the production of art, or the economic conditions under which art is produced, are downplayed by all actors of the field of restricted production. In contrast, in the field of large-scale production, strategies are developed with these economic and efficiency-related aspects expressly in mind.

Since the 1990s, entrepreneurship research has gained increasing importance for the issue of artists as leaders. Entrepreneurship as a research area has grown exponentially since then and today embraces leadership and many other aspects of start-ups and small and medium-sized organizations. Entrepreneurial leadership has, in entrepreneur and small business research, been described as passionate and important in the start-up phase of an enterprise, but it is generally described as not suited for company growth and stabilization, where more managerial skills and orientation are needed from management. Going back to the view on leadership in management research, Weber emphasized that charismatic leadership can also be sustained over longer periods of time, since charismatic leadership is leadership for change and is unstable and transitory from an organizational perspective. This has led management scholars to conclude that charismatic leadership is more closely related to and better suited to entrepreneurial settings than routine settings.

The development of the artist role has led to leadership in the art field being closer to entrepreneurship and self-employment rather than leadership defined as management within a large organization, as is often assumed in Business Studies. Contemporary entrepreneurship research clearly distinguishes between the entrepreneur as leader of a venture and the manager as leader of or within a large organization. What is emphasized in entrepreneurship research is that entrepreneurship is transitional and temporary; it concerns the initiation of ventures, the discovery of opportunities and their exploitation, and entrepreneurship is in this sense defined as innovative. What links entrepreneurship and leadership research is that both have had a strong element historically of studies of the personal characteristics of leaders and a discussion of the relative importance for the successful enter-prising of the leader as an individual and leadership as a skill and approach, in other words, something that can be learned. The character of the entre-preneur in Business Studies has been quite similar to the character of the art-ist in art history (Lindqvist, 2011), described by researchers as an innovator and forerunner with significant impact on the structure and dynamics of an entire field. At the same time, this visionary leadership style may prove incompatible with routinization, as already described by Weber (Lindqvist, 2016). All in all, studies specifically on art and artist leadership are still few and far between. The Sociology of Art and Entrepreneurship approach leadership issues related to artistic practice in quite distinct ways, as do Art History and Business Studies. More research is needed that can approach artistic leadership practice without the stigma of desecration. Whereas this is possible within the fields (markets) of performing arts and film, which are much more collective as art forms compared to visual art, it is still next to impossible in the art field. Art Leadership Studies still needs to form as a specific research area.

Conclusion

Coming back to the two questions at the start of this chapter, it firstly remains elusive what leadership in the field of art consists of in terms of practice, as research is scarce. In Art History, leadership is defined as artistic innovation and quality, whereas organizational leadership practice is taboo. A conclusion of this exploration is that a common, but highly abstracted, feature of leadership in both business and art is the emphasis on the com-munication of visions and the importance of cooperation for achievement. Leadership as style is what matters in art, whereas leadership style is what matters in business, at least from a scholarly perspective. There is certainly leadership as practice also in art, and this should be researched much more in detail to gain more profound knowledge of successful (and less success-ful) leadership in art. Studies of leadership in art are mostly undertaken in collective art forms, in particular the performing arts, music and film. Issues related to leadership in art are discussed in Sociology of Art and increasingly in the field of Entrepreneurship research, but not yet to a similar extent as in other fields of practice. Part of the dynamics of arts organizations and artists as leaders have been described by organizational researchers like Weber and Etzioni, but contemporary practices of artists follow the development of the surrounding society, and therefore merit updated theories and perspectives. This would for sure also benefit leadership research.

Notes

1   The English term Art History as such implies a purely historical perspective on art, but the discipline also comprises general theories of various aspects of art-works and artistic production. The original German term is *Kunstwissenschaft*,

which translated would be Science of Art. History of Art constitutes a part of contemporary Art History as a research discipline (in German, *Kunstgeschichte*).
2 Discipline names in this chapter will be indicated through capital initials, to distinguish them from purely descriptive notions with the same phrasing.
3 There is no single agreed-upon definition of entrepreneurs or entrepreneurship, and different definitions emphasize different aspects of phenomena referred to as entrepreneurial (Carlsson et al., 2013).

References

Alpers, Svetlana (1988). *Rembrandt's Enterprise: The Studio and the Market*. Chicago and London: University of Chicago Press.
Alvesson, Mats (2013). *The Triumph of Emptiness: Consumption, Higher Education, and Work Organization*. Oxford: Oxford University Press.
Alvesson, Mats and Sveningsson, Stefan (2003). Managers doing leadership: The extra-ordinarization of the mundane. *Human Relations*, 56(12):1435–1459.
Backhaus, Jürgen (Ed.) (2003). *Joseph Alois Schumpeter: Entrepreneurship, Style, and Vision*. Dordrecht: Kluwer Academic Publishers.
Barling, Julian (2014). *The Science of Leadership: Lessons from Research for Organizational Leaders*. Oxford: Oxford University Press.
Barnard, Chester (1938). *The Functions of the Executive*. Cambridge, MA: Harvard University Press.
Bourdieu, Pierre (1996). *The Rules of Art: Genesis and Structure of the Literary Field*. Cambridge: Polity Press.
Bourdieu, Pierre (1985). The market of symbolic goods. *Poetics*, 14(1–2, April): 13–44.
Calinescu, Matei (1987). *Five faces of modernity: Modernism, avant-garde, decadence, kitsch, postmodernism*. Rev. ed. Durham: Duke University Press.
Carlsson, Bo Braunerhjelm, Pontus, McKelvey, Maureen, Olofsson, Christer, Persson, Lars and Ylinenpää, Håkan (2013). The evolving domain of entrepreneurship research. *Small Business Economics*, 41:913–930.Chandler, Alfred D., Jr. (1984). The Emergence of Managerial Capitalism. *The Business History Review*, 58(4):473–503.
Chang, Woong Jo and Wyszomirski, Margaret (2015). What is arts entrepreneurship? Tracking the development of its definition in scholarly journals. *Artivate: A Journal of Entrepreneurship in the Arts*, 4(2):11–31.
Chell, Elizabeth (2013). Review of skill and the entrepreneurial process. *International Journal of Entrepreneurial Behavior and Research*, 19(1):6–31.
Coget, Jean-François, Shani, Abraham and Solari, Luca (2014). The lone genius, or leaders who tyrannize their creative teams: An alternative to the "mothering" model of leadership and creativity. *Organizational Dynamics*, 43(2):105–113.
Coles, Alex (2012). *The Transdisciplinary Studio*. Berlin: Sternberg Press.
Conger, Jay A. (1993). Max Weber's conceptualization of charismatic authority: Its influence on organizational research. *The Leadership Quarterly*, 4(3):277–288.
Costas, Jana and Taheri, Alireza (2012). 'The Return of the primal father' in postmodernity? A Lacanian analysis of authentic leadership. *Organization Studies*, 33(9):1195–1216.
Cunliffe, Ann L. and Eriksen, Matthew (2011). Relational leadership. *Human Relations*, 64(11):1425–1449.
Danto, Arthur (1981). *The Transfiguration of the Commonplace*. Cambridge, MA: Harvard University Press.
Denis, Rafael Cardoso and Trodd, Colin (Eds.) (2000). *Art and the Academy in the Nineteenth Century*. New Brunswick, NJ: Rutgers University Press.

Emison, Patricia (2004). *Creating the "Divine" Artist: From Dante to Michelangelo.* Leiden and Boston: Brill Academic Publishers,

Etzioni, A. (1975). *A Comparative Analysis of Complex Organizations. On power, involvement, and their correlates.* New York: Free Press

Goldstein, Carl (1996). *Teaching Art: Academies and Schools from Vasari to Albers.* Cambridge: Cambridge University Press.

Grint, Keith (2001). *The Arts of Leadership.* Oxford: Oxford University Press.

Gyllenpalm, Bo (1995). *Ingmar Bergman and Creative Leadership. How to Create Self-Directed Peak Performing Teams.* Stockholm: Stabim.

Ibbotson, Piers (2008). *The Illusion of Leadership. Directing Creativity in Business and the Arts.* Basingstoke: Palgrave Macmillan.

Jacob, Mary Jane and Grabner, Michelle (Eds.) (2010). The Studio Reader: On the Space of Artists. Chicago and London: University of Chicago Press.

Jensen, Robert (1994). *Marketing Modernism in Fin-de Siècle Europe.* Princeton, NJ: Princeton University Press.

Karlholm, Dan (1996). *Handböckernas konsthistoria: Om skapandet av "allmän konsthistoria" i Tyskland under 1800-talet.* Stockholm/Stehag: Symposion.

Koivunen, Niina and Wennes, Grete (2011). Show us the sound! Aesthetic leadership of symphony orchestra conductors. *Leadership,* 7(1):51–71.

Krauss, Rosalind E. (1985). *The Originality of the Avant-Garde and Other Modernist Myths.* Cambridge, MA: MIT Press.

Lacy, Suzanne (Ed.) (1995). *Mapping the Terrain: New Genre Public Art.* Seattle: Bay Press.

Lindqvist, Katja (forthcoming). Art ventures as hybrid organisations: Tensions and conflicts relating to organisational identity. *International Journal of Entrepreneurial Venturing.*

Lindqvist, Katja (2011). Artist Entrepreneurs, in: Ivo Zander och Mikael Scherdin, (eds.). *Art Entrepreneurship,* pp. 10–22.Cheltenham: Edward Elgar.

Menger, Pierre-Michel (2003). Sociology of Art, in: Ruth Towse, (ed.). *A Handbook of Cultural Economics,* pp: 415–430. Cheltenham: Edward Elgar.

Parush, Tamar and Koivunen, Niina (2014). Paradoxes, double binds, and the construction of 'creative' managerial selves in art-based leadership development. *Scandinavian Journal of Management,* 30(1):104–113.

Pointon, Marcia (1994). *History of Art: A Students' Handbook.* 3rd ed. London and New York: Routledge.

Ropo, Arja and Sauer, Erika (2008). Corporeal Leaders, in: Daved Barry, and Hans Hansen (eds.). *The SAGE Handbook of New Approaches in Management and Organization,* pp: 469–478. London: Sage.

Sullivan, Graeme (2005). *Art Practice as Research: Inquiry in the Visual Arts.* Thousand Oaks, CA: Sage.

Swedberg, Richard (2006). The cultural entrepreneur and the creative industries: Beginning in Vienna. *Journal of Cultural Economics,* 30(4):243–261.

Tanner, Jeremy (Ed.) (2003). *Sociology of Art: A Reader.* London and New York: Routledge.

Taylor, Steven (2012). *Leadership Craft, Leadership Art.* Basingstoke: Palgrave Macmillan.

Tengblad, Stefan (2012). *The Work of Managers: Towards a Practice Theory of Management: Towards a Practice Theory of Management.* Oxford: Oxford University Press.

Tengblad, Stefan (2006). Is there a 'New Managerial work'? A comparison with Henry Mintzberg's classic study 30 years later. *Journal of Management Studies,* 43(7):1437–1461.Vasari, Giorgio (1991). *The Lives of the Artists.* Oxford: Oxford University Press.

Weber, Max (1968a.) *Economy and Society: An Outline of Interpretive Sociology (1–3)*. New York: Bedminster.

Weber, Max (1968b). *On Charisma and Institution Building*. Chicago and London: University of Chicago Press.

Wittkower, Rudolf and Wittkower, Margot (1963). *Born under Saturn: The Character and Conduct of Artists. A Documented History from Antiquity to the French Revolution*. London: Weidenfeld and Nicolson.

Wolff, Janet (1981). *The Social Production of Art*. Basingstoke: Macmillan.

business-minded experimentation. Early stage entrepreneurs are character-ized by the small-scale nature of their business and are often self-funded, domestically or locally based, with a small number in their workforce. Typi-fied more by passion than profit, at this stage, their hope and ambition are nearly limitless. Later stage entrepreneurs may have to scale their business in workforce numbers, profits or scope, and most wear the badge of success alongside the scars and stories of failure.

Irish economist Richard Cantillon (1680–1734) is widely credited as the first to describe market processes as driven by entrepreneurship. He recog-nized the vital role of perception, risk taking and 'vigour' as key entrepre-neurial traits necessary to drive market economies in *Essai sur la Nature du Commerce en Général* (1755). For this, he is often described as the founding father of modern economics. Cantillon identified the willingness to bear personal risk as a defining characteristic of an entrepreneur.

French economist and journalist Jean Baptiste Say (1767–1832) described the process of 'entrepreneurship' as one designed to yield profit for individu-als. According to Say, this is a process of unlocking the capital or wealth that has been tied into land and which can be redirected and used to greater effect in an area of greater potential:

> The entrepreneur shifts economic resources out of an area of lower [productivity], and into an area of higher productivity and greater yield.
> (Say, [1800] 2010)

John Stuart Mills (1806–1873) further popularized 'entrepreneurship' in his 1848 book *Principles of Political Economy*. Stuart Mills highlights the role of the entrepreneur as one comprised of focusing on the creation of value. He makes a clear distinction between entrepreneurs and other busi-ness owners, whom he views more as shareholders. According to Stuart Mills, entrepreneurs are individuals who assume a greater risk and financial and personal burdens as well as potential profit.

Joseph Schumpeter (1883–1950) has become synonymous with the idea of 'creative destruction' and was the first to highlight the role that invention held in theories of entrepreneurship. Schumpeter stressed the importance of creation and innovation as a crucial facet of capitalist economies and noted that this was a two-sided affair which triggered radical change from within (1942/2009). On the one hand, creative thinking in business brings about positive change through product and process innovation, but this 'disruption' also captures the phasing out of outdated goods and services in the creation and replacement of new ones. For Schumpeter, we are actively destroying the old and incessantly creating anew.

And so, as we move towards 20th-century considerations of entrepre-neurship, we start to trace understandings of the entrepreneur as a person of discovery and learning. Hayek (1937), Mises (1949) and Kirzner (1997) articulate the entrepreneur as an individual who uses their inherent talents and abilities to discover previously unnoticed profit opportunities and who then act on their ideas in the marketplace, while Sarasvathy (2001) understands that 'entrepreneurial thinking' has an innate tendency to apply 'effectual reasoning' and 'a distinct form of rationality'. This understanding of the entrepreneur as someone who possesses innate abilities akin to a natural disposition for entrepreneurship underpins much of our understanding of the term today.

This perspective on entrepreneurial thinking has grown throughout the 20th and 21st centuries. And in many ways, this focus on entrepreneurship runs parallel to the increasing refrain of 'individualization' and 'individualism'. The emphasis on the individual as an independent centre of consciousness grew out of philosophies originating in Europe in the late 17th century, and soon became a major social and cultural principle encompassing the burgeoning ideas of the Enlightenment.

As society has moved to favor the rights of the individual, the ideological conceptualization of man as the determining force of his own destiny has become a central premise. And even in the collectively focused ideologies of Marxism and Socialism, the individual is recognized as an important cog in the wheel of the collective order. Weber, in *The Protestant Ethic and the Spirit of Capitalism* ([1930]2016), strongly links advancing capitalism with an individualized work ethic and draws a distinct correlation between a profit and goal-oriented mindset and the common good. Scholars note the greater salience of the processes of individualization and highlight how this has become conducive to the emergence of a 'risk society' and the rise of the expert and the specialist (Giddens, 1991; Beck, 1992). Beck, Giddens and Lash go further and note the influence this has had on society: where once we had 'trace memory', integrated networks, tradition and a stablizing influence, we now have disembedded, 'open' and disruptive mechanisms (Beck et al. 1994:67).

These disruptive and open mechanisms destroy previous static and institutionalized frameworks and allow new, dynamic and innovative methods and processes to respond in a more agile fashion to the market. With the rise of the free market, competitive national agendas and neo-liberal thinking, we witness an increased focus on entrepreneurship as a policy consideration and as an aspirational way of working (Department of Jobs, Innovation and Enterprise, 2014). The entrepreneur as a creative force has begun to seamlessly meld with the creative force of artistic practise as the frame of entrepreneurship slips towards the creative. This has led to emergent discourses of 'creative' and 'cultural' entrepreneurship and a reframing of what it means to be an individual engaged in creative production and practice.

Tracing Creative and Cultural Entrepreneurship

Creative entrepreneurship sits at the heart of what we now call the creative and cultural industries. Often used to describe those engaged in artistic, cultural or creatively focused activities, creative entrepreneurship is most often typified by the self-employed, portfolio or freelance worker realizing creatively focused ideas. Creative entrepreneurs, it is suggested, use creativity to unlock the potential that lies within themselves as distinct from external capital resources (Howkins, 2002; McGuinness, 2015).

Like business entrepreneurs, creative entrepreneurs are engaged in the development of new ideas, goods or services. Not necessarily a 'for-profit' endeavor, creative entrepreneurship realizes a creative idea using creative talent, creative skills or creative labor. The realization of this idea—its artistic vision, creative unity, aesthetic coherence and authentic voice—can often be of greater importance to the creative entrepreneur than any commercial profit.

While our usage and familiarity with the term is relatively recent, creative entrepreneurs have been around for a long time. There is evidence that as humans, we have used creative talents in artistic, cultural or creatively focused activities since we first started wearing clothes, making tools and creating jewelry over 110,000 years ago. The artisans of medieval Europe were skilled craftsmen, using their creative talents and intellectual capital in the provision of goods and commodities for their communities. The wandering minstrels and troubadours of the Middle Ages performed songs, told stories and entertained with dramatic tales of mythical or distant places in exchange for food and accommodation. In pre-Norman Britain, travelling professional poets were known as 'Scops'. Bards in Gaelic culture carefully crafted poems and songs to reinforce the status and power of the ruling families of the land who acted as their patrons. In Ireland, a long tradition exists of storytellers, known as 'Seanachaí', who traveled, telling tales of epic battles and local folklore.

Thinking about these practices gives access to how the artist's value is recognized. In pre-monetary society, currency centred on the bartering and exchange of labor or goods for a purpose such as patronage, protection, accommodation or provisions. Marcel Mauss (1954) and Annette Weiner (1992) demonstrate how cultural goods and the products of artisanship were used for barter and exchange and were imbued with a value which would often grow. Weiner called these 'inalienable possessions', as the value and worth would perpetuate for generations. Creative skills were thus used in an exchange process, much as Adam Smith outlined in *An Inquiry into the Nature and Causes of the Wealth of Nations* (1991[1775]):

> . . . and thus the certainty of being able to exchange all that surplus part of his own produce of his own labour, which is over and above his own consumption, for such parts of the produce of other men's labour as he may have occasion for, encourages every man to apply himself to a particular occupation, and to cultivate and bring to perfection whatever talent or genius he may possess . . .
>
> (Smith, 1991[1775]:14–15)

With the advent of the Industrial Revolution and an increased focus on a market economy, the idea of artists and creative practitioners as outside the language, and the logic, of the market grew. With emphasis placed on European Enlightenment concepts of *bildung* and 'otherness', the artist as a romantic genius was considered as working at a remove from society. Concerned with lofty thoughts and aesthetic ideals, artistic work and creative labor was placed in direct contrast to the overtly positivist logic and discourses of 'truth' and science. Arts and culture became synonymous with the symbolic realm of artistic expression and the transcendent and mystical realm of the artist.

In the United States, the 'mixing up' of genres and cultural forms was commonplace until the mid- to late 19th century, with musical hall tunes running alongside classical music, in the same venue, on the same evening (DiMaggio, 1982). An individual was as likely to encounter a Shakespearean actor as a Shakespearean clown, delivering lines of the Bard's work.

The fracture between popular culture and the more exclusive high arts became most apparent in the 20th century. Carey (2005) clearly articulates the fear felt by British elites and intellectuals such as Mathew Arnold and Virginia Woolf as the 'rising faceless mass' threatened their preserve and domain of privilege. Elites established monopoly and control over certain artistic and cultural tastes and ideas of 'high art' were developed and differentiated from the emergent 'popular' culture.

In the early 20th century, Walter Benjamin (1936) welcomed the possibilities of these more available and more popular cultural experiences, suggesting that the forms of mass spectatorship that were required would foster a new sort of social and political experience of art. In response, critical theorists Horkeheimer and Adorno (1972) were vociferous on the retrogressive nature of 'mass' culture offered through the popular culture industry, emphasizing how individuals were subservient to the dominating logic of market capitalism.

The establishment of key institutions for arts and culture in national galleries, museums, concert halls and theatres and the provision of distributive funding for the professional arts through state agencies such as national Arts Councils and ministerial departments of culture saw the development of 'culture' as a catch-all term for high arts and legitimated, professional creative practise, with policy makers largely operating on this narrower definition.

Since the 1980s, the focus in Europe has been on what culture can do for places—urban regeneration and the establishment of flagship projects such as the Guggenheim in Bilbao, Las Ramblas in Barcelona, Temple Bar in Dublin or the Potsdamer Platz in Berlin (Bianchini and Parkinson, 1994). The 1990s onwards has witnessed an increased focus on the social benefits of arts and culture in areas such as personal development, health and well-being, community empowerment and social cohesion emphasized (Matarasso, 1997). This narrative has more recently morphed into one of entrepreneurial discourses, and we are witnessing the term 'culture' emerge into the 'creative and cultural industries', with the role of cultural and creative entrepreneurship taking hold as a distinct area of economic development (Dublin City Council, 2010). Pick (1991) highlights that there is nothing new in governments finding uses for culture in positive or negative ways, and indeed, the proliferation of cultural intermediaries and the increased emphasis on the creative, economic imperative has become a defining feature of our times (Hesmondhalgh, 2013; O'Brien, 2013; Stevenson and Matthews, 2013; Maguire Smyth and Matthews, 2014).

The Artist as a Cultural Entrepreneur?

Of course, distinguishing between the value of things and the price of things is a complex business, in both business and the arts. Defining a cultural entrepreneur is no more straightforward. Are the artist and the cultural entrepreneur one and the same? Cutting through philosophical reflection, Grant (2011) invokes a helpfully nuanced and practical distinction from the unusual source of the U.S. Internal Revenue Service. Rather than separate the artist from the entrepreneur, the key distinction looked for by the IRS is between the hobbyist and the professional artist. Among the acid tests applied are:

1) is the activity carried on in a businesslike manner?
2) does the artist intend to make the artistic activity profitable?
3) does the individual depend in full or in part on income generated by the artistic work?
4) are business losses to be expected, or are they due to circumstances beyond the artist's control?
5) are business plans changed to improve profitability?

(United States Internal Revenue Service, cited in Grant, 2011).

Certainly, taxation policy is a telling indicator of cultural values and what is valued. In Ireland, for example, self-employed artists can avail of tax exemptions for work that is original and recognized as having cultural or artistic merit, such as the sale of a book or other writing, a play or music composition. Using this rubric, the distinction between the artist and the cultural entrepreneur involves subtle adjustments at the surface of things, but underneath, a more fundamental shift in motive from the work itself the profitability of that work.

We live now in an era of the enterprising self. Emphasis is increasingly placed on the entrepreneurial aspects of creative talent with the artist and cultural producer encouraged to find a niche, fill a gap, know their audience, innovate, promote, package, brand and sell him/herself and their work. Many creative and cultural workers now grapple with cash flow projections, evaluative metrics, goals and strategic statements. The tools and language of the marketplace have firmly entered the sphere of the artist, and this has now become a distinct aspect of creative working lives, viewed as a necessary paradigm in order to sustain creative and cultural practise. But the blending and combining of artistic and business mentalities and perspectives can be difficult to negotiate, and even more difficult to successfully fuse.

A stark cultural gulf between policy discourse and the nature of creative working asserts itself when the grounded and individuated experiences of cultural workers are taken into account. In reflective discussion, artists and creative practitioners contributing to this research articulate the pressure to become cultural entrepreneurs, or 'culture-preneurs' (Lange, 2006), for example, to think with a business mindset, to develop strategies and brands and place importance on networking, digital dissemination and profiling of work. Creative and cultural entrepreneur discourses can prove uncomfortable for many contemporary artists and cultural workers who self-identify as the 'creative', and many require *"others to do the business side, others with the different mindset"* (Anna, fashion designer). Still others question why business and creative perspectives should be separate and critique the education system *"which forces people to be one of the other—never both"* (Clare, jeweler). Making money for many is not easy, and even amongst the successful cultural entrepreneurs interviewed, it is rarely the main focus: *"I don't think you go into any type of craft or design led industry for the money. You go into it because you love it"* (Anna again).

Creative workers point towards a 'Trojan horse'-type approach to cultural entrepreneurship, where *the language of business has been appropriated by individuals for 'best effect'* (Tom, musician, broadcaster) as a means to secure funding, income and other professional activities and opportunities. For many, this language has become the wooden horse that those engaged in creative work have learnt to manoeuvre in order to appropriate the benefits associated with creative enterprise and cultural entrepreneurship discourses. Akin to a *'coping strategy'* (Sarah, sculptor), their professional identity and livelihoods often depend on becoming familiar with business terminology and a successful ability to manage various stakeholders, income streams, grant and funding applications and seek promotional or sponsorship opportunities.

Undoubtedly, the idea of the artist as solitary genius feels outdated in the global reality of today's competitive market economy, and perhaps the language and rationality of business and market discourses can help artists create and sustain a viable career, audiences for their work and a livelihood. Indeed, Isar (2008) highlights the capacity for cultural enterprises to make an impact on the lives and livelihoods of both the creative producers and consumers of cultural services and products, and this is a highly attractive proposition. But as we become inured to language of the market and entrepreneurial principles being applied to the management of creative and artistic activity, many artists wonder: can we reasonably expect creative workers to function as entrepreneurs, and what is the meaning and effect of the 'cultural enterprise' discourse in cultural and creative work today?

In business, as a typical starting point, we talk of values, risk and purpose distinguished through the basics of strategy, mission, aims and objectives, resource provision, outputs and bottom lines. How does this work within the sphere of the artist? And what can we say is the 'purpose' and 'bottom line' of artistic activity? DeNora and Ansdell (2014) argue, for example, that culture, in and of itself, does not have productive intent—and many artist and cultural workers do not set out to 'do' anything with their work; rather, they paint, sing, play, perform, because that is their identity as an artist, rather than with the intention of a business entrepreneur. Indeed, Caves (2001) sees the values and motivations of creative and cultural practice as fundamentally different from the business frame. For him, artists are driven to create not by enterprise, but by the creativity itself.

This distinction runs deep and suggests itself as the defining line between creative and commercial entrepreneurialism: when the underlying drives to create or profit make are set alongside each other, when they fall into tension, how is that navigated? As we wrote this chapter, we attended a talk by Justin Vivian Bond, a successful New York performance artist who created a show and audience that easily filled Carnegie Hall. Bond spoke about the moment of being offered a lucrative commercial deal that would bring her to the heart of the mainstream, incorporating a high-profile national stadia tour, and the whole package of media, merchandise and endorsements that go with that. She described her reasons for the decision to turn down what she recognised would be a transformative financial opportunity: *"I'm an artist; I'm not in it for the money. The reasons for creating that show were done. I'm well known, but to become famous would mean that show would define me forever more. It would be the end of me as an artist. It would make me a machine".*

So in this case, we see an artist look their productive capacity and choose to continue to create rather than effectively 'cash in' on that creative potential. This is not to say that all artists will make that choice or that the choice for profit makes one no longer an artist. However, typified by a need to express and articulate through creativity, creative and cultural workers are singularly unique in their perseverance and focus on the expression of their talent.

In the same moment, the artist exists in a dynamic space, occupying fringes, edges and confronting the future as well as the past. The growth and availability of digital technology has not only enabled more flexible and mobile work practices, it has been the birthing pool for a proliferation of new cultural forms, from YouTube creators, to bloggers, gamers, digital artists and makers. Indeed, perhaps in many ways, older notions of the 'bohemian' who sets oneself somewhat outside society have now been re-imagined as a value-adding creative mirror, reconnecting society with itself. In these ways, artists move between cultures, bringing their aesthetic and symbolic skills out of imagined private sphere of lofty reflective and creative expression, and into the realm of connecting people, feelings and ideas.

This has inevitably resulted in the creative producer or cultural worker becoming the "fixer of the service and culture- based economy" (Banks, 2006:457), with the innovative solutions and creative enterprises they represent creating value and wealth for producers and consumers of cultural services and products as well as society at large (Aageson, 2008). The positivity embedded in these discourses tends to give affirmation not only to the image of the singular creative self, but also to the "illusory glamour of the cultural industries [that] has rendered Western societies insensible to fundamental exploitative relations" (Miller, 2004:59, cited in Godwyn and Gittell, 2011:340).

However, cultural work has long been insecure work, and this remains a persistent 'subject of concern' (McRobbie, 2002), not least because the cultural worker anticipates 'the model figure of the new worker', embracing flexible and portfolio working practices and their associated insecurity of employment (Menger, 2002:10). So for all its abundance and hope, cultural work also takes place in 'an environment of increasing precariousness and constraint' (Oakley, cited in Bilton and Cummings, 2014:145), and the hidden costs of cultural work can include peripatetic working conditions, uncertain payment and the transfer of risks and burdens of cultural work from the organization to the individual.

Many core cultural industries—for example, in media and entertainment— have been subject to a rationalization of workforce within institutions, as well as a 'contracting out' and a casualization of formally secure employment (Oakley, 2014). Oakley highlights how there is a lot of 'bedroom entrepreneurialism' and also 'forced entrepreneurialism' from the wider structural changes and 'vertical disintegration' in society (2014, in Bilton and Cummings 2014:146).

Oakley (2007; 2009; 2011, cited in Oakley, 2014) calls this the 'paradox of independence':

> Issues such as unpaid work, long hours and absence of standard work benefits are justified by cultural entrepreneurs on the grounds that, essentially, if they had to pay and provide benefits commensurate with other industries, they would not be in business at all.

The precarious nature of this work is often considered as offset by the benefits of an autonomous, flexible and creative existence. McRobbie notes the 'passionate' attachment that such people have to their work (2007:1), while Gill (2007) cites the 'extraordinary passion and enthusiasm' that cultural workers have. And combined with the symbolic benefits of working within the creative sphere, workers are considered to be engaged in creative labor for 'the love of it' (Hesmondhalgh and Baker, 2011). Scholars believe "a different set of personal motivations—autonomy, creativity—than in other allegedly more commercial sectors" are present (Oakley, cited in Bilton and Cummings, 2014:149). Banks (2014) has articulated this as 'Being in the Zone', with cultural workers believing that "ordinary human capacities are transcended to produce work of excellence beyond convention" (2014:242). This is well articulated in the words of a well-known filmmaker we spoke to: "I do what I do because I express my vision, it's my way of making a contribution to the world. Through my work, I feel connected to others, I feel alive and connected. It's an exhilarating experience and a privileged way to live".

Echoing Marx, San Juan Jr. (1995), suggests that "art and labour are . . . creative acts that express humanity through the objects man makes and endows with purposes, objects that satisfies his needs". Therefore, creative and cultural entrepreneurship isn't solely focused on the pure creation of aesthetic goods or services in a '*l'art pour l'art*' sake scenario, but is also about a contribution to society in which man produces objects and experiences which express him (Vasquez, 1973:63). Legacy and footprint in the world are part of this, too. The jeweler we spoke to, when thinking about what drives her on, said that it was because "nothing is ever exactly as I want it to be, it drives me on, putting it out there into the world and trying again. I want to do something I care passionately about, something that will last".

Talking in terms of growing a business, craftsperson John is conscious of diversifying his brand and keeping his customers coming back. He regularly updates his Facebook profile and ensures a quality of standard across all platforms. His phone jingles, as we talk, with Paypal payments as people download his instructional videos in wood turning. For John, the recession "helped his business. It's just evolving all the time". But he is happiest when he is on his own making bowls: "for a very niche craft, there is a huge amount of interest out there. People love the idea of my craft and my life".

Many creative workers acknowledge this relationship and find ways to sustain a livelihood. The jeweler we spoke to sells her work in 65 countries, the woodturner is soon to tour the United States, giving workshops and doing bowl signings, yet unlike business entrepreneurs, many state that money and financial gain are not the driving forces behind what they do. Entrepreneurial ventures in the arts, media, craft and design sub-sectors provide valuable opportunities for engagement with particular communities and consumers, but entrepreneurship in creative work involves unique values and motivations typified by a need to achieve, self-belief, willingness to exploit a challenge and perseverance in their practice allied with the ability to weave cultural traditions through their work.

Earlier, we referenced Howkins's belief that the difference between creative entrepreneurship and business entrepreneurship is that "entrepreneurs in a creative economy . . . use creativity to unlock the wealth that lies within themselves . . . they believe that this creative wealth, if managed right, will engender more wealth" (2002:129). At their most successful in career, peer and financial terms, the creative workers we spoke to appeared to have unlocked a wealth within them which had brought great happiness. When explored, this happiness appears rooted in the need to create, while the financial gain of a successful business emerges as a spin-off benefit rather than a raison d'etre or modus operandi.

However, we cannot get too rosy. Entrepreneurialism is about creativity, but it is also about risk. The risk borne by businesses is very often through venture capital, while in the arts, through much smaller budgets, it might be seed capital, or for an established or recognized emerging talent, perhaps an advance, but more often than not, the artist's own labours as subvention. While the artist and arts organizations learn the tools and language of the market in order to develop sustainable livelihoods, we should consider if the rigors of business and professional thinking need to be applied to the treatment of artists and cultural workers. Recently, one well-recognized academy artist, in order to create a large work for delivery to a national cultural institution, spoke publicly about having to take a loan out to pay for childcare, as no advances were forthcoming. Another artist, popular by today' standards of sales, Internet profile and peer critique, articulated hunger, poverty and inability to meet regular household bills. One wonders if the same would happen with a business entrepreneur.

Underlying this is the very essence of arts' and business' ambivalent relationship with each other. The colonization of the arts misses its value. And there is a lot to learn from the arts about getting things done, about experimentation and improvisation, but also about the triumvirate of doubt, hope and persistence. What we get most clearly from looking beneath the surface and past our sometimes-romanticized notions is the understanding that creative work is difficult, and that it is indeed work.

So where does this leave us? In tracing the story from the premodern to the now, we have seen there has always been a blurring of boundaries between the worlds of art and business and the artist and the creative entrepreneur. These blurred boundaries at times seem to lose sight of the essence of the things that make art and business different. When this difference is lost, it can seem that the ethos (and not simply the discourse) of enterprise begins to assert itself: in what is valued, the approach to managing people and resources, understandings of capital and purpose and the evaluations and metrics for success that come to apply. Actor Brenda Fricker recently put it thus, when reflecting on one art form: "the problem with the film industry today is it wants guarantees: you can't guarantee creativity, it has to be loose". Artists are artists because of this knowledge, this preparedness to live the risk.

So for artists to be true cultural entrepreneurs, it cannot be just about surviving but finding the means to thrive. An extractive approach to the artist—the search for idea, insight and glow—has a short-term sensibility that cannot be sustained. The portrait of the precarious and risk-filled world of the cultural entrepreneur mirrors patterns of contingency and precariousness in the wider sphere of work and society (Bolton et al., 2012). However, among business too, desires for a more human-sized economy and more sustainable future are growing loud. Perhaps as we reach the end, the stereotypes of both business and artists begin to wear thin. As we turn to the next generation, we see new recognition that business is embedded in a moral economy of interdependence, and that for business to thrive depends on a thriving society and mutual, shared value. A moral economy lens offers an antidote to relentlessly economic analyses of enterprise and recognizes the generativity and containment of culture. New models of enterprise that weigh the value of culture in non-economic terms are the route to enabling artists and creative entrepreneurs to fulfil the purpose of their art, which as deBotton has both grandly and simply described, might well be understood as helping us to find the means to both live and to die.

References

Aageson, T. (2008). Cultural Entrepreneurs: Producing Cultural Value and Wealth, in: K. Helmut Anheier and Yudhishthir Raj Isar (eds.). *Cultures and Globalization: The Cultural Economy*, pp. 92–107. London, UK: Sage.
Banks, M. (2014). Being in the zone of cultural work. *Culture Unbound: Journal of Current Cultural Research*, 6: 241–262.
Banks, M. (2006). Moral economy and cultural work. *Sociology*, 40(3):455–472.
Beck, U. (1992). *Risk Society: Towards a New Modernity*. London: Sage publications.
Beck, U., Giddens, A. and Lash, S. (1994). Reflexive Modernization: Politics, Tradition and Aesthetics in the Modern Social Order. Stanford: Stanford University Press.
Benjamin, W. (1968 [1936]). *Illuminations: Essays and Reflections*. Berlin: Schocken Books.
Bianchini, F. and Parkinson, M. (1994). Cultural Policy and Urban Regeneration: The West European Experience. Manchester: Manchester University Press.
Bilton, C. and Cummings, S. (2014). *Handbook of Management and Creativity*. Chichester, UK: Edward Elgar Publishing.
Bolton, S. C., Houlihan, M. and Laaser, K. (2012). Contingent work and its contradictions: Towards a moral economy framework'. *Journal of Business Ethics*, 111(1):121–132.
Cantillon, R. (1755/2013). Essai sur la Nature du Commerce en Général. *History of Economic Ideas*, 21(2): 1303–1.
Carey, J. (2005). *What Good Are the Arts?* London: Faber and Faber.
Caves, R. E. (2001). Creative Industries: Contracts between Art and Commerce. Cambridge, USA: Harvard University Press.
DeNora, T. and Ansdell, G. (2014). What can't music do? Psychology of Well-Being, 4(23): online open access.
Department of Jobs, Enterprise and Innovation (2014). *National Policy Statement on Entrepreneurship in Ireland*. Ireland: Government Publications. Retrieved from <https://www.localenterprise.ie/Documents-and-Publications/Entrepreneurship-in-Ireland-2014.pdf>.
DiMaggio, P. (1982). Cultural Capital and School Success: The Impact of Status Culture Participation on the Grades of U.S. High School Students. *American Sociological Review*, 47(2): 1892–01.

Dublin City Council (2010). *Defining and Valuing Dublin's Creative Industries*. Retrieved 02.11.2015 from <https://www.dublincity.ie/sites/default/files/content/Planning/EconomicDevelopment/Documents/Creative_Industries_Final_Report._05.05.10.pdf>.

Galloway, S. and Dunlop, S. (2007). A critique of definitions of the cultural and creative industries in public policy. *International Journal Of Cultural Policy*, Feb:17–31.

Giddens, A. (1991). *The Consequences of Modernity*. Stanford: Stanford University Press.

Gill, R. (2007). *Technobohemians or the new Cybertariat: New media work in Amsterdam a decade after the Web*. Report prepared by Rosalind Gill for the Institute of Network Cultures. http://networkcultures.org/_uploads/17.pdf

Godwyn, M. and Gittell, J. H. (2011). *Sociology of Organizations: Structures and Relationships*. Thousand Oaks: Sage Publications.

Grant, D. (2011). How do you define 'Artist'? *Huffington Post*. Retrieved 28.02.2016 from <http://www.huffingtonpost.com/daniel-grant/how-do-you-define-artist_b_582329.html>.

Hayek, F. A. V. (1937). Economics and Knowledge. *Economica*, Feb 4:33–54.

Hesmondhalgh, D. (2013). *The Cultural Industries* (3rd ed.). London: Sage.

Hesmondhalgh, D. and Baker, Sarah (2011). *Creative Labour: Media Work in Three Cultural Industries*. London: Routledge.

Horkheimer, M. and Adorno, T. W. (1972). *The Culture Industry*. New York: Herder and Herder.

Howkins, J. (2002). *The Creative Economy: How People Make Money From Ideas*. London: Penguin.

Isar, Y.R. (2008). The Intergovernmental Policy Actors, in: K. Helmut Anheier and Yudhishthir Raj Isar (eds.). *Cultures and Globalization: The Cultural Economy*, pp. 108–120. London, UK: Sage.

Kirzner, I. M. (1997). Entrepreneurial discovery and the competitive market process: An Austrian approach, *Journal of Economic Literature*, 35(1):60–85.

Lange, B. (2006). From cool Britannia to generation Berlin? Geographies of culture-preneurs and their creative milieus in Berlin, in: C. Eisenberg, R. Gerlach and C. Handke (eds.). *Cultural Industries: The British Experience in International Perspective*. Humboldt University Berlin, Edoc-Server. Retrieved 12.09.2015 from <http://edoc.hu-berlin.de.>.

Maguire, Smyth, J. and Matthews, J. (2014). *The Cultural Intermediaries Reader*. London: Sage.

Matarasso, F. (1997). *Use or Ornament? The Social Impact of Participation in the Arts*. Stroud, UK: Comedia.

Mauss, M. (1954). *The Gift*. Glencoe, IL: Free Press.

McGuinness, M. (2015). *The 3 Critical Characteristics of the Creative Entrepreneur*. Lateral Action weblog.Retrieved 20.10.2015 from <http://lateralaction.com/articles/creative-entrepreneur/.>.

McRobbie, A. (2007). *The Los Angelisation of London: Three Short-Waves of Young People's Micro-Economies of Culture and Creativity in the UK*. Retrieved from <http://eipcp.net/transversal/0207/mcrobbie/en>.

McRobbie, A. (2002). Clubs to companies: Notes on the decline of political culture in speeded up creative worlds. *Cultural Studies*, 16(4):516–531.

Menger, P.M. (2002). Portrait de l'artiste en travailleur: Métamorphoses du capitalism. Paris: Éditions du Seuil et La République des Idées.

Miller, T. (2004). A view from a fossil: The new economy, creativity and consumption – two or three things I don't believe in. *International Journal of Cultural Studies*, 7(1): 556–5.

Mises, L. V. (1949). *Human Action*. New Haven: Yale University Press.

Oakley, K. (2014). Good work? Rethinking cultural entrepreneurship, in: Chris Bilton and Stephen Cummings (eds.). *Handbook of Management and Creativity*, pp. 145–159. Chichester: Edward Elgar publishing

O'Brien, D. (2013). *Cultural Policy: Management, Value and Modernity in the Creative Industries*. London: Routledge.

Pick, J. (1991). *The Arts in a State: A Study of Government Arts Policies from Ancient Greece to the Present*. Devon: Short Run Press.

San Juan Jr, E. (1995). *Hegemony and Strategies of Transgression: Essays in Cultural Studies and Comparative Literature*. New York: SUNY Press.

Sarasvathy, S. (2001). *What Makes Entrepreneurs Entrepreneurial?* University of Washington Working Paper. Retrieved from <http://www.effectuation.org/sites/default/files/documents/what-makes-entrepreneurs-entrepreneurial-sarasvathy.pdf>.

Say, J.-B. (2010, [1800]). *A Treatise on Political Economy*. Memphis, TN: General Books LLC.

Schumpeter, J. (1942/2009). *Can Capitalism Survive?: Creative Destruction and the Future of the Global Economy*. London: Harper Perennial Modern Classics.

Smith, A., (1991, [1775]). *The Wealth of Nations. [Adam Smith, 1723–90, Inquiry into the Nature and Causes of the Wealth of Nations]*. London: Everyman.

Stevenson, D. and Matthews, A. (2013). *Culture and the City: Creativity, Tourism. Leisure* (eds.). Oxon, UK: Routledge.

Vasquez, A. S. (1973). *Art and Society: Essays in Marxist Aesthetics*. New York: Monthly Review Press.

Weber, M. (1930/2016). *The Protestant Ethic and the Spirit of Capitalism*. CreateSpace Independent Publishing Platform.

Weiner, A. (1992). *Inalienable Possessions: The Paradox of Keeping While Giving*. Berkeley: University of California Press.

13 The Conundrum of Power

Sintering Structural and Relational Perspectives in Business and Arts Organizations

Yuliya Shymko and Alison Minkus

Introduction

The title of our chapter points to a conundrum of power in organizations, which we disentangle via the opportunities afforded by theoretical cross-fertilization between business and the arts. In approaching power as *structural* (power manifested in structurally enabled individual action over others) and *relational* (power manifested in the circulation of actions), we emphasize the dynamic nature of this social phenomenon and its unavoidable dialectics that result in an inescapable conundrum—a story of power in organizations is simultaneously a story of disempowerment and the responsibility of taming, impeding or softening the destructive impulses of certain structures and individual tyranny.

The format of the chapter is an unfolding dialogue, debate and reflection on conceptualizations of power in the organizational literature and beyond. While our respective roles reflect both business (Yuliya) and arts (Alison) contexts, it is not a purist approach, but one that already embraces a common ground (Yuliya's research includes Russian theatre, and Alison's training includes studies in organizational analysis). In part, historical trajectories prompt our search for common ground, as academic areas that shared common roots—arts and sociology (Tanner, 2003) and music and sociology (Devine, 2010)—were transformed into 'autonomous domains' over time (Tanner, 2003). While recent work has sought convergence, progress has been elusive (Tanner, 2003; Martin, 2006). Further, we also acknowledge important transformations from the late 18th to 19th centuries, whereby the social and artistic were 'emancipated' from powerful political and religious institutions, only to be absorbed by a new "rationalised and mechanistic capitalist 'cage'" (Tanner, 2003:1).

Our dialogue is first set in Max Weber's (1946) first formal attempt to describe the 'modern organization', characterized by technical/functional rationality and disembodied forms of authority, and thereafter, in Weber's (1978) conceptualization of charismatic authority and political/relational sources of power. In particular, bureaucracy has become a dominant structure of modern economic organization, gradually infusing other social domains, including the arts. This leads to two key questions. First, *do modern business organizations still cling to a bureaucratic rationality, or has there been a notable shift over time?* Second, *what does the injection of bureaucratic formalism mean for the arts?*

Dialogues on Bureaucratic Sources of Power

> The fate of our times is characterized by rationalization and intellectualization, and, above all, by the 'disenchantment of the world'. Precisely the ultimate and most sublime values have retreated from public life either into the transcendental realm of mystic life or into the brotherliness of direct and personal human relations.
>
> —Weber (1918:20)

YS: Today, we are asked to endorse a new liberating narrative that claims a time of great transformation—the gradual dismantlement of bureaucratic organization galvanized by technological progress and market liberalization. A recent article in The Economist ('Death and transfiguration; Schumpeter', 2015) proclaims the inevitable decline of the post-WWII Western corporation, comparing it to the fall of the Roman Empire. The authors envision the future belonging to a new type of global company—agile, idea driven and led by a charismatic founder. Space and materiality, as defining conditions of bureaucratic structures, no longer matter as organizations transform themselves into weightless, mobile and virtually connected networks of projects and cooperating individuals. Hierarchy is dead—or irrelevant—and the doors of the 'iron cage' are wide open. In my view, this burial of bureaucracy as an antiquated and near-extinct form of organizational reality is very premature.

Despite creativity-centric rhetoric around the techno-utopian spirit of our times, the question of organizational structure (or to put in more infatuating terms organizational design) still addresses sources of power in a canonical bureaucracy. Re-invention of structures does not eradicate power; it rather shifts its source from one structural position to another (supported by a similarly novel, stylish label). With the sharp decline of labor unions around the world, modern business organizations are increasingly created and maintained as structures of crude power differentials, sustained through the practices of managerialism. Therefore, the bureaucratic essence vividly described by Max Weber more than a century ago remains intact, despite the fact that modern organizations present themselves as an antithesis to bureaucratic order. Many associate the grave sin of inefficiency with public management, as represented by the state, an entity that currently finds itself out of fashion. As such, it is useful to reflect on why bureaucracies are persistent and why this may be a positive turn for the modern business organization.

Structures for Efficiency

Bureaucratic sources of power are faceless, disembodied forms of authority derived from a position in an organizational structure. Position provides its holder with a mandate of governance and administrative resources to exercise influence and control over other organizational members. Structure, therefore, imposes a particular pattern of interactions between organizational members and defines the domains of accountability. Structure also creates intra-organizational social classes and provides a set of rules for the distribution of power. Power becomes an obtainable resource (but not possessed *a priori*) by virtue of belonging to a distinct organizational class. In modern business organizations, these classes are presented in a generic typology of internal stakeholders along the lines of bureaucratic subordination—directors, managers, employees and workers, the amalgams of structural power endowments.

Max Weber (1946) positioned bureaucracy as a universal phenomenon that codifies its experiences, converting them into rules of behavior. He also first offered structural subordination—the 'iron cage'—as a primary condition for organizational efficiency. It is important to mention that Weber's ideas were influenced by the initial context of his study—the Prussian army, which may explain his proclivity for machine metaphors. Efficiency rhetoric rests on what Weber called 'functional rationality' and requires a stable and continuous pattern of interpersonal relations where decisions are taken, goals are set and orders are issued and followed. Such order requires an elaborate system of monitoring and control built around measurable metrics of performance. Consequently, the exercise of bureaucratic power is an objective evaluation of one's service, contingent on organizational class membership. Similar to Hobbes' project in *Leviathan* (Hobbes, 1909), organizational members are transformed into bureaucratic subjects when they voluntarily deprive themselves of some (and sometimes all) freedom of discrete action in the name of organizational functionality and order.

Despite control, bureaucracy protects individuals from corruption and wilful misuse of power, therefore representing "the most formally rational mode of exercising political domination" (Clegg and Lounsbury, 2009:119). The impersonal and inflexible rules and regulations of bureaucracy provide relief from whimsical powers of arbitrary rulers and help alleviate the concerns of organizational endurance and stability. Broad and complex tasks require similarly broad and complex organizations characterized by predictability and consistency. As much as Max Weber decried the dehumanizing nature of bureaucracy for individual souls, he also considered it indispensable for the administration of complex human affairs.

In a similar fashion, German sociologist Georg Simmel (1968) contended that subordination to authority allows groups to remain intact as they expand in size and diversity. Simmel (1968) posited a pyramid—a hierarchy—as the ultimate form that emerges from most social relations, but noted that coercion or dependence is rarely sufficient for the realization of group purpose. It is noteworthy that he was one of the first social thinkers to point out the primacy of aesthetic drive in the design of organizational structures. The balanced and symmetrical structures of hierarchies emerge through man's form, giving power to "the confused character of mere nature" (Simmel, 1968:71). Thus, aesthetic effort is a foundation for intelligible social organization, and hierarchy is viewed as an 'aesthetic redemption' from natural forces of life that are affective, instinctual and irrational. However, Simmel (1968:71) also acknowledged the dialectical side of aesthetically formed and rationalized power structures at the moment when life becomes overly rationalistic: "Once intelligence, reckoning, balance have penetrated it, the aesthetic need once again changes into its opposite, seeking the irrational and its external form, the asymmetrical". Consequently, structural sources of power in organizations are doomed to wrestle with instinctual and creative urges of surpassing or transforming these same structures. The unstable condition of hierarchy highlighted by Simmel is especially relevant when one considers the instrumental nature of individual tasks and talents in the realization of organizational goals.

Considering these points, *how indispensable are bureaucratic sources of power for arts organizations driven by substantive rationality and a sense of institutional mission that surpasses the calculative ethos of efficiency and profit making? Can they be sintered to give space for individual empowerment? What does art reveal in terms of individual power that goes beyond structures so cherished in classical management theories?*

> When it was born in the late seventeenth century the orchestra was a novelty . . . represent[ing] a new kind of social organization: a large number of people doing the same thing at the same time in precisely the same way.
> —Spitzer and Zaslaw (2004:507)

AM: A new liberating narrative may well be premature in the modern business context; however, a focus on freedom and empowerment in the arts is also problematic. The arts are imbued with hierarchical (and historical) configurations, in large part determined by institutional trajectories. For example, the symphony orchestra has not been characterized by a gradual dismantlement of bureaucratic organization as part of its institutionalization (or modernization), but rather by an active creativity and freedom amidst structure. Therefore, the burial of bureaucracy would fracture a bureaucratic essence (to borrow your phrase), as well as important relationships within and between institutions.

Sintering the Iron Cage: Structures for Artistry

While the literature on artistic cultural institutions (Arian, 1971) has been largely mute on the nature of bureaucracy, structure and power are indispensable in problematizing the arts. I point to art in the broadest sense: visible (or audible), of extended tradition and involving a viewer (or listener). Employing the example of the symphony orchestra, we are able to observe the relevance of hierarchy in the arts (Spitzer and Zaslaw, 2004). Several significant structures appear at various levels of this art form. For example, at the micro-level, the notated score is at the heart of musical expression, while the concert hall provides a space and materiality for its expression and reception. These 'structures' are embedded, integral and indispensable, creating an institutional home for successful production, interpretation and reception. At the organizational level, institutional structures offer rigorous training for aspiring musicians and long-held practices associated with rehearsal and performance. Further, culturally specific structures express unique entanglements of power and hierarchy, from state control (typical in Europe, Latin America, the UK), to not-for-profit organizations (the United States, the UK) and cooperative structures (the Vienna Philharmonic). While bureaucratic sources of power are typically cast as faceless, disembodied forms, the orchestra provides a particularly public face, including the orchestral conductor and the virtuoso soloist.

From these varying expressions of structure springs an 'artistic efficiency', unique patterns of interpersonal relations and associated powers—from composer, to score, conductor, orchestra, audience reception and critical mention. While protection amidst control is a significant consideration, extracting an arts institution from such an entangled 'iron cage' may not necessarily signal freedom, but rather expose it to significant disruption. In the musicological literature, two sources point to such a conundrum of freedom and restraint. Arian (1971:121) traces the Philadelphia Orchestra's bureaucratization from its inception in 1900, noting the double-edged sword of structuring art, which can enable financial survival but also impose costs—"artistic, social, and individual" that Arian (1971:121) argues are "unaccounted for in Weber's theory". Mangset, Kleppe and Røyseng (2012:173) focus on structural surprises in Norwegian performing arts institutions—i.e., theatre actors in an "iron cage of charismatic leadership" and orchestral musicians afforded freedom within "soft bureaucratic organization[s]". These findings emphasize that categories are relevant, but hybrid realities are apparent.

These highly visible manifestations of power complement others that point to Weber's substantive rationality, whereby "behaviour can be shaped by ultimate values that are difficult to calculate" (Clegg and Lounsbury, 2009:126). For example, Judy (1998:43) argues that the orchestra "has no 'owner'"; here, aesthetic impulse or creative genius is situated *beyond structure*, infusing artistic activity with a powerful and personal directive. Further, while Khodyakov (2014) places 'aesthetic leadership' on equal terms with individual and relational approaches, Ziarek (2002:175) notes a "mistrust of art's aestheticizing power", pointing to varying and conflicting understandings of power and its application in the arts.

How indispensable are bureaucratic sources of power for arts organizations? I argue that they are *inextricably* entangled, and if extracted, would leave some sort of institutional 'scar'. In practice, we see artistic forms realizing inspiration amidst restraint, in part via the power of creative genius, a position that first emerged in the philosophical works of Kant and Schelling on aesthetics. Considering these observations, *what is the actual reach of bureaucracy in the modern business organization? What relational powers might infuse the visibly (and perhaps stereotypically) bureaucratic day-to-day workings of individuals and organizations in these contexts?*

Dialogues on Relational Sources of Power

> 'Charisma' will be applied to a certain quality of an individual personality by virtue of which he is considered extraordinary and treated as endowed with supernatural, superhuman, or at least specifically exceptional powers or qualities. These are such, as are not accessible to the ordinary person, but are regarded as of divine origin or as exemplary . . . [However], what is alone important is how the individual is actually regarded by those subject to charismatic authority, by his 'followers' or 'disciples'.
>
> —Weber (1978:241–42)

YS: Your detailed account of structures as an enabling and simultaneously restraining force resonates with Anthony Giddens' (1984) theory of structuration that positions individual action as either reinforcing or altering organizational realities represented by material and cultural structures of power. Your description of different forms of artistic bureaucracy also evokes a dynamic and agentic approach to power that arises as a reaction to bureaucratic disciplining or what Foucault (1982) coins 'relational power'—an action upon action. Mainstream management literature pays relatively little attention to this type of power, while the prevalence of a functionalist approach inadvertently seeks to approve rather than to problematize the deployment of power engendered in hierarchical organizing. In other words, management scholars rarely investigate the ontology of structural sources of power because they perceive them as fixed and essential attributes of legitimate organizing. However, I argue that such an approach limits our understanding of modern business organizations.

Political Power: Conflicts, Structural Frictions and Uprisings

The tradition of modern organizational theory that traces back to the scientific management of Taylor (1911) and Fayol (1949) places organizational classes into a presumed state of unitary value consensus, whereby those at the top of the hierarchy acquire a right to manage those at the bottom to reach commonly shared goals. Weber (1946) refers to this right as 'authority'—the legitimate form of power. Obedience is assumed, since all organizational members pursue the same goal with agreed-upon means. Hence, formal authority is treated as a relatively stable and defining force of organizational life. In the popular business literature, this consensual and unified vision of organization is often articulated via poetic metaphors of captains, ships and oceans, which focus exclusively on the prerogative of power allotted by bureaucracy to the management class. This offers a leadership paradigm with neat categories of leaders and followers accompanied by a myriad of techniques and discourses that apply a human face to the exercise of formal authority.

In particular, social media have functioned as a catalyst to propagate the stories of modern business 'heroes' who are increasingly portrayed as artists, enjoying a celebrity status that was previously reserved only for artists. The narratives of their success often rely on accentuating their 'creative genius' and ability to resist conventional power holders—governments, bureaucracies and conservative corporate elites. Companies in Silicon Valley are notable in that they construct their public image through founding CEOs and their disruptive visions. Arts scholars' focus on the dynamic and alluring nature of creative genius is especially helpful in understanding the celebrity-centric leadership of a new type of technocratic rationality, as observed in organizations such as Google, Amazon, Facebook and Tesla. A common feature is consistent aestheticization of power, whereby power appears to surpass mere bureaucracy, forming a visionary organizational force. This new siren song of leadership with vision typically seeks to eradicate organizational conflict and disguise structural oppression directed at individuals set to efficiently perform a concrete task. Overall, the principle of efficiency, as a defining feature of good organization, has never been more pronounced and pervasive than it is today. This condition precipitates antagonisms in the pseudo-progressive ethos of visionary leadership and the stable practices of efficiency-driven exploitation of labour.

While structural power sustains unity and provides meaning and direction for followers' actions, this bureaucratic unity, or what Daniel Bell (1978) calls 'techno-economic order', is often irreconcilable with broader social norms, values and beliefs that inform individual action. Likewise, James March (2007) insists that given the complexity of firms' social environments, it is not clear if a unitary organizational purpose is actually shared amongst all participants. Thus, what management literature tends to present as a value consensus is just a fiction. For its own epistemic convenience, this literature ignores sublime, informal and antagonistic relations between formal authority and individual resistance. Consequently, reducing the manifestation of power in organizations to purely structural properties of functional rationality leaves no space for organizational politics with all its conflicts, structural frictions and uprisings. Further, it does not explain why structural and technocratic sources of power and authority so often become irrelevant, only to be replaced with politically complex relations between organizational members.

Max Weber was the first to recognize the strength of 'charismatic authority' over formal constraints in binding people together. Charisma requires no consensus over an abstract goal of collective excellence—it enchants, inspires and unites around the strength and authenticity of individual moral character. Charisma provides an aspirational ideal of social life that people are willing to share. The continuity of collective action and the power of charismatic leadership depend on how morally binding and genuine the ideal is, and how well the tension between performed tasks and held beliefs is mitigated.

Bell (1978), for example, discerns two structural sources of tension in organizational reality: 1) between an organizational structure that is bureaucratic and hierarchical, and a polity that believes in equality and participation; and 2) between an organizational structure that is constructed fundamentally in terms of roles and specialization, and a culture that is concerned with the enhancement and fulfilment of the whole person. These tensions often provoke resistance against individual disempowerment implicit in the exercise of formal authority and create arenas of political bargaining available to various contending groups. As pointed out by Scottish sociologist Tom Burns, modern organizations are designed as systems of simultaneous competition and collaboration, where structural forces of power focus on the accomplishment of a common task, and where social and cultural norms drive competition for limited resources, status and career advancement (Burns et al., 1979). A hierarchical organizational chart emerges as a double-faced Janus of competition and cooperation upon which organizational politics thrive and where power is lost, acquired and contested in formal and informal individual exchanges, interactions and identity reconstructions.

In conclusion, I believe that accommodating political and relational accounts of power within a bureaucratic ontology provides a much richer understanding of organizations, breathing life into the 'iron cage' and restoring the importance of agency, individual action and emotion. *What political tensions do you see in arts contexts that arise from the inherent antagonisms between structural and relational sources of power? How do scholars in the arts approach the problem of 'competition vs. cooperation' in creative processes?*

> The age of baroque music, when the first violin could from his desk gently lead the small band, is gone. In music since about 1800, the number and complexity of the efforts to be unified require a host of decisions by one mind. As on a ship, the course must be set by a single intelligent will . . . what justifies a particular commander is, once again, the integrity of his aim and the merit of its result.
>
> —Bernstein and Haws (2008:13)

AM: Your defense of both relational and bureaucratic accounts of power resonates deeply with institutional, musicological and historical approaches to the orchestra. For example, while an orchestra's structure is quite bureaucratic in nature, it is also characterized by deeply embedded interactions at the institutional, organizational and individual levels. Tensions (contrasts) infuse this structure, from music's reliance on contrast (loud-soft, fast-slow) to the interplay between exogenous and endogenous actors (conductor-orchestra, soloist-critic).

Contrasts at the Core: Creative Strength in Conflicts, Structural Frictions and Uprisings

Weber's authority of a highly positioned bureaucratic class is expressed in the arts, from the orchestra's conductor to the ballet's artistic director. While management scholars tend to preference a fixed and essential nature of structural sources of power, my research reveals a *malleable yet essential* nature, in part derived by an inherent human face in performative and organizational aspects of expression. In the case of the orchestra, poetic metaphors have also been used to highlight hierarchical and fluid manifestations of power. Early metaphors from the late 1700s highlighted the orchestra's structure as a consensual and unified vision—i.e., as an army, choir of angels or single instrument; however, from the 18th and into the early 19th centuries, a duality of conception appears—i.e., the orchestra as well-functioning machine and as a living organism (Spitzer and Zaslaw, 2004). These contrasting (if not contradictory) realizations point to a foundational duality and a dialogue of contrasts in the literature, which reflects a spirit of contrasts that is at the heart of artistic expression. Therefore, considering the orchestral context, James March (2007) is justified in doubting the unitary nature of organizational purpose. The various actors that assemble for performance may well have varying goals—for example, the conductor hires the favorite soloist, the soloist performs for virtuosity's sake and the orchestral musician executes a role.

Following your discussions of creative genius, my reading of the musicological and arts management literatures shows no lack of expressions of the sublime, informal and antagonistic, as well as colorful examples of Weber's charismatic authority, often observed in roles such as the conductor and virtuoso soloist (Shanet, 1975). Your description of Bell's (1978) tensions between bureaucratic structures and a sense of equality/participation, and between roles/specialization and fulfilment of the self, are also immediately applicable. While the orchestra is based on defined hierarchical (and historical) configurations of power, it is also characterized by actors who are simultaneously dedicated to the highest levels of artistic expression during public performance—i.e., individuals become part of a whole. Further, while all players are set within distinct, highly specialized roles, individuals are also fulfilling their own personal trajectory as musicians. This latter case points to Burns' (Burns et al., 1979) focus on simultaneous competition and collaboration, whereby orchestral players compete for positions within their respective sections, but also collaborate in the day-to-day interactions of rehearsal and public performance (the most visible common task). Indeed, Burns' (Burns et al., 1979) conceptualization of exogenous sources of structural power inciting accomplishment are apparent in orchestra settings in such roles as conductor and reviewer; however, endogenous sources of power, such as the call to become a musician, are also relevant and *powerful*.

The arts management literature complements the tensions between bureaucratic and relationship sources of power with several instances of shared power in the arts. As confirmed by de Voogt (2006) and Landry (2011), dual (vs. 'duel') leadership has also been observed in various forms and fields; however, in the context of arts, shared power is understood as a common practice. For example, negotiation is a defining characteristic of the troupe Cirque du Soleil, where power from the top is viewed as blocking innovation and change (Morency and Needles, 1998). Further, the singular creative genius is challenged by Soila-Wadman and Köping (2009:38–39), who argue for relational aspects of leadership, whereby "negotiation, communication . . . and coming into being" are given precedence over a "person/hero who possesses special traits or knowledge and the power to influence others". In such contexts, the 'lone, heroic leader' is *insufficient*.

To conclude, I conceptualize the creative process as a *negotiation of tensions*, amidst performances that convey a *unity of expression*, or what I term the institutional core (Minkus, 2015), a higher-level 'essence', accessible and reconcilable by all actors. Therefore, the call of the profession, and the expression of creative genius, points to why Nureyev danced, why the Beatles sang and even why Babe Ruth got up to bat, time and time again. Considering our conversation thus far, *are there key differences emerging in the relative balance of bureaucratic and political manifestations of power in business and the arts? Further, are bureaucratic structures and relational/political accounts of power expressed differently in business and the arts?*

Postscript

Our interdisciplinary dialogue sets a new direction for articulating the nature of power as a social phenomenon and social practice in two very different—if not antagonistic—activities: business and the arts. Sociological tradition helps establish the collective and cooperative nature of these activities and outlines a fundamental principle of organizing: the division of labor requires structural order for the fulfillment of collective purpose (for example, efficiency and high standards of musical performance). The imposition of structure creates a legitimate form of power or a formal authority that instructs, monitors and constraints individual action. In the case of modern business organizations, hierarchy, as a materialized structure of formal authority, is a common phenomenon. Since the manager's knowledge power is emphasized, class-related competences and financial rewards are less likely to evolve into more democratic forms of collective life. Hierarchical structures sustain managerial (formal) authority by granting access to all types of material and non-material resources, which may be used later to combat internal stakeholders, such as unionized employees, who may seek to contest managerial power.

Further investigation, employing the lens of aesthetic theories, uncovers important myths and misconceptions concerning the expression of authority in organizational contexts. First, the tendency for all-or-nothing thinking often positions a structured modern business organization against a free artist. To be sure, hierarchy and structure also infuse art; however, artists are able to create amidst structure. Extracting structure from artistic organizations would fracture flows of bureaucratic (and relational) powers embedded in and between institutionalized forms. That said, further analysis reveals two points of difference between business and the arts: 1) faceless, disembodied forms of authority in bureaucratized modern business contexts are set against the typically public faces of comparable authorities in the arts, and 2) concentrated power in most modern businesses contrasts the dominance of shared power in arts settings.

Aesthetic theory also allows us to offer creative genius or aestheticizing power as a relatively new expression in modern business organizations whereby relational authority is woven into the bureaucratic fabric of power. The growing allure of entrepreneurship and disruptive innovation—constructed around and nourished by the collective beliefs in a power of creative genius—creates space for a personal source of power in a canonical bureaucracy. Charismatic and bureaucratic sources of authority mingle and give birth to new practices of management and subjugation. Ironically, this hybridization of techno-utopian charisma and hierarchy in the very same bureaucracy that sought to remedy arbitrary power of celebrity creates a new type of aristocracy—a creative organizational class—that leads many modern business organizations. Their power risks becoming incontestable and in some cases leans toward absolutism. The cases of Jeff Bezos, Steve Jobs and Elon Musk are very telling in this regard.

What distinguishes arts organizations in this respect is that the power of creative genius is not reserved for the exclusive use of managerial class. Talent gives one a legitimate right to oppose formal authority regardless of one's structural position in an organization. Therefore, key dyads such as freedom-restraint, informal-formal and collaboration-competition are active at all levels, as part of a constant flow of creation, negotiation and resolution. The laxity of rules and regulations affords opportunity within structure, instigating dialogue and movement through contrast and via tension and release. Overall, we believe that the fluidity of power relations and the possibility of creating beyond inhibiting structures are key issues that have not been fully explored and critically addressed in the organizational literature, nor parallel literatures in the arts.

Finally, by drawing attention to the *multi-dimensional nature of power* that characterizes both business and the arts, we also highlight its consequences for individuals. Our chapter does not aim at providing a cure for—or liberation from—power. Rather, we position power as a key building material of the human condition and self-realization. The study of structural and individual sources of power unveils the essential aspects of human and societal development and astutely reveals the strategies by which "people are made subjects" (Foucault, 2000:526). However, power relations presuppose resistances, which are fundamental for the possibility of art and social progress. A key conundrum of the nature of power, therefore, concerns *freedom within restraint*, and its corollary, *restraint within freedom*. Any conceptualization of a better, more benevolent and more creative organization should build and nourish itself on the recognition of the importance of power as an enabling force of individual self-realization. Once we envision an organization as a space of colliding and colluding creative energies, rather than a place of enlightened leaders and obedient followers or creative managers and unimaginative employees, we are able to provide a compelling account of the 'art' of business and 'business' of art.

References

Arian, E. (1971). *Bach, Beethoven, and Bureaucracy: The Case of the Philadelphia Orchestra*. Tuscaloosa: University of Alabama Press.

Bell, D. (1978). *The Cultural Contradictions of Capitalism*. New York: Basic Books.

Bernstein, B. and Haws, B. B. (2008). *Leonard Bernstein: American Original. How a Modern Renaissance Man Transformed Music and the World during his New York Philharmonic Years, 1943–1976*. New York: Collins Publishers.

Burns, T. R., Karlsson, L. E. and Rus, V. (1979). *Work and Power: The Liberation of Work and the Control of Political Power*. London: Sage Publications.

Clegg, S. and Lounsbury, M. (2009). Weber: Sintering the Iron Cage Translation, Domination, and Rationality, in: P. Adler (ed.), *The Oxford Handbook of Sociology and Organization Studies: Classical Foundations*, pp. 118–145. Oxford: Oxford University Press.

de Voogt, A. (2006). Dual leadership as a problem-solving tool in arts organizations. *International Journal of Arts Management*, 9(1):17–22.

'Death and Transfiguration; Schumpeter' (2015), *The Economist*, 8956, p. 66, Academic OneFile, EBSCOhost, viewed 4 December 2015.

Devine, K. (2010). Music and the sociological gaze: Art worlds and cultural production by Peter J. Martin. *Canadian Review of Sociology*, 47(2):207–210.

Fayol, H. (1949). *General and Industrial Management*, trans. C. Storrs. London: Sir Isaac Pitman & Sons.

Foucault, M. (2000). *The Essential Works of Foucault, 1954–1984, vol. 3, Power*, ed. J Faubion, trans. R. Hurley. New York: New Press.

Foucault, M. (1982). The Subject and Power. *Critical Inquiry*, 4:777–795.

Giddens, A. (1984). *The Constitution of Society: Outline of the Theory of Structuration*. Cambridge: Polity Press.

Hobbes, T. (1909). *Hobbes's Leviathan. Reprinted from the Edition of 1651, with an Essay by the Late W. G. Pogson Smith*. Oxford: Clarendon Press. Retrieved 04.11.2015 from <https://archive-org.login.ezproxy.library.ualberta.ca/details/hobbessleviathan00hobbuoft>.

Judy, P. R. (1998). The leadership complexity of symphony orchestra organizations. *Harmony*, 6:41–44.

Khodyakov, D. (2014). Getting in tune: A qualitative analysis of guest conductor-musicians relationships in symphony orchestras. *Poetics*, 44:64–83.

Landry, P. (2011). A conceptual framework for studying succession in artistic and administrative leadership in the cultural sector. *International Journal of Arts Management*, 13(2):44–58.

Mangst, P., Kleppe, B. and Røyseng, S. (2012). Artists in an iron cage? Artists' work in performing arts institutions. *Journal of Arts Management, Law & Society*, 42(4):156–175.

March J. G. (2007). The study of organizations and organizing since 1945. *Organization Studies*, 1:9–19.

Martin, P. J. (2006). *Music and the Sociological Gaze: Art Worlds and Cultural Production*. Manchester: Manchester University Press.

Minkus, A. C. (2015). *Maintaining the Institutional Core: A Case Study of Disruption and Repair at the New York Philharmonic Orchestra (1842–2012)*, PhD thesis, University of Alberta. Retrieved 18.11.2015 from ERA (Education and Research Archive), <https://era.library.ualberta.ca/>.

Morency, G. and Needles, J. (1998). Company profile: Creative management—Focus on the creation collaboration. *International Journal of Arts Management*, 1(1):62–70.

Simmel, G. (1968). Sociological Aesthetics, in: P. K. Etzkorn (ed.). *The Conflict in Modern Culture and other Essays*, pp. 68–80. New York: Teachers College Press.

Shanet, H. (1975). *Philharmonic*. New York: Doubleday.

Soila-Wadman, M. and Köping, A. (2009). Aesthetic relations in place of the lone hero in arts leadership: Examples from film making and orchestral performance. *International Journal of Arts Management*, 12(1):31–43.

Spitzer, J. and Zaslaw, N. (2004). *The Birth of the Orchestra: History of an Institution, 1650–1815*. Oxford: Oxford University Press.

Tanner, J. (2003). *The Sociology of Art: A Reader*. London: Routledge.

Taylor, F. W. (1911). *The Principles of Scientific Management*. New York: Harper.

Weber, M. (1978). *Economy and Society: An Outline of Interpretive Sociology*, eds. G. Roth and C. Wittich. Berkeley: University of California Press.

Weber, M. (1946). *The Theory of Economic and Social Organization*, ed. and trans. A. M. Henderson and T. Parsons. Oxford: Oxford University Press.

Weber, M. (1918). *Science as a Vocation*, ed. and trans. H. H. Gerth and C. W. Mills. Oxford: Oxford University Press.

Ziarek, K. (2002). Art, power, and politics: Heidegger on machenschaft and poiêsis. *Contretemps*, 3:175–186.

14 La fileuse de Reims, a Place Where Artists Can Work

A Dialogue Between the Founder and One of the Residents

Elen Riot and Pauline Quantin

Introduction

This is my story of la Fileuse, an ex-textile factory in Reims, a middle range city east of Paris, in France, suffering from economic stagnation, as most industrial activities stopped in the 1980s. In 2011, after twenty years of inactivity, la fileuse was transformed into a friche artistique, which literally means wasteland. Yet in English it means a land, whereas we are in a deserted factory, also a storage place for toothpicks and pills, between the time the machines were gone and the artists got into the place. Now about twenty artists work in parallel, occupying the three floors of the vast and sonorous cement concrete building. The term 'friche' was used by the 2001 landmark report by Fabrice Lextrait, which launched the national initiative and offered a key source of inspiration for Pauline during the first phase of prefiguring la Fileuse (Quantin, 2010). There is an interesting specificity in this mix of French institutional official support and non-French grassroots anti-system form of occupation of space, creating a series of original and unique 'free spaces', quiet shelters and hidden places for social groups to prepare for action.

Because each space is specific in its choices and balance between individual freedom and collective rules, I also like to use the name we use every day with great pride and pleasure, 'La Fileuse', which means, in English, the seamstress. The whole experience felt to me like learning to choose the threads and create links through time and space with some sort of weaving loom I would need to invent and reinvent, with the help of Pauline.

I have been in fact a participant observer as an artist in residence at la Fileuse since December 2014, as well as an ethnographer and organizational scholar. My mission as an artist consists of writing about the place, based on collective memories, by bringing together threads and by looking for images, objects and ideas that may connect the place with other times and places, nearby or at a distance. I have been wondering about the role of time in shaping the process of transformation at la Fileuse and about the balance between collective memories and oblivion. This chapter attempts to provide an account of what the place feels like by alternating my voice with Pauline's, with my voice as an echo, but also as a counterpart of Pauline from partly a different field, that of ethnographic and organizational research. In taking up a reflexive role here, I redeploy my experience as an ethnographer; only the writing has to be different, and for it to be different, it seems more and more obvious to me that it has to be anchored in different experiences and feelings than the kind of material I mobilize for my research. I want it to meet artistic expectations, to be more pleasant, if less scientifically grounded, than when I usually do research.

The chapter is structured in three sections. First, I contextualize and personalize the story of la Fileuse by relating it to its district and to my own memories. Second, in a dialogue with Pauline, I write about the development of an artistic wasteland, specifically concentrating on its foundation, its material organization, its individual and collective balance and finally, its ability to bring together utopian views and practical, handy solutions. Finally, I reflect on my role as a researcher at la Fileuse.

Contextualization and Personalization: La Fileuse in Orgeval and My Own Memories

There are a few insights I need to share with my reader before I can even start. First, I need to tell how I came across la Fileuse and how I got involved in the project. Then I need to explain what the French terms 'friche artistique' mean, in simple terms. Finally, I should provide basic information about Orgeval, our neighborhood in Reims, and what we are doing here.

How I Engaged in the Project, on Pauline's Call

I met with Pauline Quantin, who founded 'La Fileuse, friche artistique de Reims' four years ago, when the place had just opened. At the occasion of the European performing arts festival, Reims scène d'Europe, the Swedish collective Simka was already working there, together with a dozen artists. At one of our many exchanges, Pauline suggested that it would be a good idea for me to apply for an artistic residency myself, and so I did. I got a two-year residency in December 2014, just before Pauline left, and we decided to work together from a distance, using writing and collecting material between Reims and Tours, where she and her family were now based. In this paper, I focus on 'La Fileuse, in Reims' and the role of Pauline Quantin as an initiator of the whole adventure.

So far, I have been collecting material about the past and present of this ex-factory. La Fileuse (the seamstress) is situated in a district called Orgeval. One of the characteristics of districts like Orgeval is that memory feels like sand in one's hand. In recent years, Orgeval was identified by the city authorities as 'in need of urban integration' because of social exclusion and incivilities. People who live here are poor: many families correspond to immigration waves from the 1960s. Inhabitants are very young, 40% are less than 20 years of age, and there is a 30% unemployment rate (the average rate in France is a little more than 10%) and a high rate of mono-parental homes. At the time, choosing to locate the artistic workplace in an ex-factory in that district made it clear to all that city hall had in mind to support a large construction project by having artists bring back some cultural animation to the neighbourhood. It was part of a larger urban project with a series of similar installations in similar districts. Yet La Fileuse was specific: it was not meant to be a public place, but a shelter with twelve studios for painters, printers and sculptors who needed room for their work and their tools. There was also space devoted to rehearsals for performance artists.

The Personal Side of the Preamble: What an Ethnographer Experiences at the Occasion of an Artistic Residence

Pauline invited me, and I applied for that residency. To make sense of why I did that and why I work now, I take my inspiration from a friend (Kunda, 2013) telling us "how an ethnographic sensibility emerges and develops". So there are three key dimensions related to sensibility and experience that appealed to me: the figure of the seamstress, the old factory and the void of wastelands and finally, the Orgeval district itself.

The Seamstress: A World of Patterns

The textile factory where the artists work was closed some twenty years ago. It was called 'La Fileuse' (The seamstress), and the production was good-quality knitting, mostly sweaters and skirts. There used to be a factory store inside the factory.

When the activity stopped, the sewing machines, large steam machines, were pulled out, and for a while, the ex-factory was used as a storehouse for toothpicks and medicine. Now about twenty artists work in parallel, occupying the three floors of the vast and sonorous cement concrete building. One of the goals of my residency was to document the history of the factory at la Fileuse and the past importance of the textile industry in the region. It was interesting to observe its development since the Roman times, the influence of the Church and ecclesiastic dressing as well as trade fairs in the Middle Ages, then the growing industrialization of the processes of transformation and finally, in the last 40 years, a large process of delocalization.

I find the figure of the seamstress particularly appealing to me because it brought up family memories. My great-grandmother used to sew and make clothes, and for a long time, I wanted to become a fashion designer. I like the universe of cloth. I collected samples and books and made drawings; I especially like books about patterns from all around the world. I tend to believe I went from cloth to text and ideas via the same process of matching the patterns in samples.

The Void of Wastelands

Another personal interest in the place, apart from the industrial field (textile), is the physical nature and state of the place. I would define it in reference to a void. And because of that void, I find yet another reason to study and write about a reconverted, recycled place, collectively occupied by an artistic community.

As part of the 1968 movement, my parents left Paris to settle in central Brittany; my mother's family originated from there, in the Trégor. This region had been very much transformed at that time by a massive rural exodus. Now the youth who would 'go back to the land' claimed that land, as if it were another country. My parents and my uncle wished to create an alternative way of life in a large farm near the woods. My parents wanted to create an alternative school in the fields (Neill and Lamb, 1995). My uncle, who was a potter, bought an ancient mill and used the turbine from the river for his wheel and kiln. As they went, they abandoned parts of the utopia, but some of it is still alive and the transformative power of arts and crafts in that period is still a very great influence. This movement of appropriation of rural abodes is well described both from an ethnographic, local point of view (MacDonald, 1989) and from a more sociological, generational standpoint (Linhart, 2011). I believe this childhood experience framed later experiences in the United States (Ohio) and in Russia (Carelia), where I lived in environments shaped by a recent and radical change: the collapse of the Soviet system and the end of the steel industry.

To me, there is a particular way of occupying abandoned places, material remains left after the social frame is gone. The specific joint of time and space corresponds, in my view, to some very specific kind of collective life after the death (or maybe I should instead say disappearance) of a social frame. Precisely, it felt like the two dimensions met—the world of patterns and the void of wastelands—when Pauline invited me over to La Fileuse. That explains my initial interest and my commitment to the project. Then the chance of being selected as a resident made it possible to learn more, to go from where I knew to where I could discover. I discovered Orgeval, and I am still struggling to grasp the specific, original dimensions of that district.

Orgeval: A Modernist District Ex-Post

La Fileuse is located in Orgeval. It is a district of Reims, the twelfth largest city in France in terms of population. It is about ten minutes from the cathedral and the historical centre, now that the tramway has been built—it has been four years now. Yet symbolically, the distance is much longer: there is a wide gap between this district built as a modernist ensemble for workers in the 1960s, and the city of Sacres, the heart of Christian and monarchic France since King Clovis, in the Middle Ages.

Generally speaking, the interface between different spaces in the city is a complex one. Reims is what I would call a dislocated city, because of the war and the successive reconstructions. All I know comes from the archives collected by my friend Khalid Ramali, who founded an association, Creadev, and collected archives on an otherwise blind area, scattered in city, regional and national archives, with no fixed identity since it stopped being fields and small clusters of houses back in the 1950s. Khalid shared his research and told me a detail that I find meaningful. When the district was built as a vast, cement, integrated complex, the people living there were asked, via a referendum, to pick a name on a list made by one of the local politicians who supported the project. The name they picked was 'Orgeval' (literally: the barley vale); it sounded well, a pastoral enough choice. Here is the rub. In fact, the name was that of a chevalier d'Orgeval, a virtuoso pioneer aviator who practiced in the military camp nearby. Now the air base and the aviators were delocalized, and no one remembers the name.

Today, major building renovations did not really change the fate of the neighborhood: the people who live here are not very rich; many families come from successive waves of immigration since the 1960s. The inhabitants are very young: 40% are less than 20 years of age, there is a 30% unemployment rate (the average rate in France is a little more than 10%) and a high rate of mono-parental homes. In that district, artists play a role in terms of creating exchanges and contributing to social life, when authorities are worried about seclusion and outbursts of radicalization. Yet, the role of artists as representing society is an interesting one, because although artists often come from privileged background (inheriting at least cultural capital (Bourdieu, 1979)), most artists in France have a very low income for most of their career and their public might be like them (Becker, 1982). Besides, the artistic residency in la Fileuse provides a workspace, a kitchen, free space to work and socialize, but artists also need to make a living, so they often look for alimentary jobs elsewhere.

I work in a different way than artists, and in a sense, part of my job is to create a thread that they can use in their own way so our workplace is in relation to people living in the steets around us.

After this very personal take on the context of our dialogue, I think we can go further in the approach of the artistic wasteland. In this new perspective, the focus is more on our collective work in the city, on the process of transformation collective memories with everyday events and practices and on combining material reality with reflexivity and dream. This is what the dialogue with Pauline is about.

What La Fileuse Turned Out to Be

There are many debates regarding the official mission of 'friches/artistic wastelands' (Kahn, 2005; Lextrait, 2001), and these debates have a direct influence on what we do in la Fileuse. As an artistic wasteland, la Fileuse organizes itself and operates in mediation as a place meant for artists to be able to work on individual and collective projects. Four dimensions make this mediation work and are pillars for Pauline's initial idea of what 'La Fileuse' would be and her present view of what it has become. Firstly, it is a place that had been initially engineered and materially built so as to offer a home and a shelter for artists to work on their projects. Secondly, it is a place of transformation from factory to art and crafts workshop, keeping in touch with its industrial past in an age of industrial decline and unemployment. Thirdly, it is a place with collective rules aimed at organizing independent and shared experiences, mainly in relation to work. Finally, it is a place that exists between worlds, one of which is very material, dealing with everyday logistics, and another that is rooted in utopia and imagination. Once again, this creates a tension between what there is and what could exist, and that creates a constant process of transformation that gives its life to the place, in relation to social events and the somehow uneventful course of everyday life.

To show the specific role of each of these dimensions, I chose to quote Pauline and provide some complementary accounts of specific situations in La Fileuse. I illustrate the four dimensions I just mentioned with Pauline's testimony and my comments. The four dimensions act together, bringing some form of creative tension in what we do as creators in that specific place. What it is today, and what it used to be before, forces us to look beyond, and the future proves to be not so easy to come by. In alternance with Pauline's voice in italics, I discuss each of these dimensions below.

1) "Hopes, worries and an empty factory" (Pauline)

> *La Fileuse, the physical place, was initially called Société rémoise de bonneterie (the seamstress society in Reims), then Timwear, then Stradis . . .*
>
> *La Fileuse the mental place was initially called Friche culturelle pour jeunes artistes (artistic wasteland for young artists), then la Friche (the wasteland).*
>
> *Finally, on November 17, 2012, la Fileuse, Friche artistique (the Artistic Wasteland of Reims) was officially born.*
>
> *It was a project-program that became a space-project . . . in three years and a few more months, more than 300 interviews-meetings took place during the diagnosis and multiple milestones with public servants while the place was being fixed following the norms, and since that time, three more years elapsed, with more than 120 artists staying every year . . .*
>
> *I was there in the beginning . . . I mean when people in city hall and at the head of the direction were there too, but I was in charge of stirring collaborations and initiating a dialogue on new issues as I came across them.*
>
> *For a while, I sailed on my own, only halting at friends for trust and food for thought. After a long period of intense talks, meetings, readings, I moved into a mental space meant for creation, all disciplines, with a free space of its own, involving trustees from different local instances and political institutions. There one could find resources, contacts, also complexity and movement, as life itself.*

In Pauline's words, I read the energy and determination of a founder, an individual or a team, looking for the place and asking for people's contributions. In a sample of 18 friches artistiques in France, Gazeau and Kahn (2013) found that nearly all of them had a very determined founder. It so happens that after a while, the trust that helped the founder build the place and collect ideas may transfer to the place itself, as an act of allegiance. Yet the choices made in the beginning determine the later transformations.

2)   From factory to arts and craft workshop

> After a While, a Place and a Material Organization was built as an operational shelter.
> After a while, and day after day, resources are being gathered so as to make it easier for many artists to work there and co-construct a collective movement.

One of the many influences of Pauline's decisions as a founder was the choice of a place for the project. The place to be offered to the artists had to be spacious, but its capacity had to come from another source as well, its amplitude had to come from the past, and Pauline made her choice with a keen interest in the industrial past of the city of Reims.

> Then, an island appeared at bay: industrial buildings of the Schweitzer activity centre, buildings where an idea could become a reality, buildings that made it possible for artists to become involved not only in ideas, but also in terms of material input.
> The buildings were far from empty . . . and many a firm member, as they were leaving it, transmitted bits and fragments of the history of that site, a living history, with no gap or lapse between us, only a few breaks.
> And so we took possession of the building, which had been used for other purposes than the initial ones, the seamstress factory, pharmaceutical conditioning, toothpick packaging, at the head of Stradis. As we moved in, a woman, as if to remind us of all the seamstresses who had worked there, a businesswoman, Josette Mayeur, offered us a long interview, telling us her own story and that of Stradis.
> Us? Who was that, us? Me, interns, colleagues in the cultural department of the city office, artists from the collective Tentative, the AMPFUL project, Stéphane, the civic services (young people applying for the equivalent of military service, it no longer exists in France except as civil services), Yvon (who is in charge of all material and logistic aspects of La Fileuse), many artists, past, present and future, working in that place.
> La Fileuse can now be defined as a place meant for research, experimenting and production in all art disciplines.
> It is a workplace (not meant for diffusion but all the artistic work before that).

The old factory, with its empty walls, tells us less and less about the present material installation where people can come and go and work as they please. In a place where there was practically no zone where people could be on their own, as part of the Taylorian factory system, there are now intimate and collective spaces articulated in a new way. Yet there are two key dimensions in terms of organization that make 'La Fileuse' what it came to be. It is multidisciplinary, and it is in constant relation with the city council.

It is a place where all disciplines are allowed and encouraged to meet (comedians, dancers, sculptors, writers, painters, cartoonists, movie makers, photographers, doing circus, making costumes, settings and design).

Threads can exist between single artists and structures from other horizons in terms of discipline, of geography, both artistic structures and other structures dealing with complementary dimensions (social workers, architects, school teachers, students . . .).

Another important dimension is the principle of residency for work, offering a specific time and place setting for all projects during a period that may be stretched but has to end at one point.

The specificity of la Fileuse, our artistic wasteland here in Reims, was that it was directly commanded and engineered by the city council and more specifically, the direction of culture. It could have meant a highly institutionalized place, some form of rigidity, but this was avoided by bringing people together and paying attention to the variety of artistic processes of creation so that it would remain adaptable to all of them.

The implication of the public authority resulted in bringing in a large panel of artists, a mirror of society, more than a co-optation or a decisive aesthetic choice. This is one of the important factors in La Fileuse: its identity changed with the artists working there at every moment.

The terms 'threads' and 'cloth' come easily to us artists at la Fileuse, just as web and network are an obvious reference for digital art today. The fact that threaders make cloth, working with threads to create textiles, creates a form of tradition that provides a common inspiration, possibly a style that goes with the place and with everyday exchanges and new encounters within this material space. It feels as if the specific work culture of the textile factory was shaping the artistic collective in a symbolic way, more like a collective memory than just an impression (Halbwachs, 1997; 1994) of something we can directly experience in the walls of the factory. It is different, though, from a conservatory approach, that of a museum, devoted to textile and its patrimonial conservation.

The coexistence of visual and living artists tells us about the present state of arts in France. Most creators tend to have a multidisciplinary approach to their work, especially when they launch their own project. A theatre company needs to design the stage, whereas a painter or a sculptor may work with a singer or an orchestra. Such projects can either grow in la Friche or begin there, via encounters. What makes it easier is the public support. If the heater does not work, if the walls needs to be painted again, if we need cars to bring new chairs for Frichorama (when the doors are open to the public), the initial contract between Pauline and the city still holds. We have the logistic support of the city. This support goes to La Fileuse only; still, it benefits all of our projects singularly. In this temporary system of residencies, all the input that would be devoted to keeping the place going is spent on our own projects. That makes it easier to leave la Fileuse once our residency is over, because our charge, as far as the collective organization is going, was only partly weighting on our shoulders. Pauline says this is my impression now because I am still far away from the end, but the closer you are to leaving, the more difficult it gets, in her experience. A few testimonies from artists I befriended confirm that, and so, soon, I might be dreading this moment too.

3)   Collective rules for independent and shared experiences

A Specific Organization with Rules of the Game
to Deal with different Types of Situations

Pauline knew from the beginning that if they wanted the place to be a safe heaven, it needed a clear set of rules so everyone would be able to work in peace and each artist could weigh his or her involvement in the collective structure. Artists are aware of the balance between individual and collective because they have experienced it for a long time, and they have the ability and the desire to make it possible for others.

> And this is precisely what I like the most in la Fileuse: the individual mingling with the collective and the other way round. Each and every one comes into la Fileuse with his or her artistic concerns, possibly artistic obsessions . . . and meets with peers working in the same direction to give life, colors, letter to concerns and obsessions of their own. Elective affinities can develop, contrasts and contraries meet and ways of expression can become like a keyboard, a kaleidoscope for the world. Each has his or her experience in La Fileuse, where a place of one's own was built, shared in the collective space, and that collective can have different reaches, specific geometries . . .
>
> This is what touches me in the world I contributed to creating . . . because I grew up in collective places where each and every one had to invent a way of one's own, with the care, help or neutrality of others, collective places where, to the nuclear family, other affective family, from social movements, unions, work, holidays added up . . .

Pauline is explicit about the need to create a space with no pre-set or ready-made rules of the game, yet to decide on rules. One of them is related to the need to have people come and go in and out of La Fileuse, with no one 'owning the place'. To me, that mutual understanding of time and space helps artists act as representatives in a public sphere and be in line with the public investment in the place.

Catherine Leconte, founder of another friche in Anis Gras, near Paris, defines her role as opening the doors and deciding the rules of the game in relation to the collective identity of the place: *"[This place] is public and must provide an intimate but ephemeral shelter for artists to stay at, so no one feels this is his or her home. The logic of privatization in cultural institution[s] is a real problem, people forget about the general interest, just to keep their job"* (in Gazeau and Kahn, 2013:56). It is important to keep things both formalized and informal, and the ways to maintain this free style are very much related to the organization of time and space. I find the way la Fileuse works as both a home and a workshop quite similar to what happens in Anis Gras.

The founder says: *"People give a lot because I share the place and the power with them"* (Ibid.). However, when I read these testimonies as an organization scholar, I want to challenge them, because I know many places where such good intentions (generously sharing one's project) simply does not work out well for people. The ambition is huge, especially when a project involves creativity and people who need to devote most of their energy to their own plans.

Sometimes, it works. When it does, it involves a great deal of bricolage and no unanimous voice to say: "Bravo!" When power is shared, the need for action and the ability to manage new projects autonomously involve the 'practical reason' evoked by Flyvbjerg (2001) when he uses the Greek term 'phronesis'. Although he was thinking of the role of social science and social scientists, I believe his view is adequate to describe a certain kind of skills. Here, because it is both a social and an artistic project, it should be used in complement to 'patterns of intention', the ability to invent new forms and shape the real in a sophisticated way, combining one's present emotions and feelings with the inventions of artists and practitioners transmitted through history.

4) A place to deal with both logistic problems and utopian ideas

In a place meant to favor creation, different expectations arise, depending on the context and the situation. When you arrive, you may have very ambitious ideas in terms of changing the way things work for you and others, and as you go, because there are so many things to do, you lose that interest for change, and you only want to be able to solve your everyday logistic problems. This is a typical pattern one should have in mind when having various people come and go in the same place. However, for people to be able to stay together for a reason, one needs to share and warrant a common ground, what Maurice Halbwachs once defined as the beating heart of society, 'a firecamp'. This is what I read when I read Pauline's. In Pauline's words about on what la Fileuse has become, she pictures a place where both utopian views and everyday logistics can be envisioned at the same time, as the material for building something together, making it possible to keep our initial 'grand vision' alive when dealing with the demanding problems of everyday. Pauline says:

> I would also say, for the underlying collective memory here, that I discovered about a year after the installation in Timwear that the home and workplace of my grandfather's threading workshop, where the family lived for 30 years, was located two streets from la Fileuse. A few months ago, I learned that one of my best friends had grown up with her parents, schoolteachers, in the Jean Macé school buildings, from the years 1950 to 2000, this adds value to the place in my eyes.
>
> La Fileuse represents today in my own trajectory what I would call a realized utopia, for this place, which had all the chances never to be, is growing every day. It is engaged in making artists better known, as an inhabitant and as a worker in a specific territory. What with its structure and history, the young Fileuse is already a place where many (un)defined possibilities exist, a collective artwork of people with individual pieces, all works in progress and also, and most of all, humans, always on the move.

In what Pauline tells here, I find many reasons to identify and support her vision. First, the encounters, rooted in the present, coming from the past, come as a surprise encounter. In la Fileuse, a place chosen because of its capacity and some kind of mysterious quality, Pauline found some of her roots. She discovered that, and yet, she was ready to leave when life called. This is what we shall all do one day, for multiple reasons, one of them being that we have other projects to build elsewhere, some of them with the skills we learned in la Fileuse. This dissemination, the ability to be on the move, is one of the great qualities that make artists interesting for the rest of society. That quality explains why they can represent it.

I also want to insist on what Pauline says about this problematic issue of representativeness because she has the ability to make it simple. Anyone who knows about contemporary art and the speculation going on with artists' brands is left confused with what artists are supposed to represent. La Fileuse has, so far, been of a non-speculative nature; namely, artists work and what they do remains outside of the realm of the sort of frozen restless jests one may contemplate in museums and art galleries. This allows us all to be interested in the outside world, to try and represent it, instead of representing ourselves, in the role of artists. Still, I would say there are areas that we need to investigate more, and this will be the end of this chapter based on a fieldwork I am a participant observer of.

Concluding Notes in Reference to Three Future Areas of Research

The experience at la Fileuse is for me rather new and beneficial, since I think exchanging with Pauline made it possible for me to change my perspective and adopt a role as an artist, part of a collective with different rules and purposes than the organizations I had been a part of before. However, I think there are three dimensions coming from my world of organizational researcher that can make it easier for me to explore, share this experience and contribute to a better understanding of how artistic collectives work: reflexivity, collective memory and cultural heritage.

I have been doing research on reflexivity and reflexivity in art for the past 10 years or so (Riot, 2009, forthcoming). However, working at La Fileuse made me experience a phenomenon that I am only beginning to encompass and that I would like to analyze and interpret from now on. When writing texts, especially inspired by visual impressions and physical sensations, being a researcher can become an embarrassment: you are analytic when maybe you should not be, you just cannot let go. As visual artists tend to tell you in their own way: "you don't have to explain". So, how can reflexivity bring something here? In my specific case, I think reflexivity is required when interactions take place in relation to representations in art pieces. They offer an occasion for people with different background to meet, and as crowds, we all have ready-made ideas about others in terms of values and expectations.

Besides, unwanted reflexivity is far from limited to the world of scholarly social sciences. On many occasions, I lived through the experience of artists explaining in detail their artistic process and intellectualizing their experiences using philosophical references. Some of it has to do with the genre; for instance, socio-art or even any art installation involves such reflexivity. Artistic wastelands are places where such approaches find their place: the 60s, Fluxus and Warhol are common references. There is a common saying (possibly legendary though) that Duchamp used to say 'dumb as a painter', reflecting the opposition between two types of artists, those who are fluent with words and ideas, and those who use visual language. In la Fileuse, just as in many artistic collectives, the different profiles work together, and at least they are part of the same project. So my interest here lays in the combination of phronesis (practical reason) with something like 'imago' or 'teckné' in art, bringing in design and aesthetics as 'patterns of intention', both abstract views and practical solutions.

The second dimension I would like to explore is the role of collective memory. Here my reference is a French sociologist, Halbwachs, who incidentally also worked in the textile working class in Reims in the 1900s. Writing in times of war and political extremes, Halbwachs (1997; 1994) opposed 'collective memories' as the source of the great social fireplace around which all gathered to other types of memories: official memory (history) and individual memory. The superiority of collective memories, such as those shared by small circles (families, profession cluster, a group of students) comes from the ability to cross-check the information and also rejuvenate the richness of the past, by bringing back memories in relation to specific circumstances. Official history is more rigid, and controversies are limited to a small group of experts: they can be used wrongly and become part of the propaganda of an authoritarian regime (such was the case of World War I and war memorials for veterans in Europe). Individual memories are often distorted and they can hardly be shared with others: to be shared, they often require the skills of an artist. Yet in this transformative process, they lose their specific quality and become something else. So of all memories, collective memories favor exchanges and give us material to frame collective projects involving a plurality of actors.

In Orgeval, our 'Seamstress Project' somehow plays that role of changing the nature of the present. Based on a contemporary creation, the weight of the cultural heritage may possibly be levied (Barruol, 2014; Moureau, 2009). Symbols are very present, for still to this day, the way from Orgeval, the modernist city of the 1960s with no past to the cathedral, the heart of the Monarchic City of the Sacres is much longer than the actual 30 minutes walk, and, what with unemployment and social problems, all paths may seem more difficult to thread together. One interesting option for us is to use art pieces and their visual appeal so as to open the magic box of memories. Opening the doors of la Fileuse and sharing common experiences is a long process, yet this is why the place is sponsored as a contributor to the social life of the city of Reims. Sharing collective memories is a comprehensive way of understanding our present, and this is something I would like to be more engaged in.

The third dimension is the common cultural heritage. Many art pieces and projects are incubated at la Fileuse, and they often influence each other to the extent that, during shows, the audience seems to perceive what they see as one and the same art. Yet, as artists, we all know we have different views, and we are also aware that some views tend to have more appeal, be more influential, last longer than others, that they will sustain something of our present age in the future and capturing that moment is not so frequent. Also, one of the many discussions we have had at the kitchen table is our own change of vision, the works we discard and the views we have gone beyond. Something in this change is atmospheric, and something has more to do with deliberate choices we can explain by the menu because it has to do with learning and experience. In a cultural heritage, a form of self-selection of the shapes and frames occurs, and this is a collective process.

As part of this project, I would like to investigate how 'our collective productive heritage' is part of what Elinor Ostrom (1990) referred to as 'commons', a sum of resources for collective action. More traditional views of heritage in reference to tourism and museum science already exist. My view is more directed towards contemporary work and production today.

All artists are, at present, faced with the difficulties of the market; namely, very few of them can make a living with their art. Today, the art market is an especially fascinating one, because of its mysteries on the one hand and because of its extreme scales of valuation on the other hand. The problem of valuating art goods in relation to art works is, to us, both a personal and a general problem, a problem both material and abstract. This is something progressive movements, such as Arts and Crafts and the Bauhaus had also dealt with in the past, involving all kinds of practitioners with various stakes and different positions. The various dimensions of work, from sensations and intuitions to the chain of production and the social interest for all of art production and artists for patrons of the arts and for people whose presence is all they have to give, are something to work on today.

References

Barruol, A. (2014). *Regards sur le patrimoine des fêtes et des spectacles*. Arles: Actes Sud Babel.
Becker, H. S. (1982). *Art Worlds*. Berkeley: The University of California Press.
Bourdieu, P. (1979). *La Distinction*. Paris: Editions de Minuit.
Flyvbjerg, B. (2001). *Making Social Science Matter: Why Social Inquiry Fails and How It Can Succeed Again*. Cambridge: Cambridge University Press.
Gazeau S. and Kahn, F. (2013). *In Vivo: Lieux d'expérimentation du spectacle vivant*. Genouilleux: Editions la Passe du vent.
Halbwachs, M. (1997). *La mémoire collective*. Paris: Albin Michel.
Halbwachs, M. (1994). *Les cadres sociaux de la mémoire*. Paris: Albin Michel.
Kahn, F. (2005). *Nouveaux Territoires de l'Art*. Paris: Editions Sujet objet.
Kunda, G. (2013). Reflections on becoming an ethnographer. *Journal of Organizational Ethnography*, 2(1):4–22.
Lextrait, F. (2001). *Friches, laboratoires, fabriques, squats, projets pluridisciplinaires. Une nouvelle époque de l'action culturelle*. Retrieved 28.02.2016 from <http://www.culture.gouv.fr/culture/actualites/rapports/lextrait/volume1.pdf>.
Linhart, V. (2011). *Le jour où mon père s'est tu*. Seuil.
McDonald, M. (1989). *We Are Not French!: Language, Culture, and Identity in Brittany*. London: Routledge Publishing.
Moureau, E. (2009). *Regards sur le patrimoine textile*. Arles: Actes Sud Babel.
Neill, A. S. and Lamb, A. (1995). *Summerhill School: A New View of Childhood*. Macmillan.
Ostrom, Elinor (1990). *Governing the Commons: The Evolution of Institutions for Collective Action*. Cambridge, UK: Cambridge University Press.
Quantin, P. (2010). *Rapport d'étape Friche artistique à la demande des élus de la ville de Reims* (six mois de diagnostic). Retrieved from <http://www.reims.fr/culture-patrimoine/structures-culturelles/fileuse/la-fileuse-presentation-histoire-et-genese-du-projet—2167.htm>.
Riot, E. (forthcoming). Bernard Arnault as a CSR Leader: The Opening of the Louis Vuitton Foundation and What It Represents. In R. Bathurst et al., *CSR and Leadership*.
Riot, E. (2009). *Le petit monde du Cube. Etude ethnographique d'un centre d'art numérique à Issy-les-Moulineaux*, these presented in HEC (Greghec Ph-D program).

Section V

Learning, Knowledge and Thinking

The fifth section of the book focuses on the question of how learning is understood in the fields of business and the arts, both in the contexts of education and research. It includes three chapters, all of them based on the authors' personal experiences and experiments of learning, education and researching in between the two fields.

The first two chapters reflect on experiences of education between the two fields. Art school rector **Andrew Power** and former business school dean **Michael MacDonnell** reflect on their experiences with education programmes which are mixing business and arts disciplines both at the Institute of Art, Design and Technology and at Quinn Business School, in Dublin, Ireland. The second chapter reports on the experience of designer **Dorina Coste,** management scholar **Isabelle Né** and marketing scholar **Marianella Fornerino** in using graphic arts to allow management master students to reflect on their future profession as manager.

In the third chapter of this section, innovation management scholar **Nina Bozic** and musician and art scholar **Elisabeth Helldorf** develop a dialogue on patterns of thinking from a business and an arts perspective. Their text is a dialogic journey which develops in two dimensions: the voice of business vs. arts studies, and inner vs. scientific voice. The two dimensions do not run perfectly parallel, but only at times intersect and coincide. The result is a very fascinating writing and researching experiment on changing patterns of thinking and practicing research in new ways.

The dialogue between Nina Bozic and Elizabeth Helldorf is a beautiful ending of our collection of texts and a challenging opening to many discussions to be had in the land between arts and business. Its new format and its non-linear development speaks well to the opening chapter of this volume, that of Guillet de Monthoux and Mairesse. In many ways, this volume ends where it began: there is no linear progression, but many going back and forward and in all directions, full of fragments. The story remains unfinished and open for continuation.

15 Valuing the Other
Exposing Undergraduates to the Art of Business and the Business of Arts

Andrew Power and Michael Macdonnell

Introduction

This chapter is co-authored by Dr. Andrew Power, head of the largest art school in Ireland, the Institute of Art, Design, and Technology (IADT) and Dr. Michael Macdonnell, the former dean of Quinn Business School, the leading undergraduate business school in Ireland at University College Dublin (UCD).

IADT attracts students seeking careers as filmmakers, artists and designers, Quinn Business School is populated by students ambitious to make an impact in business. These may appear to be separate worlds, but there is a well-researched benefit to interdisciplinary work, for example, between art and science (Gurnon, 2013). These links have been explored by UCD and IADT on projects such as the Imagine Science Film Festival, which linked scientists and student filmmakers together to create new Irish science films (UCD, 2012; 2013).

IADT students gain admission by a combination of academic achievement, submission of a portfolio of work and performance at an interview. At UCD, admission is based solely on performance on the annual Irish state examination, the Leaving Certificate. At IADT, assessment is by exhibition, critique and project work; at UCD, assessment and progression are by examination and continuous assessment. The class size at IADT is typically between twenty-five and thirty students, whilst at UCD, the class size for first-year business is over four hundred. Students at IADT work in a studio setting and have a large degree of autonomy over the space they occupy while staff members move between spaces. At UCD, learning and teaching are timetabled to lecture theatres, and it is the students who move from location to location.

IADT recognized that graduates emerge from their studies with considerable skills in their discipline but perhaps lacking some of the practical skills of business in order to get and maintain work. It was also recognized that a 'one size fits all' business studies module would not be appropriate. Bridgstock et al. (2011) notes that "while the majority of creative, performing and literary artists are self-employed, relatively few art schools attempt to develop capabilities for venture creation and management and still fewer do so effectively".

At Quinn Business School at UCD, the possibility that the arts could make a contribution to enriching the experience and skills of their graduates was also recognized. A number of subjects, principally in the area of creativity and design, were considered by the authors as beneficial to the undergraduate business student experience. Increasingly, business students need to speak the language of design. Rapid prototyping, digital modelling, data visualization, are all subjects that business students need to understand.

The national context for reviewing the way in which a range of disciplines is constructed is that, like many countries, Ireland has seen a proliferation of degree offerings in recent years. As a result, public sector policy in recent years has been to encourage third-level providers (both universities and institutes of technology) to reduce entry options. UCD, as the largest university in the state, has played a leading role in this and has brought a number of (but of course not all) programmes together into four major entry points of Engineering, Science, Commerce and Arts. Students specialize within their degree, for example, entering Engineering and selecting as they move through their program of study greater degrees of specialization to emerge as civil engineers or chemical engineers. The long-term consequence of a drive to reduce the number of entry routes to undergraduate studies gives the potential for students to mix their subject choices more widely. At IADT, as a considerably smaller institution, the goal of clarifying and simplifying programme selection for the incoming student is achieved by sticking to the core competencies and mission of the institute in arts and technology; any tendency to mission creep is thus avoided. This has meant that new course development has largely been in the provision of postgraduate provision in existing disciplines rather than a broadening of subject choice.

This chapter outlines how the Faculty of Film Arts and Creative Technologies at IADT provides students in a diverse range of programmes with the necessary business skills appropriate to their discipline. It goes on to look at how students in the Quinn Business School are provided with opportunities to develop skills in creativity, visualization and innovation. Education in this context is not just about seeing the arts as another vertical business discipline like agriculture, aviation or manufacturing, but rather, as a horizontal, cross-cutting approach to seeing the world in order to better solve problems and communicate ideas.

There is a fundamental difference in undergraduate curricula between European and North American university traditions, whereby on the one hand European universities tend to operate discipline-based degrees within faculties, while American universities promote either a 'Liberal Arts' foundation or a strong Arts core in any other degree. This varies between institutions, but often takes the form of the first two years of an undergraduate degree containing a majority of subjects classed as Arts, with the final two years providing more specialization. Supporters of this tradition argue that it offers a broader education, while the obvious downside is a lower degree of specialization for those who want it. A lesser version of this tradition requires students to enroll in an undergraduate business degree to complete a comprehensive range of 'General Electives' or 'General Education' requirements. It is not clear that the North American tradition is better for students, either in terms of their interests and broad education, or for their suitability for employment opportunities.

Preparing Creative Professionals for the Workplace

In the Faculty of Film Arts and Creative Technologies at IADT, there are thirteen undergraduate programs and six taught postgraduate programs. Although each has their own approach to addressing the issues discussed in this chapter, for brevity, three representative programs are discussed: Film, Photography and Model Making.

The three-stage approach as outlined by Bridgstock (2012) provides a framework for considering the staging of business knowledge into an arts program. In first year, the iterative and reflective process of adaptive career identity building can begin alongside the development of foundational disciplinary and technical skills and knowledge. Students are supported through a highly scaffolded process of induction known in IADT as First Year Matters. This leads on to a one-semester five-credit module which exposes the students to all the disciplines of the Faculty and to their fellow students across the range of programs as they work through projects in multidiscipline teams. The second phase exposes students to multiple types of arts ventures. This is addressed in part by the elective program in second year, which allows students to select a module from a course other than their own to experience a different approach to the arts or technology. The third phase involves experiential project-based work. These are the kinds of projects that students co-create and pursue in conjunction with various facilitators (teaching staff, senior recent graduates and industry professionals). This is the type of 'business' module described below in the programs indicated.

Film

IADT's focus is on the advancement of practical filmmaking and television production skills, as well as developing strong creative storytelling abilities. Extensive practical tuition in Production, Script, Direction, Camera, Lighting, Sound and Editing, Television Programming, Drama, Documentary, Commercials, Experimental and Educational Programming are all key to the programme. Practical work and small class sizes promote a strong spirit of collaboration, a good level of interaction with tutors, easy access to facilities and hands-on production experience.

In the third year of the program, there is a module called production focus: the main thrust of this is to help students forge connections with industry, to get out, use their skills and build a network. It is critical that they absorb the working environment, calibrate their current skills and see how they are applied in industry. The third year was selected, as it is a time when they have developed some real and marketable skills; they have identified which specialism they wish to major in (cinematography, direction, editing, sound etc.); it is before the major production project which they will be absorbed with in their fourth year.

The student meets with a tutor to discuss their chosen area of speciality. The tutor will look at their work plan for the year to see the range of activities they will be involved in and identify any gaps. Each student has a calendar of work, and they are scheduling their own work plans. There is an active film industry in Ireland, and there many opportunities to gain experience in film production, television and in the production of commercials. A major learning experience for the students is the changed timeframe from an academic environment to a production environment. For example, the editors may have excellent technical skills but find they don't edit fast enough or that they are not decisive enough. This is very valuable feedback and exposure. On some occasions, it is appropriate to place a student in a role where the experience is complementary rather than a replication of their work at IADT. For example, a student majoring in cinematography may benefit from working with a theatrical lighting company.

If a student is unable to secure a placement, there is a research option. If this option is selected (or becomes necessary), the student writes a report based on research relating to industry but demanding that they connect with industry personnel at some level and research a specific aspect of the business.

Photography

The art of photography is evolving across a wide range of cultural industries. IADT explores photography primarily within the context of art, communications and the moving image. Students study photographic theory, history and practice and reflect on the changing demands of the communications and cultural sectors. For much the same logic as described above for Film, the third year was selected as the appropriate stage to have a module which is about entrepreneurship or business skills. The purpose of this module is to build professional life skills, to give students practice at the things they will need to know.

The module is made up of three components: a sequential, practical, outcome-orientated series of mini projects, business modeling and guest lectures. Students start with a project based on *National Geographic* magazine which is called 'Local Geographic'. *National Geographic* regularly has calls for photographers who, in partnership with a scientist, develop a photo essay or feature. For the students, replicating such a call gives them the practical experience of documenting a project proposal. They imagine a suitable project and take a week to research the idea: what kind of environmental or scientific project they would like to pitch for photographing, and what kind of scientist they might like to team up with. This involves them in thinking about budgets, the use of plain English, presenting themselves as photographers, describing themselves, their work and so on.

The outcomes from the 'Local Geographic' project become the model for an actual application to the Dublin City Council for Arts funding. This allows them to see what a Dublin City Council application form looks like, and what they begin to see is a pattern or consistency in the sort of skills required in terms of writing, depiction of themselves, their art and their project.

The final part of this sequence is a discussion and review with the curator of a photography gallery which widens out the requirements still further and deepens their knowledge of what is expected from them beyond the quality of the images they produce. This process, or series of mini projects, often results in successful submissions.

To address other aspects of the business of arts, the 'Business Model Canvas' is used to help students define their business proposition (Osterwalder, 2004). Business development representatives from the community also come in to speak to the students and discuss their business plans. This gives them a sense of what the local amenities and resources are in their area and what the networks are for accessing them. Visual arts organizations come in to talk to the students about how they can provide practical support to artists in all art forms throughout their careers.

The creative industries are often characterized by portfolio employment, sole practitioners, freelancers and the self-employed, micro-businesses and SMEs (McConnell, 2010). Working in this way needs to be anticipated and prepared for, as a successful career may consist of a series, or patchwork, of grant-based, commercial, project or educational working experiences, perhaps supplemented by additional concurrent work activities (Bridgstock, 2012). Most visual artists engage to some extent in portfolio careers (Mallon, 1999). The concept of a business portfolio is discussed so they are not just thinking linearly about one exhibition after another.

A series of guest lectures are provided to the photography students to help them prepare for the business environment. Issues relating to taxes and the business of operating as a sole trader are dealt with by a guest lecturer and provides them with resources where they can learn more about the details of this area when they need it. Guest lectures are also provided by professionals in media law, who talk about intellectual property and the responsibilities of photographers. The curator of the Photography Gallery in Dublin also comes in to talk about the responsibility of the curator and the process of staging an exhibition from their perspective.

Assessment for this module is done in one of two ways at the discretion of the student. Either they do a funding application, or they prepare a proposal for a photography curator in a particular exhibition space. A professional photographer or curator is then invited, along with the academic team, to form a panel, and the students pitch their proposal and submit the accompanying paperwork and portfolio of images. In this way, we attempt to roleplay a real situation.

Model Making

Students taking our BA in Three Dimensional Design, Model Making and Digital Arts (Model Making) are likely to work as sole traders but contracted on a project basis to larger companies in the worlds of film and theatre.

By the third year of the program, the students have acquired significant skills and are preparing for work placement or taking on small projects themselves. The kinds of questions students have are: how do I get a job? Once I get a job, how do I invoice? How do I get paid? When I get paid, what do I do with it? How do I pay taxes? To address these questions, a module on business was developed in the third year to try and address these very practical learnings. Another question it tries to address is how to get their name known in the industry. Students are given advice on networking and using social media to build a network with each other and their growing base of contacts.

The module provides very practical advice key to the nature of the work they are being prepared for. Students are given lists of materials and providers, in effect, a starter contact list of people and suppliers they will need to build relationships with. Students are helped in creating a website so that they all have an online presence. Some are more tech savvy than others, but it is important that they can build an online 'shop window' to establish themselves. Students are taken through the process of doing quotations, the cost of running a workshop, issues about employing people, at what point you need a bookkeeper or an accountant and so on. How to get credit, how to create an account, the importance of managing cash flow when they are managing multiple or large projects. Students discuss the protections offered by a limited company and the consequent obligations. In addition to presentations and in-class exercises, a resource pack is developed and evolves each year which students can access anytime and which provides information like where they can get various registration, tax and regulatory forms and how to fill them out.

To assess the learning of a module as diverse and dynamic as this, a number of strategies are employed. Technical questions about tax and VAT are taught and assessed through a quiz. Like an open-book test or a game that students play, they can access the information online and discuss it in groups. This is a very interactive series of classes where they are replicating real-life questions like what is the VAT rate for various items or questions like is model making a good or a service. A second assessment strategy is to give students a pitch or a business request and they have to come up with a quotation. A number of these are done during the year, and both the complexity of the job and the length of time they have to complete the quote get more challenging as the module progresses.

Students are also given practical guidance about how to find work. Developing a portfolio and making it available is the first key step. The portfolio is not a physical portfolio anymore: it's all digital. In the past, making contact with the head of a certain workshop would have been difficult; now, via social media, it is easier to identify who the key people are and how to make contact. Exposing students to online groups is also valuable. The business they are entering is not nine to five but twenty-four seven, so anything they do or build needs to be accessible to anyone all the time in whatever format they need. The onus will be on them to repeatedly obtain or create employment and to manage their own career progression (Arthur et al., 1999). Building networks and contacts is vital; work is frequently obtained by 'who you know', more formally described as 'informal social and professional contacts', and offers are made on the basis of the quality and success of previous work rather than on an application or interview process (Throsby, 2010). Students are introduced to national directories for film and theatre. Film, for example, is usually unionized, and each country will have a list of members in the relevant craft. There are certain things that all productions will have: they will all have a production office and an art director. Students will have to go out and fight for work. We mock these situations of making contact with potential employers and role-play these kinds of meetings.

The ability to introduce business thinking into the arts programs at IADT has been made possible both by the introduction of some formal elements (placement, teaching, assessment) and the informal input of staff who have worked as practitioners and can bring their experience to the classroom and studio. These practices led staff bring a real-world understanding of the role that teaching and learning have on the successful development of emerging artists.

Broadening the Business Studies Curriculum

The Quinn School of Business at UCD admits some 500 new students each year, almost all of whom are coming directly from secondary education. Such a large group of entrants contains quite a diverse range of profiles. Rather than being avidly focused on the world of the business professional, many students choose undergraduate business studies because they have a wide range of interests and wish to preserve flexibility when it comes to possible career paths. Thinking further about the motivations for choosing an undergraduate business degree, we can generalize some characteristics of the entrants. First, many school leavers do not have a strong vocational leaning toward professions like medicine, law or engineering, but have an ambition to develop a successful and rewarding career. Many students also show a range of abilities in subjects at the secondary level—it is significant that in the Irish secondary system, high-achieving students will study as many as eight or nine subjects to completion. Thus, high-performing students will show equal success in subjects that may be quite diverse compared to university offerings, ranging from languages to sciences and arts. Thus, school leavers experience a sharp change toward specialization moving into university.

Based on the authors' many interactions with potential students in the recruitment process, many students experience difficulty in choosing the best degree for them. The general nature of the Irish second level education system (most students do eight subjects for the final examination, the Leaving Certificate) means that the choice of the third-level course is likely to be the first occasion when they exercise a meaningful choice of discipline. In addition to those students who choose a business degree because it is their passion, many will see it as a good general degree. Some will select on the basis of what they are advised is a more materially rewarding direction. This thinking is reinforced by the recruitment practices of large employers, who seek graduates with education geared toward their activities, in areas like finance and marketing. Further factors in a student's choice of degree programme are reported and perceived changes in the workplace—there are popular claims that many of today's existing job types will be obsolete in a short time and that a large portion of the workforce is tending to become self-employed, calling for flexibility and the ability to think in innovative and creative ways.

Many students entering business degrees have a strong interest in including the Arts in their studies wherever possible: in the case of the Quinn School, this can mean taking a double-major degree in business and language or choosing electives in Arts subjects. The UCD Horizons electives system allows all undergraduate students across the university (with limited exceptions) to have a free choice for one course per semester (Purcell et al., 2014). With a typical workload of six courses, this means an enterprising student will complete their degree with one-sixth of the credits gained outside their discipline area (although they are free to choose electives in their home faculty). This allows business students to broaden their university education with limited involvement in the creative arts, humanities and sciences. Feedback from employers shows that choosing 'interesting' electives helps to distinguish a job applicant's profile. While business students may opt for electives outside their discipline, the traditional structure of UCD, like many large universities, means that students interested in the Arts will tend to have the most access to subjects in the humanities and little access to creative arts.

IADT and UCD have been working closer together as a result of a number of sectoral and structural initiatives. In 2013, the institutions signed a memorandum of understanding, and also in 2013, the Minister for Education in Ireland announced the grouping of all higher education providers into regional clusters, which again provided further encouragement for

IADT and UCD to deepen their cooperative relationship. This relationship has found expression in the development of joint projects and programs. In the case of the Quinn Business School, guest lectures in Data Visualization, a key component in IADTs Visual Communication and Creative Computing programs, being delivered to business undergraduates is one example. It is the authors' strong hope that there will be reciprocal movement of students or staff between the institutions to offer IADT students access to a wider offering of business experiences and to provide options for UCD business students to experience in the creative and applied arts.

A strong and recurring trend across the business school sector lately is a focus on innovation and enterprise, often attempting to span disciplines. While this is good for interdisciplinary collaboration, it is not clear that the study of innovation results in innovative thinkers. Further, it can be argued that true entrepreneurs are not informed by teaching, but follow their own ideas and initiative. Innovation needs to be broken down and systemized in a way that can be communicated to business students so it has both meaning and impact in their work. The language used to describe the skills of both business students and art students needs to be democratized and shared in a more inclusive way. Does innovation as a term, so common in business schools, have relevance in the arts? Innovation can be defined at its simplest as something new that is put into practical use (Fagerberg, 2005). What we understand by innovation is expanding into non-economic change processes in public, private and non-profit organizations (Gulbrandsen and Aanstad, 2015). The arts foster innovation, and arts-based training can teach communication skills, problem solving and product and systems innovation (Nissley, 2010).

Similarly, creativity is not a word that belongs to the arts: business students respond well to opportunities to engage in collaborative creative activities for the development and presentation of business ideas and analyses. Good ideas are discipline independent, as illustrated by a few well-known but still surprising examples. The data encryption technique, data hopping, was invented by composer George Antheil and actress Hedy Lamarr, the system of red, green and blue dots that displays the images on our TV and computer screens was devised by painters and scientists drawing on the techniques of the impressionist Georges Seurat and the programming language used in most smartphones was derived from the work of a weaver J. M. Jacquard, who developed a programmable loom (Nissley, 2010).

There is scope to increase access for business students to engage with the arts through their studies. There is also a potential benefit to creative problem solving that will likely arise from business students engaging in the applied arts. What is helpful to the development of undergraduate business students is the promotion of teaching and student activities based on engagement with creative processes, in particular applied arts like model making, graphic design, video production and photography. As well as giving a different perspective to traditional business teaching, these activities have practical value in all walks of business and are powerful communication tools for collaboration. Borrowing ideas on assessment from the creative arts is also a potential benefit to the broadening of the skills of business students, including assessment techniques such as panel reviews, crits, peer review, exhibition and so on (Carey and Matlay, 2011). These instruments offer potential for the development of curricula but are not widely implemented at the moment.

The concept of including studio-type learning environments into a business teaching environment is well discussed by Barry and Meisiek (2015) in their article 'Discovering the Business Studio'. The pedagogical benefits seem clear, but when progressing to the next stage of having students from both disciplines working together, difficulties of engagement emerged. The problems involved in combining two different cohorts of students reveal that there is much still to be learned by educators in constructing an environment where the imagined diversity and integration is actually realized. This level of mixed curricula is beyond the current experience of the authors and presents interesting opportunities for future discussions about curriculum development.

Conclusions

Many in the arts are self-employed, so it is clear that students require a basic grounding in how to establish themselves and need some management skills tailored for the arts. Business fundamentals, arts sectorial-specific knowledge and social networking capability should form the core of the business education of art students, but specialist business topics such as taxation law or accrual accounting should not (Bridgstock, 2012).

Case studies may be an interesting way to address these learnings are an area where business studies programs have a great deal of experience. The potential use of case studies presents an interesting opportunity to evaluate novel curricular designs in the future. By bringing in professionals from the arts industries to work through case studies, students would benefit not just from the information, but from meeting people not too far ahead of themselves that have gone through the process.

We have compared two distinct discipline areas in higher education; however, there are elements of both that would appeal to many potential students. The current choice of programs of study forces students to specialize to a level that may be beyond their preference: there may be broad scope to give more flexible access to combinations of arts and business studies to suit individuals' interests. These interests may be a balance of personal desires and pragmatic career ambitions.

Where a student pursues a course of study in arts or business, it would be very desirable for them to have reciprocal exposure to the other areas: a graduate in the creative arts should have some business fundamentals to enhance their workplace capability, while a business graduate would benefit from a broadly based education including the arts. In any case, feedback from employers remains unambiguous: graduates must bring skills to the workplace which help them become productive quickly.

In order to develop more interdisciplinary avenues in higher education, it is first necessary to propose better collaboration between individual academics, their departments and larger organizational components (faculties, schools, colleges, institutions). This is seen as an endemic need in higher education institutions and needs action at the policy level, with suitable incentives for academics to work across disciplines.

A further systematic problem within the university system is the tension between teaching and research: the development of interdisciplinary teaching calls for individuals to invest in developing novel approaches to their courses, which is both risky and takes time and effort away from the academic's research work. For this to change, we must rely on colleagues' vocational beliefs that diversifying and innovating in teaching are the best courses of action for them in order to facilitate the best outcomes for their students. Perhaps in time, institutions will create incentives and rewards for changing approaches to teaching and to enable structural changes in how programs are designed and delivered, but in the first instance, it falls to motivated individuals to lead by example.

Given that the two organizations discussed in this chapter are linked at a high level with an inter-institutional agreement (in principle, if not in detail), there is an opportunity for the authors to take some deliberate steps in the direction of shared learning experiences for their respective student cohorts. Possibilities include the exchange of staff members, reciprocal or shared teaching workloads, joint student teams for project work, elective modules open to each other's students and off-schedule course offerings. These could comprise intensive courses delivered outside the standard term calendar, possibly blended delivery with asynchronous learning material coupled with team projects. The softest approach to delivering courses across establishments calls for credit awards to be retained where they are so that existing credit may be awarded to a student for delivering work in collaboration with the related institution. The work carried out to date serves as a practical base on which to build more innovative mixed curricula.

References

Arthur, M., Inkson, D. and Pringle, J. (1999). *The New Careers: Individual Action and Economic Change.* London: SAGE.

Barry, Daved and Meisiek, Stefan (2015). Discovering the business studio. *Journal of Management Education*, 39(1):153–175.

Bridgstock, Ruth (2012). Not a dirty word: Arts entrepreneurship and higher education. *Arts & Humanities in Higher Education*, 12(2–3):122–137.

Bridgstock, Ruth, Dawson, S. and Hearn, G. (2011). Cultivating Innovation through Social Relationships: A Qualitative Study of Outstanding Australian Innovators in Science, Technology, and the Creative Industries, in: A. Mesquita. (ed.).

Technology for Creativity and Innovation: Tools, Techniques and Applications, pp. 104–120. Hershey: IGI-Global.

Carey, Charlotte and Matlay, Harry (2011). Emergent issues in enterprise education: The educator's perspective. *Industry & Higher Education*, 25(6) December:441–450.

Fagerberg, J. (2005). Innovation—A guide to the literature, in: J Fagerberg, D. C. Mowery, and R. R. Nelson (eds.). *The Oxford Handbook of Innovation*, pp.1–26. Oxford: Oxford University Press.

Gulbrandsen, Magnus and Aanstad, Siri (2015). Is innovation a useful concept for arts and humanities research? *Arts & Humanities in Higher Education*, 14(1):9–24.

Gurnon, Daniel, Voss-Andreae, Julian and Stanley Jacob (2013). Integrating art and science in undergraduate education. *PLOS Biology*, 11(2): e1001491. doi:10.1371/journal.pbio.1001491.

Mallon, M. (1999). Going 'portfolio': Making sense of changing careers. *Career Development International*, 4(7):358–369.

McConnell, Catherine (2010). Placement learning in the creative industries: Engaging students with micro-businesses. *Industry & Higher Education*, 24(6) Dec:455–466.

Nissley, Nick (2010). Arts-based learning at work: Economic downturns, innovation upturns, and the eminent practicality of arts in business. *Journal of Business Strategy*, 31(4):8–20.

Osterwalder, Alexander (2004). *The Business Model Ontology—A Proposition in a Design Science Approach*. PhD thesis, University of Lausanne.

Purcell, Patrick, Dunnion, John and Loughran, Hilda (2014). Experience of Elective Provision at UCD. *AISHE-J: The All Ireland Journal of Teaching & Learning in Higher Education*, 6(2): 1971–19721.

Throsby, D. and Zednik, A. (2010). *Do You Really Expect to Get Paid? An Economic Study of Professional Artists in Australia*. Melbourne: Australia Council for the Arts.

UCD News (2012, August 1). *UCD Imagine Science Film Festival—Science Expression Competition Winners*. Retrieved 04.07.2015 from <http://www.ucd.ie/news/2012/08AUG12/010812-UCD-Imagine-Science-Film-Festival-Science-Expression-Competition-Winners.html>.

UCD Science Expression, IADT/UCD Short Films 2013.Retrieved 04.07.2015 from<http://www.ucdscienceexpression.ie/events/iadtucd-short-films-2013/>.

16 Management

Stepping Back Through Arts

Dorina Coste, Isabelle Né and
Marianella Fornerino

Introduction

This chapter apprehends the relationship future managers, today at the level of master in a management school, have with the business environment and the way they represent this relationship through graphic arts. The students about whom we shall be talking, it is interesting to underline, all have had at least one year of internship experience. They have chosen, among specialization courses, a module in graphic arts, which was the opportunity for their arts professor to undertake a long survey on their visions as to their future profession in management. They eagerly challenge ideal visions of the work and business environments with other realities, strongly expressed through graphic arts and accompanying written discourses.

The analysis corpus consists of asking the students to give an account about their experience and forecast their vision through imaged and narrative posters using graphic arts techniques. We observe that they do express, with criticism, today's management rhetoric based on subjectivity and individualization. The graphic art tool, since it uses symbolism, definitely helps our future managers step back when considering both their experience as interns and their management position to come, with all its ambiguities.

We have chosen to divide this chapter into three subchapters concerning the business/management school student's project within their *promising* studies. We first contextualize our students' position and the existence of a graphic arts module. Then we develop what they have already experienced about motivation,[1] and then we chose to develop their views on the topic of capitalism particularly discussed in the present economic context, in which two discourses oppose each other: the need for growth and the need for another economic system. As many students of the sample are intending to develop a career in marketing, itself using the symbols of graphic arts, we also show some arguments they developed when giving it a critical look.

French business schools, classically called 'high schools of business',[2] undertake the mission to train the future 'managers' as required by their economic environment. Management training programs are indeed often discussed in comities joining companies' actors with professors. From the

Image 16.1 Promising studies aiming to stay in or reach favored social classes.

90s, some of these schools have chosen to rather be called 'management schools', since the students are trained in different aspects of management and for all types of organizations, not necessarily dealing with lucrative business.

The initial education in a management school is conventionally based on core courses in management (including project management, group dynamics, personalities and interactions, leadership, theories of organizations etc.), accounting, business law, finance, marketing, strategy, economics, human resources and languages in order to give the core tools to integrate the enterprise and fast become operational. The contents are quite similar from one school to another, and it must be admitted that even well-known researchers and professors do challenge all-in-one tools that are traditionally taught to the students on their way to become managers. Mintzberg's recent reflections as to what it means to study management issues and implement an adapted know-how in the enterprise, according to its specificities, is an example. His provocative book *Managers, Not MBAs* (2005) denounces the 'one best way' cloning students into an army of clumsy, non-legitimate, pure analysts who simply forget the most important thing: the specificities of contexts. Our students, we shall see, tackle this aspect. Mintzberg (2005) and Le Goff (2003), among others, do underline the importance of experience; the art of management is like a language with all its nuances. It cannot be taught strictly following theory, even if the theory was written out of observation.

But we are showing here that our students do not lack observation and criticism when the opportunity is given to them to express their feelings and self-projection into tomorrow's societies. Graphic arts is a means for them to show these ambivalences without being seen as deviant from the business culture.

Students choosing an education in a business/management school emphasize the instrumental relationship to the institution in considering mainly the professional opportunities and material rewards promised by a curriculum within a Grande Ecole[3] (Coste, 2013). Since the 90s, management schools have integrated courses in artistic fields—theatre, design and visual arts— and have undertaken partnerships with art schools.[4] In order to answer the urge for creativity in the 'ever accelerating innovation' wave, business/ management schools develop possibilities for challenge, critical thinking, self-development and other intelligences of the kind. It is particularly the case with the graphic arts module, even if this critical thinking is of course being tackled within other courses, such as organizational behavior, ethics, social and societal responsibility, resourceful management etc., though they are not using the same creativity approach.

Within graphic arts courses, each assignment carried out is coupled with a reflexive written work explaining the creativity approach. Definitely, graphic arts facilitates and fosters the expression of a language of interiority and reflexivity, an identity construction, and this cannot be implemented easily. A first stage consists of acquiring the expression techniques, a second stage aims to express some feelings and the third stage, in a questioning process, is the moment of reflection.[5]

It is important to have a few words about those students and their origins. Among about 850 students per year, about 10% in their second and third years of study, did register for graphic arts courses. A great majority of the school's students come from middle- and upper- social classes. The students who do register for the graphic arts module generally come from a privileged background. It includes a greater percentage of business leaders, upper managers and liberal professions.

François Dubet's (2008) studies highlight that students whose social origin and scholar situation offer the most resources generally are those who manage more easily to build their own experience and constitute themselves as the subject of their studies. They chose trainings which they perceive as socially useful and related to possible job offers. Yet we may nuance Dubet's observations, as the situation described here shows that the students who have chosen the graphic arts module, do not, for the most part, adhere to the cultural model of their business studies. They have a hard time in trying to project themselves in their future, and when they do, their vision is rather negative. They present a critical view of enterprises doing business for business. Ideal representations are indeed rare.

During the graphic arts courses, the atmosphere is relaxed. Compared to the core courses of management studies, the graphic arts courses count only 20 students per group. The necessary material is provided by the school: paper, acrylic paint and brushes, coloured pencils. It must be noted that this material, whenever it is used in other types of courses (organizational behaviour, for example) is fast considered as 'childish'. In many students' minds (and many actors in organizations), work is a 'serious' matter, not a place for 'amusing' one's mind with games, humour and paintbrushes. The work environment is too often seen as a sacrosanct, serious place (Farell and Linda, 1998) where creativity is opposite to norms and frames. But the graphic arts course itself is perceived as recreative, a break from other 'more serious' modules and a place where critical thinking is allowed and even encouraged.

The professional experience during internships[6] is the occasion for the majority of students to discover an environment that is sometimes hostile and quite disenchanting.

The setting of these experiences' stories through graphic posters and accompanying narratives expresses this disillusion. They illustrate their authors' distancing and awareness in relation to the business contexts and management rhetoric. They show that the contemporaneous work environment is characterized by a formal and explicit call for employees' subjectivity. Management now requires of its employees and trainees the total gift of

Image 16.2 Self-staging: 'motivation' and 'enthusiasm' as the inescapable injunction to find work.

themselves: their personality, their emotions, their most intimate resources, in addition to a strong cognitive involvement (LeGoff, 1999, 2003; Linhardt, 2008). This call for subjectivity at work is actually present in the majority of the students' posters. But it is not any kind of subjectivity, as it has to fit into measurement frames that formalize the selves as clones. From this material, posters and texts, several topics linked to social and societal issues are identified.

'Be motivated' is indispensable to finding a job or an internship. The arrival in the work environment is a real upheaval for a student who experiments a real loss of landmarks. Thanks to graphic arts, they can express this frustrated emotion, not necessarily using aesthetics, since this is not the point. Nicolas writes: "I found [it] very interesting to work on the concept of motivation because, after my experience of writing about 30 motivation letters to diverse enterprises, it is an expression I used to the point [that] I [had] nightmares. It is thus an issue I feel quite concerned about. I believe it is indicative of a real uneasiness in the world of work. Indeed, behind this formula is already hidden a prescription and prior maxim that requires being already motivated before joining a company. A motivation one would have for all the companies in which we apply? With just about a vague idea of the job and its environment?" Most courses on organizational behavior and theories of organizations tackle the concept of 'motivation' as a golden rule for better involvement, a better sense of belonging, better performance, to the point it may, if clumsily used, become just a fake, bearing no more sense as far as behaviors are concerned (Linhart, 2008). We find useful the graphic arts purpose to help express such disappointments and seek sense.

Since the 'scientific school' in organization theories, one generally suspects these functioning modes to have barbarized the work environment in which actors are instrumental (Le Goff, 1999). Taking the word 'actor' in its stage sense together with its general sense, we find staging practices that distribute, justify and legitimate actors' roles, some controlling others who need to be guided. These roles are accompanied by social norms for which each has to behave a certain way, according to his/her status, such as in a theatrical show (Goffman, 1973). We keep a façade, says Goffman (1974), speaking about individuals; we have to be convincing; all interaction is a drama in the theatrical sense, in which we are playing a double game, showing someone we are not. And what we are showing has to be in cohesion with the discourse, itself a sign. This anthropologic look at the everyday staging shows that each relationship is a spectacle in itself. Goffman expresses that exposed realities are just what is allowed to be seen, for the sake of reputation, to stay admissible to the spectators (consumers, controllers . . .) (Gumb et al., 2015). Our students, giving it a critical look through internship experiences and introspection, realize how much all is not simple, how much motivation cannot simply be called for, professions not being simply professions but also being interconnected with people, contexts, cultures, social and societal responsibilities, economy. They can be representing, in their graphics, society's actors with masks and puppets, underlining individuals' fragilities, power games and manipulations, which most management tools learned at the business school are not preparing them to confront. The graphic arts course is the leeway to express fears and frustrations, but also facilitates the awareness one should expect from a responsible manager.

The issue there is that normally, in the enterprise, motivation is a cause, not an end. An issue again since today, in any organization, the individual must force himself/herself to show motivation, whichever conditions in which he/she works, since motivation is also part of the evaluation processes (Le Goff, 1999; Gomez, 2013). It should look logical that it is for the enterprise to make the effort to integrate the employees, as suggested by our students, especially when one talks about loyalty and the problematic, in strategic HR, to retain talents (Bratton and Gold, 1999). The work environment, such it is taught in management, organizational theories and behavioral courses, should compound motivations and thus productivity. We see there that the ambiguity, seen by the students of the graphic arts courses, is potentially discussed elsewhere: is motivation a means or a cause? The nice environment, the 'best company to work for', is it for the employees' well-being and ultimately for the organization's competitiveness, or is motivation just a means to raise profits? "My experience in an enterprise where the resignation percentage is above 30% does show the prevailing malaise generated by the false postulate of 'motivation': 'motivation' has become an obligation, a demand, thus be motivated or shove off!"[7]

In the contemporaneous work environment, the individuals (all) must learn self-discipline by themselves. Control notions become blurred or, at first sight, they become 'softer', in what Le Goff (1999) calls a *new barbarism*. This remains the formal framework of skills assessments, to show that things are controlled, but in which we must match the expected framework. And it is known that creativity does not readily team up with standards. Actually, our students' choice is to represent, through graphic arts, very critical views on standards, management issues, innovation etc. and the Western economic system itself.

During the fall semester of 2015, the topic money crises and capitalism was suggested to the graphic arts class by a professor in economics at the same business/management school, to participate in an international conference on the same topic.[8] Like with any other topics some classes have dealt with, projecting themselves as future managers in the work environment and as active participants of the economy and of society, this year's students allowed themselves to reveal a very critical and pessimistic view of today's capitalism system. They are underlining the ambivalence between what they will professionally become, after graduating from a business school, and the economic context of today that challenges old points of view of growth being inherent to economy. Authors contesting pure capitalist approaches have been seen, before and during the business school's curricula.

Images 16.3 Capitalism ambiguities: money, capitalism and crisis.

Four main themes were identified when looking at the concept of capitalism in today's context: 1) the finance and economy profession representations illustrating adherence to the corporate and business schools' culture; those schools' messages include sacrosanct growth, it comes to the 'taking part in the role' described by Goffman (2002); 2), representations opposing themselves to this culture; described by Goffman as 'distance to the role', we recognize the feeling of manipulation in financialization (Vitari et al., 2013); 3) representations stating the ethical 'ambivalence' of the profession, in the introspection's process of presenting issues in the posters, the students lead a dialogue with their own values; and 4) the question of the 'game' emerging in these representations, illustrated by the fragility and the fall of the economy. These results illustrate how such signs are representative of the students' questioning from their representations of finance in a professionalization process, which is part of their identity-building dynamics.

Students expressing positive and optimistic representations of their future profession are to be situated within Goffman's 'taking part in the role'. According to Goffman (1991), taking part in the role is before all the production of a mental scheme built out of what he/she has observed: one must understand what occurs, then one must conform. In the same perspective, Kaufmann (2001) shows that throughout the observation phase, the actor studies the game's rules, what is allowed, tolerated, forbidden and of course what is considered as bad and why. Then the actor adapts these observations to his personal feelings according to the circumstances, so as

Images 16.4 Capitalism ambiguities: money, capitalism and crisis.

to define what could be 'good' for him in acting while staying 'normal': the normative development builds the conditions under which the 'taking part in the role' becomes possible. The graphic arts process helps to challenge consciously what is considered as a norm.

Images 16.5 Capitalism ambiguities: money, capitalism and crisis.

But for the students dealing with the topics on money, capitalism and crises, the 'taking part' would have been the deviant reaction compared to the rest of the class. Indeed, they were not in a finance class, specializing in econometrics and trading, where such representations would have been seen as irrelevant, even if bridges should be made according to all post-Keynesian economists and to business ethics professors, from which today's business schools are not devoid.[9]

The students tackling the topic on finance and capitalism do not hesitate to talk about the 'religion' of money that 'abuses', in 'lying' and 'manipulating', most actors in the economy. "My project", says Sarah (third poster above), "compares capitalism to a worship, as its goal is to satisfy and answer the worries of its believers who are blinded by the perspective of a better future: being richer. The comparison shows veneration to a divinity, Money. In this world of exacerbated capitalism, the value of individuals is being measured out of their ownings, hierarchizing them. The worshiping group believes itself to be blessed with superiority and Excellency. In the shade of the blessed group, a crowd, out of reach of the light rays, represents the left outs. Dry and cracked ground under their feet reinforces the symbolism of their poverty and misery:[the] flip side of wealth". The discourses as to finance in a business school have evolved since the revelations and consequences of the subprime crisis. Our future managers, in representing such criticism, do see themselves as social actors with responsibilities. We observe more and more of them, thanks to the graphic arts courses (and other modules tackling ethics, behaviours) daring the reflection that could be seen as deviant from the purposes of studying in business schools (in order to make businesses flourish, make money, etc.). "Money is badly used", writes Cyrielle (first poster above), "It does everything. It represents power. The raised fist shows both the crushing suffered by people and their rebellion as they aspire to more money and power". She later writes the expression of "capitalism violence", meaning at the same time that she find herself in the between of capitalism two tendencies: her choice to integrate a business/management school, and her strong desire to have professional objectives influenced by the values enhanced through her creativity.

Conclusions

Functional to the two processes presented, graphic posters and text, the identity construction integrates mental representations, thus guaranteeing the integration of lived experiences. These elements lead to formulating the following question: what are the representations business schools' students have of the different professions they might have (in finance, marketing etc.) when they get through their identity construction linked to their professionalization? The research led through the graphic arts courses aimed at identifying and classifying some representations, including the civilian position and responsibility, through an interactionist approach.

The issue of 'sense' for the future profession is manifestly present in many of the students' representations. A 'paradox' is shown: loving the exercise of a profession (with its exciting sides in terms of activity and intellect), and wondering about the sense at the same time of a professional activity that bears some negative aspects because, with marketing for example, it can lead the consumer into 'the spiral of consumption' and the future professional to no longer be 'consistent with his/her moral framework'.

This 'distance to the role' is present in the majority of the students' work, and it is indeed one of the objectives of seeing topics through the arts. According to Goffman (2002), the 'distance to the role' is a very flexible notion, empirically traceable: all forms of caricatures, mockery etc. the social actors use upon themselves or on others are illustrations of a detachment, which can be translated as a refusal of the official self, produced by the 'role'. It reveals the person behind the actor. The students chose rhetoric with signs and words, based on humor and derision, to translate the economy-related questioning. For Bergson (2012), the comic primarily expresses the unsuitability of some particular person to social norms. This unsuitability is perceptible in the business school students of our sample.

The different productions done by the students during the graphic arts courses were the occasion for expressing, in the sense of externalizing a thought, a sensation, an emotion, through the support of a graphic and a 'creation diary'. For the purpose of a PhD,[10] some discourses and graphic analyses were thoroughly deepened with sociological and anthropological approaches. We may expose here, within our conclusion, the usage of the several expressive usages:

- The students registered in the graphic arts courses have a critical view of the business school institution where the risk is to be formatted.
- The graphic arts courses are seen as an 'outlet' to 'open one's mind' within this context and get a different means to interpret and understand processes.
- They do have a critical vision about the topics taught such as 'marketing', 'finance', 'control management' and 'strategic management'. In this class, they do not feel embarrassed to say it.
- After their internship and two years' work experience, only a minority of them express an 'idealized' vision of their 'future profession'. In contrast, for the majority, contrary to any student's expectations, the internship occasion is a destabilizing factor as to the choice of a profession. Even more so, for several students, this experience led them to abandon or modify the professional orientation that had been the previous choice. Maybe the management career project was not theirs after all, and it just needed to be said, one way or another.

Notes

1 As interns but also what they have observed about other actors fully included in organizations, or about literature, medias and other specialized or core courses.
2 Ecoles Supérieures de Commerce.

3 Grande Ecole is a title allocated from the Ministry of National Education to institutions of higher education into which students get access after a competitive examination. These institutions are required to provide a high level of education.
4 For example, theatre is taught at MIP Paris (Management Institute of Paris), IESEG Lille, ESC Dijon, ESC Grenoble and Group Sup de Co La Rochelle.
5 Not mastering drawing techniques has not been an obstacle to the graphic realizations.
6 Concerning the students of the graphic arts module, the compulsory internship of 52 weeks is mostly done in fields of marketing, communication and event management, work fields where actually creativity is at the core of the profession. A small minority (5%) is oriented in finance and auditing.
7 Nicolas; extract from the narrative accompanying his poster about the topic "Me, today in the enterprise", October 2011.
8 An international post-Keynesian conference in Grenoble, December 2015,
9 The management school in which our courses are conducted hosts a research chair on "Mindfulness, Well-Being at Work and Economic Peace".
10 Dorina Coste.

Bibliography

Bergson, H. (1900/2012). *Le rire. Essai sur la signification du comique.* Paris: Payot.
Bratton, J. and Gold, J. (1999). *Human Resource Management: Theory and Practice.* London, UK: McMillan Edition.
Coste, D. (2013). Loriol (2013) L'humour au travail, dépasser les lectures fonctionnalistes et critiques. *Les Mondes du Travail.* N° 13. Juin.
Dubet, F. (2008). *Faits d'école.* Paris: Editions de l'EHESS.
Farrell, L. (1998) You've got to be kidding: Humor as a fundamental management tool. *Records Management Quarterly,* Jul 98, (32)3.
Goffman, E. (1973). *La mise en scène de la vie quotidienne.* Paris, Editions de Minuit.
Goffman, E. (1977). *Stigmates. Les usages sociaux des handicaps.* Paris. Edition de Minuit (First edition, 1963).
Goffman, E. (1979). *Asiles; Etudes sur la condition sociale des malades mentaux et autres reclus.* Paris, Edition de Minuit (first edition, 1961)
Goffman, E. (2002). La « distance au rôle » en salle d'opération. *Actes de la recherche en sciences sociales.* Vol. 143. N°. 3, pp. 808–7
Goffman, E. (1977). La ritualisation de la féminité. *Actes de la recherche en sciences sociales.* Vol. 14, Avril 1977. Présentation et représentation du corps, pp. 345–0
Goffman, E. (1991). *Les cadres de l'expérience.* Paris, Editions de Minuit.
Gomez, P-Y. (2013). *Le travail invisible: enquête sur une disparition.* François Bourin Editeur.
Gumb, B., Né, I. and Duymedjian, R. (2015). Integrated Spectacle as a Metaphor of Contemporaneous Management: Death or Rebirth of the 'Situation'? *Paper Proposal for 10th Philosophy of Management International Conference Saint Anne's College—Oxford, July 2015.*
Kaufmann, J-C. (2001). *Ego. Pour une sociologie de l'individu.* Paris. Nathan
Le Goff, J. P. (2003). *Les illusions du management.* Paris, France: La Découverte.
Le Goff, J-P. (1999). *La Barbarie douce: La Modernisation aveugle des entreprises et de l'école.* La Découverte.
Linhart, D. (2008). *Pourquoi travaillons-nous? Une approche sociologique de la subjectivité au travail: Collection.* Paris, France: Éditeur Eres, Collection Clinique du travail.
Mintzberg, H. (2005). *Managers Not MBAs: A Hard Look at the Soft Practice of Managing and Management Development.* Berrett-Koehler Publishers.
Vitari, C.; Ashta, A.; Bobulescu, R.; Né, I; Lepesant, M.; Lê, N-T.; Bloemmen, M.; Bratu, D. (2013). *Slow Management: Entreprendre la transition.* Tours. Pearson France

17 The Rag Rug
Weaving Together Artistic and Business Patterns of Thinking

Nina Bozic Yams and Elisabeth Helldorff

Introduction

This chapter is a dialogue between our inner voice and our scientific voice. The inner voice is written in the form of personal story telling, which follows experiential, emotional and intuitive principles, like artistic thinking. The scientific voice, on the other hand, is more analytical and rational, and thus closer to business patterns of thinking. To make traveling between two voices easier, we marked the inner voice in italics. When writing 'we' in the parts of the scientific voice, we refer to ourselves as the authors. Moving through the text, the reader is supposed to get an insight into what the 'rag rug thinking' can look like in practice when patterns of thinking across disciplinary boundaries are woven together.

The chapter's discussants are:

Elisabeth, 32, born and raised in Germany, started playing violin when she was five and continued playing cello when she was eight. Besides being a professional musician, she studied cultural management in Hildesheim. She is now a PhD student and researches in the field of arts and innovation at the University of Hildesheim and the School of Design Thinking in Potsdam.

Nina, 37, born and raised in Slovenia, married and currently living in Sweden. She started to dance classical ballet when she was four, but never turned into a professional dancer. She ended up studying marketing instead and working as a business consultant, trainer and entrepreneur. At a certain point of her career, she suddenly left the comforts of her management position to join a nomadic dance academy. She is currently doing a PhD in innovation management, exploring how she can combine her two passions: business and dance.

Prologue

The main point of this text is not to juxtapose business against art, or linear against non-linear thinking and to propose that businessmen should think more like artists or vice versa. It is rather about how we can all, no matter if we are businessmen or artists, in this polyphony of voices and stimulus that surrounds us, trying to penetrate our brains from all sides, demanding from us to constantly perform something that is expected of us and fulfill others' fantasies and desires, sometimes even trying to appropriate our own bodies, just stop for a second. Breathe in, breathe out and stand in silence for a while. Allowing ourselves time to find and articulate our own voice and thoughts. Not because it's cool, super arty, super entrepreneurial or because it brings us fame, money or power. But just because it is about who we are, what we need and what we truly feel is relevant for us right now.

Artistic vs. Business Thinking

Most of the authors who write about patterns of thinking refer to two predominant patterns of thinking. Depending on whether they come from psychology, management, art or some other field, they might use different terminology, but essentially, they talk about linear vs. non-linear, convergent vs. divergent or rational vs. intuitive thinking. Epstein et al. (1996) differentiated between two modes of processing information: the rational and the experiential. "The rational system operates primarily at the conscious level and is intentional, analytic, primarily verbal, and relatively affect free. The experiential system is assumed to be automatic, preconscious, holistic, associationistic, primarily nonverbal, and intimately associated with affect" (Epstein et al., 1996:391).

There are different factors that make one or the other system dominate in different situations, such as individual preferences, the type of task we are engaged with and the level of emotional engagement (Epstein et al., 1996).

Elisabeth: I remember math at school. I hated it. I could literally feel that the part of my brain where this math-thinking was supposed to be located occupied less space than the part for sports and music. Airless space as small as a pea.

Sternberg (1994) claims that a thinking style is a preferred way of using one's abilities. Our thinking styles change over the course of a lifetime as a result of different influences and role models throughout our lives (Sternberg, 1994). If we spend many years in business or on the other hand in artistic practice, this will influence our preferred ways of thinking.

Nina: I used to work in this big American consultancy firm. Everyone was thinking like mechanics. Companies were some sort of machines we were analysing and then fixing with our flashy consultant tools. The people inside were just numbers that we would move around or delete to present the best possible score at the end of the spreadsheet.

Business is usually associated with the linear models of thinking, while artistic practice is connected with non-linear thinking styles. Different studies have demonstrated the predominance of the linear thinking style in business (Bratianu and Vasilache, 2010) and the non-linear thinking style in art (Emery, 1989; Ryder et al., 2002).

When people use a linear thinking style, they mainly rely on cognitive intelligence, processing data and facts in analytical cause-and-effect manner, solving problems through linear processes of problem recognition, identification of alternatives and implementation of solutions (Wulun, 2007). On the other hand, when people use a non-linear thinking style, they rely more on emotional intelligence and intuition, solving challenges in an open-ended iterative experimental process in which the direction becomes clear through trying out different possibilities, building, testing and adapting things in an emergent process (Emery, 1989).

Elisabeth: One of my brothers loves goals. I think he is a linear type of person in many ways. He needs the proof of successfully tested formulas in order to have a sense of control over the expected outcome. He is an engineer. Basically he is interested in understanding the objective reality of things. On the other hand, I usually think more in a non-linear way. I like to be part of more open-ended processes where I can tap into my inner feelings, sensations and intuition. I enjoy being part of a discovery process where the result is not known in advance but emerges through trying out different possibilities.

Dividing patterns of thinking in this dualistic linear vs. non-linear manner is of course quite simplistic. We all to a certain extent combine the two modes of thinking, even though we probably have a personal preference. And although one pattern of thinking might on average prevail in business and the other one in art, we know that the world is more complex than that. Both in art and business, we can find a wide spectrum of personal preferences and organizational practices ranging from very traditional mechanistic models based on hierarchy, top-down planning and control to extremely innovative modes of working that are based on flexible collaborative network structures, emergence, self-organization and improvisation. Innovative high-tech companies today are probably much more non-linear in their leadership thinking style than many big traditional art institutions like state museums, theatres and orchestras.

Nina: One of my clients used to be a game-development company. I remember when I once entered their office and found myself in the middle of a battlefield. Someone was hiding in an improvised bunker, working on a laptop, fake arms lying all around, and combat music was played in the background. In the meeting I found out that the office was half empty because most of the team went on a field trip to Germany driving a tank. I almost got scared. What was happening? Well, they were developing a new fighting game and wanted to create the right conditions to stimulate their creative process.

What we propose in this text is thus not that businesspeople should think more like artists or vice versa. But since many of us get trapped in specific patterns of thinking which are expected of us based on our profession, different roles that we play in life or because of our usual habits, we suggest that it makes sense to re-think our thinking patterns, first by becoming more aware of our current patterns and then by exploring how we could change them to better fit our real needs and to stimulate our different capacities. Weaving a rag rug thinking can also help us better cope with the complex challenges of the dynamic, interconnected global environment we live in. We use the word rag rug because we think it represents the complexity behind each individual's thinking patterns more precisely than dividing people in artistic vs. business or linear vs. non-linear thinking boxes. A rag rug is messy, fluid, colorful and integrates odd scraps of fabric. We also like the potentiality of a rag rug—that each person can look at her own thinking rag rug, bring some new scraps of fabric and weave in some new patterns. So now the next question must be what this weaving process could look like.

Weaving a Thinking Rag Rug Through a Writing Experiment

We wrote this book chapter as an experiment in weaving our own thinking rag rug and trying to see what others could learn from it. We wanted to question the usual patterns of thinking about how a scientific text should look like by weaving together our different experiences and thinking styles from both arts and business.

Nina: I want to write a juicy text. A text that will awaken the body of the reader while reading it. A bodily text. A text that reflects our bodily process. This means that our inner bitches have to get room in the text, too. Not only nice and beautiful stuff, not only facts and theories and logical arguments. It has to get dirty at some point, too. Let's show that the stuff that would be considered junk in traditional scientific writing can actually create a nice choreography in the text. Text as choreography. Text as a dance performance. Text where our personal stories, observations, reflections and evaluations of ourselves in the everyday life set the stage for choreography in the text.

One core element of our approach in this writing experiment was to work in an emergent way instead of performing a predefined schedule of tasks. We tried to respond to our needs in the process and adjust the timing, activities, spaces and composition of the days to the emergent needs of our bodies. Each of us would start the day with some tuning in, taking the time to feel what we needed in that specific moment of our writing process. During the days, we experimented in different ways, trying out what happens to our writing process if we worked in different spaces and combined writing with various activities that we felt like doing. This meant that we worked in a dance studio, on a playground, in cafés and restaurants, in art museums, while walking, dancing or listening to concerts and even getting a manicure.

Elisabeth: I just had a great plate of pasta at my favorite Italian restaurant. It blows my mind and gives me the feeling that everything I will write in the very next moment is so relevant and intelligent that people will eat it like I did the pasta just minutes before. And the best thing about it is that I do it in the middle of the day instead of sitting in some meeting or answering the 154th email this day. I just took this time off from conventional work in order to be able to finally think and work as I love to do it: with loud music in the background, with pasta in my stomach and with people passing by at the window.

So why do I sit at this Italian restaurant? First of all: because I can—nobody forces me to sit at a certain desk to do my work. Second: because I allowed myself to try out working in different places in order to find the one that fits my needs. Third: because I force myself to think about why something works and something does not. Why there are days that drive me crazy because I don't find the right recipe for the workflow? Fourth: because my dear writing partner does the same. With her in person, I have somebody to share my thoughts with.

During our writing process, we had a lot of freedom to experiment, but we also established some basic routines. Every day we had to write and send each other a text. We also wrote a short reflection of the day, answering three questions: what have I done today, how does it feel and how does it make sense for my work? Additionally, we selected a picture of the day, which could be a drawing, a photograph or any other form of visualization, for example, a small installation. Since we were writing in different cities, we had daily Skype meetings to share our experiences, reflections and ideas. Each of us choose an external sharing partner in order to get some further feedback a few times during the writing process. An important external collaborator was dancer and choreographer Dejan Srhoj, with whom we had previously co-developed our research and who gave us a choreographic perspective on the text and also some tasks for the movement experimentation which resulted in a few of the personal reflections included in the inner voice in this text. The experimental writing cycles were repeated three times. After each cycle, the text was sent to the book editors to get feedback before going into the next cycle.

Key Elements of Re-Weaving Thinking Patterns

By testing the proposed model on ourselves while we were writing the chapter and reflecting about our experiences, we were able to distill four important aspects that helped us re-weave our thinking patterns in the process: the acknowledgement of the body as a thinking muscle, the role of unfocusing to focus, the importance of belief in the process and the need for individual formulas.

The Body as a Thinking Muscle

The first finding was that the body is an important thinking muscle that we often ignore at work but which could importantly help improving people's thinking. This is supported also by evidence from existing research (Steinberg et al., 1997; Hannaford, 2005; Hansen and Sundberg, 2014). The body is more than a vehicle that carries the brain to work. Even though we associate thinking mainly with the brain, we actually think and work with the whole body. Everybody owns a body that we can accept as a partner who is able to support us in better understanding our patterns of thinking and re-weaving them in new directions.

Nina: I started my day with a breathing exercise to tune in. I'm lying on the floor, breathing . . . I start breathing in through the whole body, and as I keep doing this for a while, I notice that my mind starts to wander . . . I'm planning the evening, as I'm receiving a guest from abroad, and my thoughts go to all kinds of details, from fetching the keys to the guest apartment, fixing the bed linen, to instructions about how to get to our place from the station. I suddenly remember that when I was in a Vipassana camp once, only meditating, sleeping and eating without communicating to anyone or being distracted by any activities for 10 days, I suddenly started to observe my patterns of thinking. I realized that I have a mind of a planner, which often thinks of what and how I will do in the future, but rarely thinks back into past. Sometimes my wandering mind thinks about big things, and sometimes it plans things down to every little detail. Since that experience in Vipassana, I started a little practice every time I observe that my mind wanders into a planning mode. I imagine that my mind is a white canvas and I just try to enjoy the nothingness in front of me. It always makes me feel joyful, thinking of the potential of that empty space that I can later splash with new colors and shapes.

As we started to pay attention, listening to the body during our writing experiment, we began to understand what kind of patterns of thinking and feelings connected to them were present in us. After a while, we started drawing a line between the kind of thinking and behavior that was reproduced as a matter of habit or expectation and the process that started when we directed attention to the needs that emerged from our body. This could be a walk in the morning, substituting the daily news check in the Internet. Or going for a pedicure at lunchtime instead of sitting at the computer and checking emails. Following the body's needs challenged us to test various positions and locations instead of just taking it for granted that working means sitting at a desk and typing on a computer. With the increase of movement, different thinking emerged. Research shows that even simple regular movement like walking improves memory, concentration, learning and creative thinking (Steinberg et al., 1997; Hannaford, 2005; Hansen and Sundberg, 2014). Still, the outcome is a matter of training and practice.

Elisabeth: My body (and I am talking about the body like a different person on purpose) is challenging me in a very special way. I get in touch with it not just by using it in a different way (dancing, working in a different position): it even forces me to bring my whole plan for the day in line with its moods. It is ruling me and deciding when it thinks I should work or not. I am controlled by a foreign power! This requires an extreme form of an emergent way of working. An extreme feeling for what you need in the moment. I am the boss and my body is the staff. We have a project together, and it is my task to understand what my staff needs in order to achieve the project goal.

You really need to focus on the different parts of the body one after the other to understand what they are actually doing all the time. It seems like the whole human body (including the brain) is just too much for our naive little existence. No wonder everybody prefers just working with the brain—it's simply too difficult to include the whole system.

Through our experimentation, we learned that every person needs to find out what works best for her. The starting point is to learn more about one's own body and its needs by trying out different things. After insisting with this kind of experiment for a while, one will realize that better conditions for new thoughts were created. This extreme way of emergent working is like training yourself in improvisation. And practicing improvisation has been shown to increase the ability for divergent thinking (Lewis and Lovatt,

2013). If one chooses the right motion, affirmative effects will override the struggle one had in the beginning.

Focusing by Unfocusing

Nina: I've been sitting and writing for a while, so I need to shift my focus and stretch the body. I decide to do some explorative movement exercises, beginning with an exercise in which I stretch my limbs by following an impulse that starts in one part of the body and then moves very slowly through the body as it is stretching. The movement never stops and my body is going from standing position to lying on the floor and back to standing continuously, but in an extreme slow motion. I am out of space and I forget where I am. My eyes are closed. After doing this for 10 minutes, I awaken back into the reality of my living room by the timer. It is a pity because it would be nice to stay for a while in this soft, blurry, slow-motion world in which each move takes ages. I realize this is a good exercise for me to challenge my usual patterns of thought and behavior. I am a rather active person. There is rarely a day when I don't do anything. I like to meet friends, see art, go to concerts or dance, play with my daughter, participate in workshops and conferences, read books, go for walks, work . . . But right now I feel a super nice and calm feeling in my body. I wonder how it would be if I spent one day each week in extreme slow motion.

The focus on the body as a thinking muscle leads directly to the ability to accept or even expedite detours. A mind that is focused on the one right way to reach the one goal might miss important details or even a new goal. In practice, detouring means that the body and mind are navigated into new directions on purpose. In our writing experiment, we engaged in intentional detouring by doing daily tuning in (reading an inspiring article, listening to a whole symphony while lying on the floor, taking a different way to work every day) and in form of intentional periodical experiments during the day (by using a different table, working in a fitness studio, being in extreme slow motion for a while, going dancing). These exercises made us aware of the fact that our attention constantly shifts between focus on the task and distraction. Distraction happens in those moments in between, when we take a break, lose focus, get stuck and frustrated or distracted by everyday things, like eating, gossiping, going from one place to another or wanting to go to the cinema in the middle of a work day. In our usual work, we try to push away distractive thoughts in order to focus on the task. But if you instead follow these needs and use them either for relaxation, to practice observation or to do a detour from the task when you get stuck, these moments of distraction can actually create a better flow in your creative work and bring unexpected ideas.

Elisabeth: I needed a distraction, so I decided to take a walk without heading for a certain location. I suddenly felt like getting a pedicure. I passed the first studio and entered the second one. Unfortunately, they had no free slots today anymore. Too bad. I went on and started to feel my back. I needed a break, so I stopped at a nearby café. The waitress seemed to be very slow. But I did not care. I enjoyed a beautiful view. While waiting I decided to reflect on the writing process: I just write down what comes to my mind. It is so easy. Of course it is not the most intelligent and deep shit you can find in literature. But we are reflecting on the process itself, so this must be allowed, too. I can see that writing is easy when you don't feel pressure for quality, for time, for content and (in contrast to scientific writing) no pressure for following strict rules. I think of my professor who always tells me to go to the library without any books. "You have everything in your head", she says. And of course, she is right. We are just doing it too seldom.

Being distracted at work is not at all uncommon. Taking into consideration all the hours when people work with low concentration or spend time randomly surfing on the net, they would probably account for a significant share of work time. So it is worth reflecting upon how to make use of those moments of distraction for something we actually need. And yes, this could be taking a nap or going for a walk when we are tired, or seeing an exhibition when we need inspiration.

Belief

Nina: Uuuuuffff . . . my head is spinning. My whole body is red. I sweat rivers. I am trying to catch my breath like a fish on the shore. Here is what happened. I opened the Spotify app and chose a random playlist called 'Dancefloor list'. For 10 minutes I danced like a mad woman. It was not music that I would usually listen to, and at some points I was on the border of becoming an ironic version of myself dancing on a disco floor. But every time this was about to happen, I went even harder for it, not only taking my dance super seriously but encouraging myself to go even deeper in my disco moves that were becoming something totally else. After 10 minutes of hardcore dance came 10 minutes of jumping. I was already out of breath when I started so I felt like: "Man, there´s no way I can do this!" But there was this inner belief in the task and my process that kept me going. When I thought I would collapse, I bent down to support myself with my hands on the sofa as I continued jumping small and fast jumps, lifting my feet only a centimetre from the floor. I had no idea where this was taking me, but that was exactly what excited me. Since I started this experiment with integrating body and movement in my work I always feel like a child when I know that there is a day of discovery in front of me. It is this inner drive, this joy for playing that keeps me going even if there are moments where I think: "What the fuck am I doing?" or "If anyone could see me right now, they would think I'm going nuts!" But in the end the experiments always take me somewhere, so I keep doing them.

All distraction and experimental detouring runs the risk of failing if the one who is doing it does not believe in the process. According to Emery, who writes about artistic making and thinking, "belief is not simply divine inspiration. The term belief is used to describe intensity of involvement in the artistic process. Belief is described here as the catalyst which drives the individual to want to engage in complex cognitive and sensate processes. It is difficult to imagine making art without belief, for without belief, art becomes sterile, mechanical, and often imitative. Belief needs to be present in order to activate other forms of cognitive and sensory responding" (Emery, 1989:240). This means that believing in the process and having the courage to bear uncertainty in order to come to a better result is something relevant no matter if a person tries to develop new patterns of thinking in the arts or in business. But believing in the unknown and trying out new ways of working demands from us to trust our process and needs and most probably redefine what work is.

Create Your Own Formula

When trying to adjust work to the emergent needs of the body, one will quickly realize that different people have very different needs and there is no recipe that can enable creativity at work for everyone. Due to the fact that the ways of thinking differ a lot and that everybody is unique, there is no way around individual solutions. This is a challenging fact for organizations, which still make use of very few modalities that are perceived as real work—namely sitting at a desk and working on computer, or being in meetings in conference rooms.

Even in a project like our scientific writing experiment, which was held by two people who share a similar view on work, the results were very different personal experiments and reflections about how we wanted to change our patterns of thinking and acting in the future. One of us reflected about the experience from the process.

Elisabeth: What I learned and want to keep in my work in the future:

1) change space as often as I feel bored in my body.
2) trust in the process and in myself: the moment will come where I will write down the really good shit.
3) don't stress!
4) share early and often with interesting people; choose them well.
5) write down everything that comes to my mind. I can always erase it.
6) structure every day but allow myself to change the structure as much as I want during the processs.
7) use the time in between either for relaxation or observation.
8) do everything on purpose and consciously —no matter if it is active or reflective.

Conclusions

Looking back at our process and seeing the results of our writing experiment, some reflections start to pop up. Being researchers and having quite a lot of freedom to decide how to do our work, we were able to allow ourselves to be very free in our experimentation. Still, we were facing the challenge to accomplish the given task (writing a scientific text with all its rules and restrictions) and following personal needs at the same time. Through our experimental process, two kinds of texts were produced and weaved together, supporting us to build our story. On one hand, creative ideas and material were written as a result of doing different experiments during the days, using the intuitive, experiential thinking style. These are represented as the inner voice in the text. On the other hand, we also used the rational, analytical thinking style to look at the creative material, structure fragments of text in a story that would make sense and connect our own experiences with argumentation from existing research. The result is a text that challenges the classical format in scientific writing and shows how we can combine experiences and thinking styles from both arts and business to propose something new. The text will hopefully on one hand engage the reader more personally through storytelling, and on the other hand suggest also a useful framework to apply in everyday work practices.

An important side effect of our writing experiment is also that we as authors learned a lot about our own thinking and behavior patterns and re-weaved them into a new way of working that we hope to keep in the future. This will help us create a better balance and flow in work, following our needs, daring to experiment more in the daily routines and then combine the new experiences with the linear thinking style that is also important for us as researchers.

Our experiences and the model we tested might be useful for others who would like to engage in re-weaving their thinking and acting patterns. Nevertheless, there are also limitations of the proposed approach. Changing

Image 17.1 Representing the process of composing the text, cutting different parts of texts into small pieces and weaving them together into a rag rug.

patterns of thinking takes time, and even though engaging in an experiment is fun, it is also easy to fall back into old habits once the experiment is over. The approach we tested might also not suit everyone. Not all people might feel comfortable experimenting with using body and space in new ways at work. This kind of experiment demands that an individual has an open mindset and works in an environment where both management and employees give each other freedom, trust and support in trying out new things. Nevertheless, we believe that our practice so far has shown some positive effects of the proposed approach, which encourages us to experiment and develop it further in our future studies.

Epilogue

Carl Bass, CEO of Autodesc people [. . .] strongly refuses the idea that one should (re)train people: "First we beat creativity out of people, then we hire them for efficiency, and then we try to train creativity back into them? Ridiculous!" (Schmiedgen et al., 2015:113).

This comment made us rethink our thoughts again and again. Shall we rewrite this article? Rethink our research? We know that people have their typical ways of thinking, and we experienced ourselves how hard it can be to change them. And to be honest: some days later, we observed ourselves falling back into old patterns. Everything crap after all?

But then, at the risk of being pathetic: yes, we do need all this. Because to survive and be able to cope with today's complex challenges, we need to understand different ways of thinking and the origin of people's mindsets. We need to be able to break with existing patterns of thinking in order to come up with new solutions. This implies a willingness to open up oneself. To stop hiding personal needs and thoughts—like we did with our inner voice. By sharing our experiences of good pasta and the effects of breathing exercises, we give the reader the possibility to dig deeper into the authors' minds. This text is more than a scientific text. It is an attempt to rethink scientific writing and reading in a way that fits our personal needs. We hope to encourage you, dear reader, to dare listening to your needs as well. For us this experiment was a success, because we re-weaved our personal rag rug of thinking.

Trial and error. Fail early and often.

Now it's your turn.

References

Bratianu, C. and Vasilache, S. (2010). A factorial analysis of the managerial linear thinking model. *International Journal of Innovation and Learning*, 8(4):393–407.

Emery, L. (1989). Believing in artistic making and thinking. *Studies in Art Education*, 30(4):237–248.

Epstein, S., Pacini, R., Denes-Raj, V. and Heier, H. (1996). Individual differences in intuitive-experiential and analytical-rational thinking styles. *Journal of Personality and Social Psychology*, 71(2):390–405.

Hannaford, C. (2005). *Smart Moves: Why Learning Is Not All in Your Head.* Salt Lake City: Great River Books.

Hansen, A. and Sundberg, C. J. (2014). *Hälsa på recept.* Stockholm: Fitnessförlaget.

Lewis, C. and Lovatt, P. (2013). Breaking away from set patterns of thinking: Improvisation and divergent thinking. *Thinking Skills and Creativity,* 9:46–58.

Ryder, N., Pring, L. and Hermelin, B. (2002). Lack of coherence and divergent thinking: Two sides of the same coin in artistic talent? *Current Psychology,* 21(2):168–175.

Schmiedgen, J., Rhinow, R., Köppen, E. and Meinel, C. (2015). *Parts Without a Whole? The Current State of Design Thinking Practice in Organizations.* Potsdam: Technische Berichte des Hasso-Plattner-Instituts für Softwaresystemtechnik an der Universität Potsdam (97).

Steinberg, H., Sykes, E. A., Moss, T., Lowery, S., LeBoutillier, N. and Dewey, A. (1997). Exercise enhances creativity independently of mood. *British Journal of Sports Medicine,* 31:240–245.

Sternberg (1994). Allowing for thinking styles. *Educational Leadership,* November:36–40.

Wulun, J. (2007): Understanding complexity, challenging traditional ways of thinking. *Systems Research and Behavioral Science,* 24:393–402.

Index

For Product Safety Concerns and Information please contact our EU
representative GPSR@taylorandfrancis.com
Taylor & Francis Verlag GmbH, Kaufingerstraße 24, 80331 München, Germany

www.ingramcontent.com/pod-product-compliance
Ingram Content Group UK Ltd.
Pitfield, Milton Keynes, MK11 3LW, UK
UKHW021607240425
457818UK00018B/429